S0-CDS-865

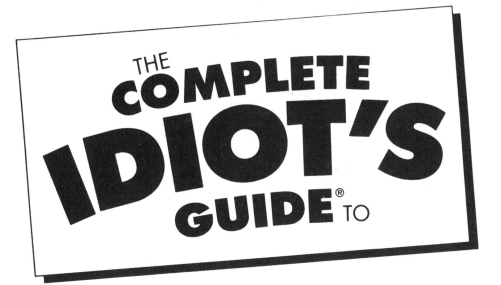

THE COMPLETE IDIOT'S GUIDE® TO

Online Investing for Canadians

*by Douglas Gerlach, Tom McFeat,
and James Gravelle*

**alpha
books**

Prentice Hall Canada Inc., Scarborough, Ontario

Canadian Cataloguing in Publication Data

Gerlach, Douglas.
     The complete idiot's guide to online investing for Canadians

Includes index.
ISBN 0-13-014585-8

1. Investments—Computer network resources. 2. Investments—Information services. I. Gravelle, James.
II. McFeat, Thomas Charles, 1954–   . III. Title.

HG4515.95.G47 1999   025.06'3326   C99-931800-4

© Prentice-Hall Canada Inc.
     Scarborough, Ontario

ALL RIGHTS RESERVED

No part of this book may be reproduced in any form without permission in writing from the publisher.

Prentice-Hall, Inc., Upper Saddle River, New Jersey
Prentice-Hall International (UK) Limited, London
Prentice-Hall of Australia, Pty. Limited, Sydney
Prentice-Hall Hispanoamericana, S.A., Mexico City
Prentice-Hall of India Private Limited, New Delhi
Prentice-Hall of Japan, Inc., Tokyo
Simon & Schuster Southeast Asia Private Limited, Singapore
Editora Prentice-Hall do Brasil, Ltda., Rio de Janeiro

ISBN 0-13-014585-8

Editorial Director, Trade Group: Andrea Crozier
Acquisitions Editor: Nicole de Montbrun
Copy Editor: Lu Cormier
Production Editor: Lori McLellan
Art Direction: Mary Opper
Cover Design: Monica Kompter
Interior Design: Steve Geiselman
Production Coordinator: Kathrine Pummell
Page Layout: B.J. Weckerle
Illustrators: Judd Winick and Kevin Spear

1 2 3 4 5 RRD 03 02 01 00 99

Printed and bound in the United States of America.

THE COMPLETE IDIOT'S GUIDE TO and Design are registered trademarks of Macmillan USA, Inc.

This publication contains the opinions and ideas of its authors and is designed to provide useful advice in regard to the subject matter covered. The authors and publisher are not engaged in rendering legal, accounting, or other professional services in this publication. This publication is not intended to provide a basis for action in particular circumstances without consideration by a competent professional. The authors and publisher expressly disclaim any responsibility for any liability, loss, or risk, personal or otherwise, which is incurred as a consequence, directly or indirectly, of the use and application of any of the contents of this book.

Visit the Prentice Hall Canada Web site! Send us your comments, browse our catalogues, and more.
www.phcanada.com.

Contents at a Glance

Contents

Introduction

Everybody loves technology, right? After all, it's what makes our lives more productive. Technology offers conveniences of all sorts, saving us time and money, whether we're cooking a quick meal in the microwave or calling for roadside car service from our cell phone.

But we can't rely on technology to take the place of good, old-fashioned common sense. With just about any new technology, there's a learning curve that we need to master to make good use of the tools at our fingertips. And there are significant problems that we might face if we get in over our head.

For instance, one newfangled gadget is finding its way into the hands of many adventure-minded people. "Global positioning system" (GPS) units interpret signals from military satellites and tell us exactly where we are on planet Earth. What's more, a GPS unit is small enough to fit into the palm of our hand, and can be accurate to within one hundred yards.

Experienced hikers, sailors, backpackers, and other outdoors enthusiasts can readily put a GPS receiver to good use as part of their essential gear, to make sure they always know where they are, no matter how thick the fog may be, or how deep into the wilderness they go. Technology has provided a new tool for navigating the seas and forests (and highways, too!).

One unfortunate side effect of the increasing popularity of GPS systems is what happens when they fall into the hands of inexperienced users—individuals who don't take the time to learn how to use the devices before they venture into the woods. News stories are appearing regularly about "weekend warriors" who venture into the mountains, armed with a GPS device and a cell phone, and end up being the subject of a search-and-rescue operation. Why? Because the batteries ran out in their GPS, or their cell phone was out of range, or they learned that knowing where they were didn't help them know where they should be. In this case, users who didn't understand the technology and its limits ended up in life-threatening situations. Lulled by a false sense of security, these people often push themselves into dangerous circumstances because of their dependence on technology.

Like all technologies, the Internet can either help us to be more productive or present hazards to our financial well-being.

Millions of people are getting online and looking for help with starting or building a portfolio. In fact, by the end of 2002, experts expect that a total of 14.4 million accounts will have been established at online brokerages, up from just 3 million at the end of 1997.

But just like with those GPS gadgets, if we don't take the time to learn how to use the Internet properly, we could very well end up getting lost. And where our finances are concerned, that could be an expensive proposition.

And that's where this book comes in. With *The Complete Idiot's Guide to Online Investing for Canadians*, you can learn the basics of using the Web to research stocks and mutual funds. You'll find the sites that can teach you about the various approaches that you can use to build a portfolio. You'll discover online tools to search for the right funds and stocks for you.

How to Use This Book

The Complete Idiot's Guide to Online Investing for Canadians is organized to help you get off the ground even if you know nothing about computers, the Internet, or investing! Like a great big lasagna, the book has a number of layers that all come together at the end to form a complete (if not delicious!) dish.

Part 1, "Getting Started on the Road to Successful Online Investing," lays out the basics of getting online, from turning on your computer to setting up an account with an Internet service provider. It also describes a few of the most important and most basic financial concepts—the knowledge you need before you start buying and selling stocks and mutual funds.

In Part 2, "Investing in Mutual Funds," you'll learn about the ever-popular mutual fund, including all the varieties from which to choose. You'll learn what to look for on a fund company's Web site, and where else you can research a particular fund.

Part 3, "Investing in Stocks," takes you into the world of the stock market. You'll learn that it's not enough to buy a stock just because you have a "hunch" that it might go up in price—you'll need a disciplined approach if you want to make money in the stock market. You'll uncover the best way to put together a balanced and diversified portfolio of stocks, and learn where to turn for advice. You'll also get a peek into the world of the online brokers—how to choose one and how to use one. Finally, you'll get the inside track on ways you can invest without using a broker at all.

Part 4, "Managing a Portfolio," describes how to use online tools to manage the stocks and funds that you own. You'll see how quote servers and portfolio trackers work on the Web, and other ways that you can keep up to date with all your holdings.

Part 5, "The Dark Side of the Web," is where you'll get the bad news that investing online isn't all sugar and spice. But you'll be armed with knowledge that can help you protect your privacy and keep your financial information secure. You'll also get an inside peek at the seedy tactics that are sometimes used online to stir up interest in stocks.

Finally, Part 6 is "Putting It Together." This is where you'll take all the knowledge you've learned in this book and put it to work toward meeting your goals, no matter if you're trying to pay for school or retire a millionaire.

Extras

The Complete Idiot's Guide to Online Investing for Canadians packs in as much information as possible, and you are presented with tips and advice as you read this book. These elements enhance your knowledge, or point out important pitfalls to avoid. Along the way, you'll find the following elements:

Money Market Speak

The language of finance and investing can sometimes be intimidating, or just downright confusing! These translations will help you learn the lingo of Bay Street.

Crash Alert

Warning! Warning! Remember, both stock markets and computers can crash! You'll learn what potential computer or investing pitfalls to look for as you surf the Web in search of financial information.

Heard It on the Street

The wisdom of Bay Street and Wall Street has been tested through the years. Here's the practical advice you need to make better investing decisions.

Net Savvy

You can increase your I.Q. (Internet Quotient) with these tips and tricks about using your Internet. You'll learn how to use your Web browser, e-mail software, and other programs to navigate the online world.

Market Stat

People in the financial markets are fascinated with statistics. Now you can learn some interesting facts about the stock market and its history, often from a numbers perspective.

Acknowledgments

I would first like to thank all of the great staff at Prentice Hall Canada for their time and effort in helping to make this book what it is. To my family, especially to my parents and brothers and sisters (including the outlaws!), who have always been there to offer their courage and support, I give you my thanks.

To James Gauthier, for his expertise and sense of humour. I couldn't have done it without you.

And most importantly, to my wife, Elaine, whose outer beauty is only bested by her inner beauty. Thanks for your patience and love. Jay.

Dedication

For the newest member of our clan, Matthew Louis Robert Gravelle.
Born August 21, 1999.

James Gravelle

Part 1

Getting Started on the Road to Successful Online Investing

That computer over in the corner is ready to be used for something more than typing letters and playing games. It is your powerful investment tool—your personal research assistant that can bring you the best financial advice and resources that are available. However, it is no substitute for financial discipline and good sense.

Chapter 1

Using Your Computer and the Internet as Investing Tools

In This Chapter

➤ The basics of the Internet

➤ How to get your computer connected to the Net

➤ The advantages of online investing

That fairly substantial piece of hardware on your desk probably cost quite a bit more than the refrigerator or air conditioner or stove or dishwasher or any other major appliance you've got in your home. So it's only natural to wonder whether it's possible to do something useful on your computer, besides using it as an expensive typewriter.

Or perhaps you haven't even taken the plunge yet, and don't own a computer. Before you make such a big-ticket purchase, you will want to make sure that you're getting the equipment you need to accomplish what you would like to accomplish.

And after you have the right computer, how do you go about getting online? What's the difference between an "online service," "the Web," and "the Internet," anyway?

Turning On, Tuning In, and Dialling Up

Although people often mean "the Internet" when they talk about "going online," they're really two separate things. Any two computers can communicate using telephone lines, as long as they're properly equipped. You could set up your computer to dial up a friend's house and "talk" to the computer on the other end, or send files back and forth. You would be online!

But the online world is more than just two computers talking to each other. Using the same sort of technology, computer systems were set up to enable many users to communicate and share information. Known as bulletin board systems (BBSs), these computers acted as a central hub where users could dial up, log on, and communicate with each other. These networks were named after their capability for users to write and respond to messages in a public forum, similar to a cork bulletin board.

BBSs often featured libraries of files that users could download (transfer to their own computer from the main computer), and ranged from networks operated out of the basement of the sysop (system operator) to full-scale commercial operations. Although many BBSs were free, others required users to subscribe for a monthly fee. Although you can still find some BBSs around, these mini-networks really hit their heyday in the late 1980s and early 1990s.

Although BBSs were great ways for users to communicate, their reach was pretty much limited by geography—users generally aren't willing to make long-distance calls to connect to a particular BBS. And so another type of online computer service became popular, the commercial online service. You will probably recognize the names of America Online, CompuServe, and Prodigy, three of the best-known computer networks. These networks were built to offer access to users all across the country—no matter where you were, there was a good chance that you could reach a network with a local or regional phone call.

Get a Complete History Lesson About the Internet

If you really want to dig into the history of the Internet, check out the various links collected by the Internet Society (http://www.isoc. org/internet/history). The Society is a not-for-profit group that works toward setting standards and guiding future development of the Internet.

After you connected to the network, however, you were routed to a main computer along with all the other users who were online at the same time—like a giant BBS! On the main computer, you could have your choice of topics that you could discuss, or vast libraries of files that you could download. No matter what your interests, you could find someone online who was also engaged by the same topics. One big disadvantage of the commercial online services was the cost. Users paid by the hour for the privilege of connecting to the network.

"Going online" took on a completely new meaning in the early 1990s, as Internet fever began to sweep North America. The Internet is truly a phenomenon of the 1990s, although its roots go all the way back to the 1960s. Just how popular is the Internet? According to Relevant Knowledge, an estimated 57,037,000 people were using the World Wide Web in 1998, up from practically zero in 1993. In fact, the World Wide Web didn't really even exist before 1993!

Nowadays, you can't watch a television commercial, drive by a billboard on the highway, look at a magazine ad, or pay your telephone bill without seeing the addresses of Web sites! But what exactly is the Internet? And is the Internet the same thing as the World Wide Web? It's time for a primer on the Internet and how it works.

The Internet is a global communications network. No one "owns" the Internet, and no single authority governs the entire Internet. In fact, a number of private companies, government agencies, and other organizations all operate pieces of this giant, interconnected network. Standards have been established to make sure all the groups continue speaking the same computer language and to ensure that data can travel anywhere throughout the network.

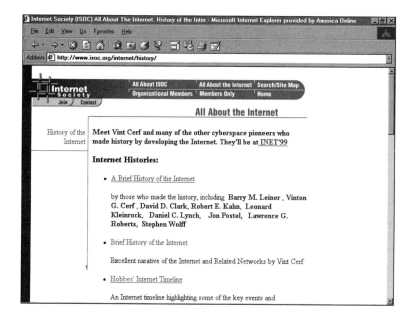

Get the full story behind the creation and development of the Internet directly from the people who created it, here at the Internet Society's Web site.

So who pays for the Internet? The Internet has a main "backbone" maintained by a handful of companies (including some familiar names such as MCI Worldcom and Sprint). These backbone providers sell access to the rest of the Internet via their high-capacity network to other companies, who sell to other companies, who sell to other companies (and so on), until, eventually, a company offers access to individual users. When you want access to the Internet, you will need to arrange it through one of the last companies in this network food chain, called an Internet service provider (ISP).

When you want to get on the Web, you will tell your computer to dial up and connect to your ISP's computer using a small dialler program. After you're connected, however, your ISP's computer isn't your final destination. Your ISP is really just your gateway to thousands of other computers, all over the world, attached to the Internet.

Where does the World Wide Web fit into the Internet? The Web is actually nothing more than a way to send information across the global network of the Internet. In

Internet-speak, the Web is a "protocol," just one of many ways that information can be delivered on the Net. If you have ever seen a Web site address, you've probably noticed that it begins with the letters *http*. This is an abbreviation for Hypertext Transfer Protocol, the exact name of the protocol for delivery of Web pages. Other protocols include e-mail, for instance, and the File Transfer Protocol (FTP). The http protocol governs how text and images are sent from a Web server. This is a computer connected to the Internet that is devoted to delivering (or "serving") the pages of a particular Web site. These days, users think of the World Wide Web as being synonymous with the Internet, but they're not really the same thing.

Getting Online in Four Easy Steps

Although all this sounds complicated, you can get online in just four easy steps! And several of these steps couldn't be any easier. After you have taken care of these prerequisites, you can begin to explore the online world.

1. **Get a telephone.** You probably already have a phone that you can use to connect to the Internet, so this step is a cinch!

If a regular telephone connection isn't fast enough for you, your phone company might offer a special telephone line called Integrated Services Digital Network (ISDN)—for a price, of course. An ISDN line can be many times faster than a regular connection, but can also carry hefty per-minute usage charges and requires some special equipment.

Call Waiting Can Disrupt Your Online Sessions!

If you have call waiting service on your telephone line, you will need to disable it before you call your online service provider. Otherwise, an incoming phone call will knock you off the line!

Another new technology called Asymmetric Digital Subscriber Line (ADSL) is also available from some telephone companies. ADSL works using your existing telephone lines, so you don't have to rewire your home!

Although the telephone will probably be your conduit to the network of the Internet, other new technologies just arriving on the scene promise to be faster ways of connecting to the Net. New cable modems can provide a super-fast connection to the Internet, and satellite and wireless systems are also becoming available in some parts of North America. These are reliable alternatives to telephone-based connections.

2. **Get a computer.** This is another pretty easy step, right? At least if you already have a computer, that is! If you don't have a personal computer, you will probably be shopping for one, at least if you want to be a regular Internet visitor.

So what kind of computer should you look for? Basically, any new computer you purchase today comes with a pretty standard array of components that is sufficient to get you online, and many even include the software you will need to get connected.

When you shop for a new computer, you should follow this rule of thumb: Either buy the biggest, most powerful computer you can afford, or buy the absolute cheapest computer that will accomplish the tasks you want to accomplish. The rationale is that a well-equipped, state-of-the-art machine will last longer, giving you years of service before it becomes obsolete. The el cheapo version, on the other hand, will quickly become outdated; but what the heck, you didn't pay very much for it, and you can buy another.

When you shop for a computer, remember this: the bigger and faster, the better. The faster your computer's processor speed, the faster your computer will work. Having a lot of random-access memory (RAM) can also help your computer work faster and let you do more tasks at the same time. While 14-inch and 15-inch monitors are standard, a 17-inch monitor might be easier on your eyes (if you find your eyesight isn't what it used to be).

You Can't Use the Phone Line in Your Office to Connect to Your Computer

The snazzy telephone system you use at work is likely to be part of a digital network and incompatible with the hardware in your computer when it comes time to connect to an online service. In fact, you risk damaging your computer if you try to plug a phone line into this kind of phone system. You will have to ask your boss to have a special line installed that will let you connect to the outside world (just make sure you have a compelling business reason before you ask!).

3. **Get a modem.** A modem is a piece of equipment that translates the digital signals of your computer into analog signals that can be sent across a telephone line. At the other end of the line, a modem converts the signals back to digital so that the computer at that end can interpret them. The word *modem* actually comes from the description of how the equipment "modulates" the signal from one format to another; "modem" is a lot easier to say than "modulator/demodulator"!

Nearly all new computers come with a modem, in either an internal version that lives inside your computer or an external version that connects to your machine via a cable. Modems are available in several speeds, rated by kilobits per second (Kbps). Currently, the most common standards are 28.8 Kbps, 33.6 Kbps, and 56.6 Kbps (also known as 56K). The same rule of thumb applies here as with the rest of your computer setup: the faster, the better!

4. **Find an Internet service provider.** Now that your equipment is set up, there's one more step before you get online: set up an account with an online service provider. Companies that specialize in providing access to the Internet are known as Internet service providers (ISPs). Usually, you can set up an account that will provide you with unlimited access to the Internet for somewhere between $15 and $25 a month.

A Noisy Telephone Line Can Cause Big Headaches

If you live in an older home or an older neighbourhood, your phone lines might sound like someone's crumpling up cellophane on the other end of the line. This noise can interfere with the transmission of data when you're online, sometimes knocking you offline altogether. If this is a problem, ask your telephone company to test your phone lines for excessive noise, and see whether they can be repaired.

Sometimes Fast Is Too Fast!

Although the latest crop of modems can receive data at 56.6 Kbps, current telephone lines can't handle speeds any faster than about 53 Kbps. And when you send data from your computer to another, your uploads will be limited to about 33.3 Kbps! Still, every bit of speed helps, so go for a 56K modem if you can.

So, how do you find the right ISP for you? Finding an ISP can be tough if you don't know where to look. If you're already online, you can consult one of the directories of ISPs on the Web. The List (http://thelist.internet.com) and ISPs.com (http://www.isps.com) are two comprehensive databases of providers; just search by your telephone area code to find an ISP near you.

Of course, if you don't already have an ISP, telling you to search for one on the Web is a bit like asking you to drive to the auto dealer before you own a car! In that case, check for ads in the business section of your local newspaper or listings in the yellow pages, or ask for referrals from friends or at the nearest computer store.

You might consider one of the commercial online services, such as Sympatico. Besides offering their own proprietary information, these services also provide access for their customers to the complete Internet. These services have local dial-up numbers all over the country, and even all over the world. If you travel outside the country frequently, an account with Sympatico can let you dial up from your laptop and check your e-mail from thousands of places on the globe!

So after you've found a couple of ISPs in your area, how do you evaluate them? Here are a few things to consider.

Does the ISP have an access number that's a local telephone call for you? You might find an ISP advertising in your area, only to learn that it's a toll call every time you dial up.

Does the ISP offer flat rate monthly pricing for access to the Internet? Is there a limit on how many hours you can use in a month?

Does the ISP offer a free trial? Many will let you try out their service for a week or two, or even a month. If they do, take advantage of this opportunity to test them. See whether you have any trouble connecting to their network, or if you constantly get busy signals when you try dialling up. If so, you might want to look elsewhere.

Remember, you can always change providers if you need to; so don't give out your e-mail address to hundreds of friends, relatives, and adoring fans until you're sure that you will be sticking with that provider!

Your ISP will probably provide you with all the software you need to get online, but here's a short list of what you might expect.

A *dialler program* does just what it sounds like: It dials your ISP and establishes a connection with your computer. Windows 95 and 98 include dialler programs, and that's all you will probably need. You will need a *Web browser*, probably Microsoft Internet Explorer or Netscape Navigator. Both can be freely downloaded from the Web from the Microsoft Web site (http://www.microsoft.com/ie) or Netscape site (http://www.netscape.com/computing/download).

An *e-mail program* is essential, and both Microsoft and Netscape include free e-mail software with their full suite of Internet tools. Eudora is another popular e-mail program, and a free version is available on the Web (http://www.eudora.com). A full-featured version of the program, Eudora Pro, can be purchased if you find yourself using e-mail a lot and might be able to use some of the software's advanced capabilities.

Can You Use Your Older Computer to Get Online?

Sure, you can log on to the Internet with a computer that's five or six years old—but you might not be happy with the slow speed and other limitations. Unfortunately, as the prices of new computers fall, it might not be feasible to upgrade your computer. But you just might be able to buy a new computer, one that's bigger, better, faster, and stronger, for less than the cost of upgrading! Before you use your old machine as a doorstop, you might consider handing it down to the kids or grandkids, or donating it to your local library or other organization.

Internet Explorer and Navigator Aren't the Only Browsers in Town

Although Internet Explorer from Microsoft and Navigator from Netscape Communications are the most popular Web browsers, you do have other options for surfing the Web. A Norwegian firm named Opera Software makes a Web browser (called "Opera") that is small and fast. The installation file is about 1 megabyte in size (compared to more than 10 megabytes for the full packages of the other browsers), and Opera can run well on slower computers (such as older 386 and 486 PCs). In nearly all respects, you will get the same features as you will find in other Web browsers—and some you won't find anywhere but in Opera. You can download the browser to try it out (http://www.operasoftware.com); if you like it, there is a nominal fee to register the program.

Search The List's database of Internet service providers by entering your telephone area code. You will find all the companies that provide Net access in your region.

You Can't Beat the Price of Free Online Access!

In many communities across the country, organizations offer free Internet accounts to local citizens. Known as "freenets," these groups provide an important public service to their communities. You can check a list of freenets around the world at http://www.lights.com/ freenet. Also check with your local library, because more and more libraries are providing free Internet access for research purposes. These tend to be popular, so try to schedule your visit at an off-peak hour.

Those are the essentials! You might also occasionally find a use for FTP (File Transfer Protocol) software, to upload and download files, or Telnet software, to connect directly to a remote computer, and those programs might be included in the software you get from your ISP.

All these new programs can take some time to really master, but the best way to learn them is to practise! Don't forget to make use of the Help file that comes with the program, too (and reading the manual is a good start!). Many developers of online software include their user manuals on their Web sites, so drop by there if you have unanswered questions.

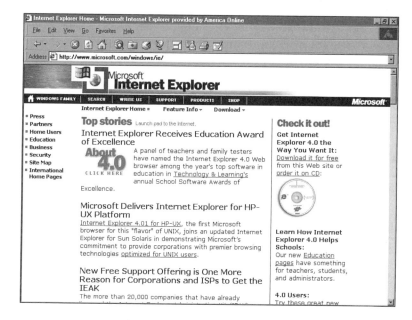

You can download Microsoft's Web browser, Internet Explorer, for free from the Microsoft Web site.

Six Reasons Why Investing Online Is Good—and Good for You

Now that you're online, what about this investing business? One of the primary reasons that individuals are flocking to the Internet is because they want to use the many tools and sites related to personal finance and investing. And it's certainly true, as you will learn throughout this book, that there are some really terrific advantages to online investing. Here are a some advantages of the Internet when it comes to building a portfolio.

➤ **The Internet can save you time.** Before the Web, if you wanted to read the filings a company made with a provincial securities commission or the U.S. Securities and Exchange Commission (SEC), you had to call the company and request that they send you a package of information. A couple of weeks later, an envelope would arrive. Today, you can go to some of those commissions' Web sites and get the information in minutes.

➤ **The Internet is very convenient.** It's hard to beat the convenience of downloading a stock report from the Web, compared to driving to the public library to make a photocopy of that same report. And the Internet never closes, so feel free to do your investment research in your bathrobe!

➤ **The Internet provides access to more information than you could get at your local library.** With tens of millions of pages on the Web, there's no way any library can stack up. And there's more information being published online every day! Much of the information that's online is only available in that medium—you won't find it anywhere else.

➤ **The Internet can save you money.** Brokerage commissions are at an all-time low, something that's made possible only by the low costs to firms of servicing customers on the Internet. It can cost less than $30 in commissions to buy or sell up to 5,000 shares of stock, if you're willing to place your orders online.

➤ **The Internet can offer you access to other investors who share your approach.** There are countless communities of investors on the Web, each one focused on a particular style or method of investing. Without the Web, you might never have the chance to meet and discuss potential investments with people who share your approach to the markets.

➤ **The Internet hosts a growing amount of educational investment resources.** If you don't know how to invest, you can learn from the many tutorials, glossaries, lessons, workshops, and seminars available online. You can learn how to start investing, how build a portfolio, or learn the lingo of Bay Street, all on the Web. And *The Complete Idiot's Guide to Online Investing for Canadians* will show you how!

The Least You Need to Know

➤ The Internet is a vast network that connects users from all over the world. There are other online services as well, but the Internet and the World Wide Web have become synonymous with getting online.

➤ All you need to get online is a telephone, a computer, a modem, and an Internet service provider. You will need to find the right provider for you, and you can often try out a company for a couple of weeks to get some first-hand experience.

➤ After you're online, you can look forward to enjoying the advantages of using the available tools to complete many of the tasks of investing.

Chapter 2

Understanding the Basics of Personal Finance

In This Chapter

➤ Understand that successful investing begins with saving

➤ Why you don't need to feel bad about not sticking to a budget

➤ Learn why it's so important to pay yourself first

➤ Discover the secret of compound returns

Now that you understand a bit about how your computer and the Internet works, you still need a few more lessons before you jump feet-first into the online world. It's time for an overview of some of the most important things you need to know as you begin a lifetime of investing.

You Gotta Learn to Swim Before You Surf

Whenever it comes to money, it's easy to feel intimidated. And with the millions of pages of information related to finance and investing out there on the Web, it's even easier to feel like you're in over your head.

Never fear! Even though you may have been taught to swim by being thrown into the deep end of the pool, most people start out in the shallow end doing the dog paddle, and gradually pick up the pace from there. In time, and with practice, you will be using the butterfly stroke or Australian crawl to swim lap after lap.

Before you start investing (and certainly before you start surfing the Web for answers to your financial questions), you need to know a few things about money.

It All Starts with Saving

How would you like to know the true secret to building wealth? The honest-to-goodness, sure-fire way to create your own million-dollar portfolio? Read carefully to learn how millionaires are made, in just two steps:

1. Spend less than you earn.

2. Invest the rest.

That's it!

Learning to be a good saver is the first part of any solid plan to accumulate wealth, whether you're looking forward to a comfortable retirement, a top-level education for your kids, or your dream home. But, finding the extra bit of money to fund your investing plan can be tough—at least until you finish this chapter!

The "B" Word: Budgeting (Yuck!)

Conventional wisdom says that you can find the money to invest just by preparing a household budget. Unfortunately, the mere mention of the word budgeting is enough to cause any reasonable person to turn and run in horror! So here's an idea that will throw most professional financial advisors into a frenzy: Forget about the "b" word entirely!

Most of the time, you probably have no trouble finding enough money to pay all your bills without going through the process of micromanaging your spending habits. It's likely you already have a pretty good idea of where your money goes each month—essentials such as rent, mortgage, utilities, auto expenses, and telephone bills; and nonessentials such as double mocha cappuccinos from your local coffee house or a newly remastered double-CD of the hits of Ol' Blue Eyes (okay, well maybe that is an essential, but you get the point). You can probably trim plenty of fat from your monthly expenses.

Throwing Out Your Budget Doesn't Mean You Can Spend Whatever You Like!

You don't need a degree in economics to understand this scientific concept: The amount of money you can spend each month is determined by the supply of money that you have access to, either money in the bank or money in your wallet. If you spend more than you have, month after month, you will be headed for just one place: bankruptcy court!

Pay Yourself First—You're Worth It!

Who's the most important person to your financial plan? You are! So instead of trying to budget all the fun out of your life and *hoping* to end up with enough at the end of the month to put into a savings plan, tackle the problem from the other direction: Pay yourself first! Each month, before you pay the rest of your bills, write the first cheque to yourself and deposit it into a special account, at a bank, a brokerage firm, or a mutual fund company.

By putting your financial plan at the top of the priority list, you will never again give yourself the short end of the stick when it comes time to pay bills. And somehow, you will probably be able to find the money to meet the rest of your obligations each month.

So how much should you put away each month in a savings and investing plan? A good goal to shoot for is to save 10 percent of your paycheque, after all taxes and other deductions. If that sounds way too excessive for you, start with 5 percent. When you get your annual raise, increase the percentage a bit more. When you get a little extra cash from a freelance job or bonus, add that to the pot. Keep working toward your goal of setting aside 10 percent of your paycheque on a regular basis, and pretty soon you will be saving with the best of them!

What would you have to give up to be able to pay yourself 10 percent each month? The Armchair Millionaire features a fun calculator that will clue you in on just how easy it is to pay yourself first (http://www.armchairmillionaire.com/fivesteps/ step_2app.html). Just enter your monthly take-home pay, and the program will list a few ways you can keep that cash in your pocket. If your monthly paycheques totalled $1,000 after taxes, for instance, here's what you'd have to give up to save $100 a month:

$ 7.00	2 video rentals
$30.00	2 music CDs
$12.00	1 large pizza with the works, delivered
$ 3.00	1 fast-food burger with fries
$ 3.00	1 pint of ice cream, the good stuff
$25.00	1 latest best-selling novel (hardcover)
$ 6.00	2 beers (at a bar)
$ 3.00	1 bag of Oreos
$ 4.00	2 muffins
$ 4.00	1 chips and dip
$ .50	1 candy bar
$ 2.00	1 cappuccino
$99.50	Total

When you really start to look at where your money goes each month, and when you realize how far your money could go if it was invested for twenty-five or thirty years, you can be inspired to change your behaviour.

Still, when it comes to writing that cheque each month, many people fall flat on their faces. Don't worry, there's another, even easier way to fund your savings plan. Nearly every financial institution offers a plan where they will electronically transfer money from an account at another firm at a specific date each month.

The Armchair Millionaire can show you how easy it can be to pay yourself first with their simple calculator.

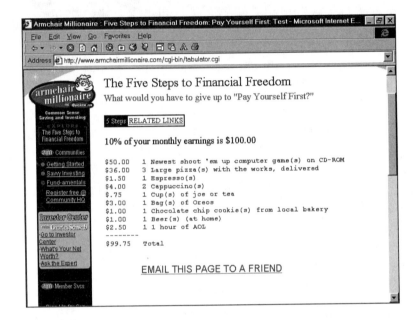

Automatic Investing Plans Have Another Advantage

If you set up an automatic investing plan with a brokerage firm or mutual fund company, you can often get around the minimum investment they might otherwise require all at once to open an account. By committing a certain amount of money to be invested each month, at least until you've reached the minimum account size, you will be paying yourself, without the need to come up with a minor fortune just to open an account.

These automatic plans may be called automated transfer programs, moneylinks, or automatic investment plans, but the concept is the same. You will have to fill out some forms (usually the company that's receiving the money will provide these) and specify the amount you would like to have transferred. Then all you have to do is remember to add the transaction to your chequebook register each month! Now your pay-yourself-first plan will be taken care of each month!

Do You Appreciate Compound Interest?

After you've found the money to start your investing plan, you can proceed to step #2 of the secret of building wealth: putting the money to work! The key to success whenever you're saving and investing to meet any goal is to allow enough time for your money to really work for you. Time is the fundamental ingredient in the plan: without time, your money just can't work at its maximum potential for your benefit.

Why is time so essential? Because of the power of compound interest, referred to by some as the "eighth wonder of the world." The power of compound interest can cause your money to multiply to amounts that you might have thought impossible. Here's how it works.

Let's say you deposit $100 in a bank, and are able to earn 5 percent in interest a year. At the end of the year, you have $105 in the bank (5 percent of $100 is $5). Now, if you leave that $105 in the bank, how much will you have at the end of the second year, assuming you still earn 5 percent a year in interest? You will have $110.25. Five percent of your original $100 is still $5, but the $5 you earned last year and left in the bank also earned you interest of $0.25, for a total of $110.25. This is compound interest, when you earn interest on your interest! Maybe this short example doesn't sound like much, but let's consider another story in which we let time work its magic.

Twins Nelson and Nellie are 18 years old. Nellie decides to start her savings and investing plan at this young age, so she invests $2,000 a year for the next four years. By the age of 21, she has invested $8,000.

Nelson is a bit slower when it comes to financial matters, so he doesn't invest anything until he's 30 years old. Then he puts away $2,000 a year, and keeps going until he's on the brink of retirement at age 64. Nelson is proud to have put $70,000 into his brokerage account.

Over the years, both Nelson and Nellie are able to earn an annual return of about 10 percent in their portfolios, the long-term average of the stock market (as you will learn later).

At age 65, Nelson smugly turns to Nellie and chastises her for neglecting her investments all those years. Nelson's account balance is $596,254, and he's feeling pretty good about it.

But Nellie produces her account statement, and Nelson's jaw drops. Her account is worth more than Nelson's: her original $8,000 has grown to a total of $615,000.

There's only one way to explain the difference in Nelson and Nellie's investing plans, and that's the power of compound returns. Nellie's account grew and grew, not necessarily because of her investing acumen. And it wasn't because she continued to put money in her account, either, but because she didn't take any money out! She left all the interest and profits she earned in her account, and that interest and those profits earned even more interest and profits, to the point where the biggest part of her portfolio by far comes from the compounding of returns.

Imagine where Nellie would be at age 65 if she had continued to invest $2,000 a year after age 21!

Time is your ally. Don't be a prisoner of time. Let it work for you and help you reach your financial goals. That means just one thing: Start saving and investing today!

Setting Goals and Meeting Them

You've probably got a lot of dreams. We all do. You want things from life, whether it's your dream house or a worry-free retirement or a luxurious sailboat. So how are you going to make those dreams become reality? You're going to stretch to fulfill your desires with a savings and investing plan.

Articulating your goals is only part of what you will need to do in order to meet your objectives.

You also need to separate your long-term goals from your short-term goals. The reason for this is simple: If you expect to be paying for college in three or four years for that future doctor you've been raising, you don't want to invest all of your money in something that carries a lot of risk. If your investment didn't work out, you would be stuck without enough money to pay the bills!

On the other hand, if your goal is to save for your retirement and you have twenty-five years until you expect to retire, you might be able to maximize the returns on your investment if you don't need to worry so much about short-term changes (as long as you know that in the end you have a good chance of ending up with a solid portfolio).

Overall, the Stock Market Goes in One Direction —Up!

Since 1928, the U.S. stock market (as represented by the Standard & Poor's 500 Index, a collection of the best-known companies from all industries) increased in fifty-two calendar years and declined in twenty years. However, the ups were much, much bigger than the downs. In forty-one of those years, the market grew by more than 10 percent, but the market fell by 10 percent or more in only eight of the down years.

These two investors have vastly different goals, so they're likely to end up with two very different savings and investing plans to meet their objectives mainly due to their different time frames.

But how do you define "short term" and "long term"? Well, experts generally agree that five years is the dividing line. If you have a need for money in less than five years, you have a short-term goal. If you don't need the money for more than five years, you've got a long-term goal.

There are big differences between short-term and long-term goals and how you meet them. Remember the story about Nellie and her not-so-bright twin brother Nelson? If you have a long-term goal, the power of compounding plays a major role in helping you meet your objectives. If you have a short-term goal, however, the only way you will be able to build up your bank or brokerage account is by putting money into the account on a regular basis. Your contributions will be the most important part of your plan.

If you have long-term goals, you should probably be investing in the stock market. Over the long term, the stock market has returned about 11 percent a year to investors. But over the short term, the stock market fluctuates—and fluctuates a lot. In a single year, it's not unusual for stocks to decline 25 percent! This kind of unpredictable decline could wreak havoc on your financial plan, leaving you short by quite a few dollars just when you need the money the most.

Building Your Plan

Later in this book, you will learn how to put together a plan on the Internet that fits your personal situation. You will learn how to balance risk and return, and discover which investments are likely to be best for your own goals. And whether you're planning for retirement, or college, or some other aim, you can find the tools on the Internet to help you reach all your goals.

The Least You Need to Know

➤ No matter how rich or poor you are, the key to building your nest egg is learning to save regularly. Pay yourself first each month, and your savings will quickly begin to grow.

➤ It doesn't take much to begin your savings and investing plan, but every day you delay starting is one day less that your money could be working for you. The principle of compound returns is the key to building wealth, so let time work on your side and not against you.

➤ You need to separate your long-term and your short-term goals, and create a plan to help you achieve both. Different types of investments are appropriate for each goal, so make sure you're investing in the right place.

Chapter 3

"Debt Is Saving in Reverse"

In This Chapter

➤ Learn why it's so important to save, not spend

➤ Devise a savings plan

➤ Build a plan online to reduce your debt

The legendary American fund manager and author Peter Lynch once wrote that "debt is saving in reverse." This is an apt description of what happens when your debts pile up. Not only are the interest payments likely to drain your wallet faster than just about any force known to physical science, but you're severely crimping your ability to save. And the one thing you need before you invest is the money to invest!

It's time to get your debt load under control. You can start today by visiting some of the Web sites that offer tools and resources to help you get back on track.

They Don't Call It "Debt Burden" for Nothing

Yep, the phrase "debt burden" is really appropriate. It doesn't matter whether it's a car loan, mortgage, student loan, home equity loan, installment loan, or credit card debt—the interest you have to pay for the privilege of borrowing money can vary from 5 percent to 20 percent, and sometimes even more.

The Difference Between Interest and Principal

Interest is any payment you make for the use of borrowed money. *Principal* is the money you actually borrowed from a lender. Any debt payment you make is made up of interest, principal, or a combination of the two.

Sure, some of this debt might be unavoidable (or so you are convinced), but consider this: If you carry an unpaid balance on your credit card with an interest rate of 18 percent, paying off that debt is the same thing as getting a guaranteed effective 18 percent return on your investment. There's no other place on earth where you can get a guaranteed rate of return of 18 percent on an investment!

Here's an example. If your credit card carries an interest rate of 18 percent, and you have a $5,000 balance, it will take you five years to pay off the balance if you make monthly payments of $128 (a little bit more than the 2 percent minimum monthly payment required by most cards). Of course, you can't make any more charges on the card, either.

In those five years, you will have paid a total of $2,635 in interest! With that kind of return, it's no wonder the credit card companies are stuffing your mailbox with offers of pre-approved credit cards.

To put your savings plan in forward gear, you need to do three things:

1. Get your spending in check.
2. Start your savings and investing plan.
3. Reduce the amount you're paying in interest on existing debts.

For help, you need turn no further than the sites and tools described in the following sections.

Not All Debt Is Evil

Of course, no one is saying that all debt is bad for you. A student loan with an interest rate of 6 percent might be a pretty good deal. And if you can get a better rate of return from a savings or investment account, say 9 percent or 10 percent, it might not make sense to pay off that loan early with other funds. You will get a better overall rate of return by making regular monthly payments on the loan and saving or investing the rest.

Spend Not, Save Lot

Sometimes the best way to tackle your debt is to figure out how you got so deep in the hole in the first place—and then figure out how to modify your behaviour so that you can avoid falling back in.

The Truth About "Frugal Living"

Although it may not seem very polite to refer to a person as a cheapskate or a spendthrift, a lot of people embrace these descriptions! It's all part of a movement that some call "frugal living." It's not about being cheap, but about living well and living within your means. One important advantage of eliminating wasteful habits and reducing your spending is that you increase the amount you're saving and investing.

For many people, this means adjusting their lifestyle to enable them to live within their means. The idea is simple: Don't spend more than you make! Putting it into practice can be a little more challenging. The folks at Cheapskate Monthly (http://www.cheapskatemonthly.com) are ready to help. Hosted by author Mary Hunt, this site is a companion to her monthly print newsletter.

Learn tricks and tips to make every dollar last longer at Cheapskate Monthly.

Although much of the site is accessible by members only (for a modest annual fee), you will find a lot of free tools and tips to explore on the site. Check out the preview issue, for instance, or the interactive tools and calculators in the Activity Center.

How Can You Start a Savings and Investing Plan When You Have All That Debt Hanging over Your Head?

One of the biggest myths about investing is that you have to have a lot of money to get started. It's just not true! In fact, you can start with just $10 or $25 a month. Even if you are mired in debt, why not start your savings plan somewhere, even if you just put away a few dollars a month on a regular basis. At the same time, continue to pay off your debts. You will reap the rewards as you begin to see your savings grow and realize just how terrible it is to let yourself fall back into the debt quagmire.

If you get the idea into your head that it's far better to save than to spend, maybe you will think twice the next time that you pull out your credit card. By cutting your monthly expenses, you will have more to contribute to paying down your existing debt and to funding your long-term savings plan.

Online Debt Reduction Calculators and Planners

After you've made up your mind to eliminate your bad spending habits, you need to make a plan of attack to pare down the debt you've already rung up. Your first stop on the Web should be Quicken.com's Debt Reduction Planner (http://www.quicken.com/saving/debt). This calculator will help you to tally up your existing debts, and then create a strategy to help you pay off your debts.

Before you begin using the planner, gather up all your credit card statements and other paperwork related to all your debts. Then enter the amounts of all your current debts in the program. This includes credit cards, mortgages, auto loans, home equity loans, personal loans, and any other debts you might have. You will need to enter the interest rate, current balance, and payment details in the program, clicking the Save button after each item. Then click the Next button to go on to the next screen.

The Debt Reduction Planner then calculates how long it will take you before you are 100 percent debt free. Don't get too depressed, however, because the Planner has a few tips for you. Click Next to go on to the next page.

The Planner walks you through strategies that can save you money and reduce your debt faster. It shows you how much you will save by paying off high-interest credit cards

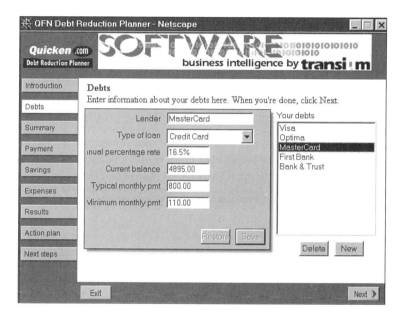

Add up all your debts using Quicken.com's Debt Reduction Planner, and build a step-by-step plan to eliminate them.

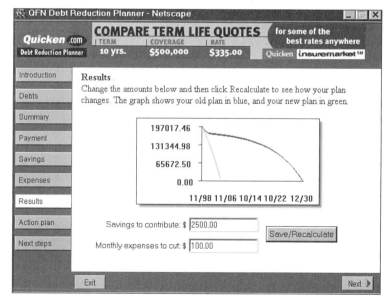

Quicken.com's Debt Reduction Planner demonstrates how quickly your action plan can get you completely out of debt.

25

first, by using some of your savings to pay down debts, and by reducing your monthly expenses. As you enter the amount of cash you can direct toward reducing your debt, the Planner recalculates your savings and the time required.

Finally, the Planner shows you a before-and-after chart, illustrating how the plan you've just created can save you money. You also get an Action Plan that details how much to pay each month to each of your obligations for the next year.

The Least You Need to Know

➤ Unless you get your debts under control, your savings and investing plan will be impossibly bogged down.

➤ Develop a plan to reduce your debt, and then stick to it. But don't put off starting a plan of regular saving: Start setting aside a small amount for your long-term savings even while you whittle away at your debt load.

Chapter 4

How the Stock Market Works

In This Chapter

➤ Why companies sell stock

➤ How the stock market works

➤ Stock exchanges and market simulations on the Web

For many years, average Canadians just didn't concern themselves with notions of investing in the stock market. Why should they have? For many, a job in a good company was a permanent position. There were no layoffs or downsizing or restructuring to worry about; and after retirement, company pensions and the Canada Pension Plan could provide for the family. Others, who might have considered investing on their own, were scared off by their childhood memories of the "Great One"—no, not #99—the Great Depression of the 1930s. If they didn't recall the hard times directly, their parents were sure to remind them of the years of suffering and hardship. And because the Great Depression is forever linked to the 1929 stock market crash, all too many individuals turned their backs on "speculating" in the stock markets. Fear drove investors and potential investors from buying stocks.

Investing for Your Future

Today, the spectre of job insecurity and a crippled social security system haunts many investors. Company pension plans (known as defined benefit plans) are going the way of Cadillacs with fins, in favour of retirement plans that employees themselves

Buy a Bunch of Stocks, and You've Got a Portfolio!

A *portfolio* is any group of investments that you own, or the total of all your investments. You can divide up your holdings into portfolios in whatever way makes sense to you; maybe by thinking of your retirement plan as one portfolio, your college savings investments as another, and your regular brokerage account as your third. Or, you could lump them all together and just call it "My Portfolio."

Investment Clubs Work!

In the U.S. in 1997, 45 percent of investment clubs surveyed by NAIC outperformed the Standard & Poor's 500 Index. In comparison, only 10 percent of all mutual funds beat the S&P's 500 in the same year.

Source: National Association of Investors Corporation

must fund (such as RRSP accounts). And with each passing generation, memories of the Great Depression are fainter, lingering mostly in the history books.

All those changes add up to a nation of investors who are afraid of never being able to retire, yet aren't afraid of the markets. Individuals are taking control of their financial destinies—by turning to the stock market.

Boy, how times have certainly changed. With the changing attitudes of Canadians, a whole new industry devoted to those individual investors has arrived. Today you can turn on the television and tune in to any number of channels devoted to the financial markets. Thousands and thousands of Web sites are devoted to financial topics. New financial newspapers, magazines, and newsletters seem to appear every week, and subscriptions are soaring. And let's not forget books that aim to help beginners get their feet wet in the stock market (like, for instance, this one).

Unfortunately, too many people are still labouring under the misconception that investing is a complicated subject. Although there are plenty of tricky concepts in the world of corporate finance, the basics of investing can be easily understood by just about anyone with a seventh grade education.

Maybe you don't even need a seventh grade education, either. In his book, *Beating the Street*, Peter Lynch immortalized the seventh grade class at St. Agnes School in a Boston suburb and their teacher, Joan Morrissey. As part of their social studies class, the students managed a hypothetical $250,000 portfolio. Although the portfolios were hypothetical, the returns were terrific. From 1990 to 1991, the student portfolios returned 69.6 percent, trouncing the 26.1 percent return of Standard & Poor's 500 (S&P's 500).

You can take a moment now to recall what you were doing when you were in seventh grade. Pretty depressing in contrast to the story of Ms. Morrissey's class, huh? But don't worry, even if you weren't lucky enough to learn about investing when you were in junior high school, there's still hope. Just keep reading.

Sometimes people confuse investing with other, more difficult subjects. Take economics (please!). Economics is hard. There's a story about a college graduate who took the opportunity of his twenty-fifth class reunion to visit his economics professor. While the two were pleasantly recounting old times, the former student noticed a test on the professor's desk and, leafing through it, remarked, "I see you're still using the same test you gave us twenty-five years ago."

"Ahhhh," the economist replied, "the test is the same, but the answers are completely different."

Yes, economics can be a difficult subject to learn. But investing can be mastered by anyone who is willing to spend some time learning how the stock market works.

It comes down to this: Investing isn't rocket science. You can invest successfully. After you believe this, you will be on your way to building a profitable portfolio.

Understanding the Stock Market

When people talk about investing, they usually mean the stock market. You probably can name several stocks without much difficulty: Nortel, IBM, BCE, Coca-Cola, and Chrysler. These are all publicly traded companies, corporations that have issued stock that investors can buy and sell in the open market.

A stock is nothing more than a share of ownership in one of these public companies. So how does the stock market work, and how do investors buy and sell these shares? These are a couple of the questions that you will need answered before you start investing.

Why Do Companies Go Public?

When a company sells shares of stock to investors through a stock market (a process known as *going public*), they're no longer privately owned, and become what's known as a *publicly traded company*. So why does a company go public? To answer that question, consider the following: Let's say that you are the manager of a department store, and one day you decide to go into business for yourself and open your own store. It takes money to start such a business, to acquire or lease or rent a building, to stock inventory for your shelves, to hire personnel, to advertise your new business, and to pay the myriad other costs involved with the operation of your business.

Where do you get the money to pay all those expenses? You have a couple of options:

➤ You could use your own savings.

➤ You could borrow from the bank, friends, or family and pay back the loan with interest.

You Can Find Many Public Companies on the Web

More than 5,000 publicly traded companies have sites on the Web. These companies typically publish information about their products and services, and many offer specific information for investors.

➤ You could sell a stake in the business to a partner who would run the business with you, sharing in any profits (as well as any losses).

These are all sources of capital, and are essentially the same ways that corporations such as McDonald's, Exxon, Nortel, and Bombardier get their hands on money for their operations, but on a much bigger level.

You can get your new business up and running with your own savings and a little from the bank. Business is good, and your new store is popular. In a few years, you can build and operate a few more stores until finally you are sitting on a little retail empire. It's clear you're on to a big new concept in retailing. Now, you're ready to take your chain to a national level. As you look at the costs of building hundreds of stores across the country, however, you are amazed at how much more capital you need.

Although you could go back to the bank and ask for a big, fat loan, you see a couple of problems with that plan. First, banks want a solid business plan; then they want some kind of repayment guarantee and collateral. That is a lot of leverage for a bank, giving them the ability to foreclose on your loan if you fall behind on payments.

Companies Like to Get Their Hands on Other People's Money

Going to the trough is the term sometimes used to describe what companies do when they look for outside financing, whether from venture capital sources or in a public offering.

A few bad months, and the bank could be knocking on your door with a foreclosure notice. Banks also charge interest—that's how they make their money, after all—but those interest payments could have a serious drain on your cash flow in the crucial expansion stage of your business.

So what do you do? The next step is to turn to people outside your company and ask them to invest in your business. In return for their investment, you will give them a piece of your company. If the company were profitable, they would be eligible to share in those profits with you. They would also have some say in the operation of your business.

When it comes time to look for outside investors, you could turn to the private firms and individuals that specialize in helping businesses to grow. These investors provide what's known as *venture capital*, and will put up millions of dollars in return for a stake in the company.

You could also go public. You will offer shares of your company for sale to the general public, in the form of stock that trades on a stock exchange. This sale of stock is your *initial public offering*, and the proceeds from the sale go into your company's bank account (after you pay the investment bankers who helped manage the offering).

Your new shareholders each own a piece of your business, and can elect a board of directors to oversee the management of your business. (Of course, you will probably maintain a majority stake in your business and have some pull in the nomination and election of the board's directors and officers.)

By going public, not only have you raised money for your company, you've also raised money for your own wallet! Because you were the owner of the business, the shares that were sold to investors belonged to you.

A Stock Is Born

An *initial public offering* (also known as an IPO) is the first issue of stock to the general public.

By the way, the preceding story is essentially the tale of how a pickup truck small business owner in Arkansas named Sam Walton turned a small chain of stores into one of the biggest companies in America—Wal-Mart Stores—with sales of $119 billion in 1997. Wal-Mart was added to the Dow Jones Industrial Average in 1997, representative of its ascendance to the pinnacle of American business.

Inside a Stock Exchange

If you'd like to buy a share of stock in BCE—or any publicly traded company—you will most likely need the services of a brokerage firm. Although it's possible to buy and sell shares of stock on your own, this approach risks some practical and legal problems. The securities industry is highly regulated, so you can't just hang a shingle and start selling stocks to the general public unless you're properly registered and licensed.

When you want to buy groceries, you go to a grocery store. When you want to buy a sofa, you go to a furniture store. And when you want to buy stocks, you need to do business with a brokerage firm.

A *brokerage firm* is a dealer of stocks and other securities that acts as your agent when you want to buy or sell stocks. (You will learn more about brokers in chapter 14.)

Most trading of stocks happens on a stock exchange. These are special markets where buyers and sellers are brought together to buy and sell stocks. There are four main stock exchanges in Canada. They are the Toronto Stock Exchange, the Montreal Stock Exchange, the Vancouver Stock Exchange, and the Alberta Stock Exchange.

What's a Security?

A *security* is anything that represents ownership in a company (such as a stock), a debt that is owed (such as a bond), or a right of ownership (such as an option).

When most people think of a stock exchange, they picture a scene of frantic activity, with traders in funny-looking jackets simultaneously jostling for position, shouting commands, making strange hand signals, and writing up orders.

Behind this frenzied spectacle, however, is a methodical and organized system of trading in which the price of any stock is set purely by rule of supply and demand in an auction setting. Specialists help match buyers and sellers, but shares are always sold to the highest bidder.

How a Trade Is Made

From the perspective of an investor, buying and selling stocks seems pretty simple. If you use a full-service broker, just call her up on the phone and place an order for one hundred shares of Nortel. Within a few minutes, you will receive a confirmation that your order has been completed, and you will be the proud new owner of Nortel's stock.

Behind the scenes, however, a lot of action takes place between your order and the confirmation. Here's what has to happen before you actually become the owner of Nortel stock:

1. You place the order with your broker to buy one hundred shares of Nortel.
2. The broker sends the order to the firm's order department.
3. The order department sends the order to the firm's clerk who works on the floor of the exchange where shares of Nortel are traded (the Toronto Stock Exchange).
4. The clerk gives the order to the firm's floor trader, who also works on the exchange floor.
5. The floor trader goes to the specialist's post for Nortel and finds another floor trader who is willing to sell shares of Nortel.
6. The traders agree on a price.
7. The order is executed.
8. The floor trader reports the trade to the clerk and the order department.
9. The order department confirms the order with the broker.
10. The broker confirms the trade with you.

That's how a traditional stock exchange works, but much of the action that takes place when you buy or sell a stock is being handled with the assistance of computers. Even if you bought a stock that trades on a stock exchange, it's possible that your order could be executed with little or no intervention by humans. You can log on to a brokerage firm's Web site, enter an order, have the trade executed, and receive a confirmation, all within sixty seconds or less!

A Tour of Stock Exchanges on the Web

There are stock exchanges all over the world and across Canada and the U.S., from Boston to Vancouver to Montreal to California. Most offer tours to groups of visitors, and these can be educational and entertaining events.

But it's also possible to visit stock exchanges without leaving your desk. Many exchanges produce full-featured sites on the Web, providing a glimpse into the workings of the financial markets.

The Toronto Stock Exchange (http://www.tse.com) is Canada's biggest stock exchange. Its Web site is loaded with information and tools, as well as the all-important fifteen-minute delayed ticker of any stock on the TSE. You simply enter the ticker symbol of the stock you want quoted and it produces a time-sensitive quote.

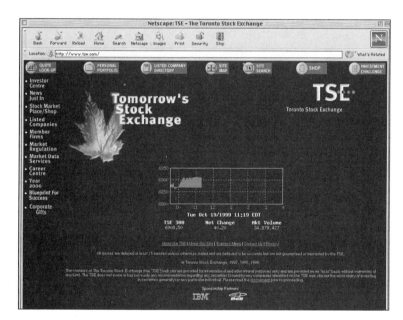

You can get a glimpse of the financial markets at the Toronto Stock Exchange Web site.

The ABCs of Ticker Symbols

Ticker symbols of stocks on most exchanges have three letters or less. Single-ticker symbols are the most prized, but the New York Stock Exchange is holding two such symbols, I and T, in the hope that it can someday lure from NASDAQ two big companies to list on its exchange. The companies? Tech giants Intel and Microsoft!

The Montreal (www.me.org), Vancouver (www.vse.ca), and Alberta (www.ase.ca) exchanges all have their own informative Web sites as well. It's a good idea to visit a given stock exchange site (especially the smaller exchanges) before you invest with a company that is listed there, so that you can get an idea of what standards and regulations are followed on the exchange.

In the U.S., the New York Stock Exchange (http://www.nyse.com) is known as the Big Board because it's the preeminent stock exchange in the world. Its Web site provides plenty of information about the exchange and the stocks listed on it.

Start your exploration of the NYSE site by selecting the Education link and reviewing the online publication "You and the Investment World." In seven chapters, the tutorial describes how companies raise capital in the stock market, how the market works, and why stocks go up and down.

Another type of exchange is the NASDAQ. NASDAQ is the abbreviation for the tongue-twisting phrase "National Association of Securities Dealers Automated Quotations." NASDAQ is not a stock exchange, however. It's a completely electronic market. Known from its advertising campaign as "the stock market for the next generation," trading on NASDAQ is done by computers over a vast network that connects brokers and investment banks.

The NASDAQ system connects "market makers" of NASDAQ stocks. Market makers are brokerage firms that agree to maintain an inventory of shares of stock in a particular company. They are always willing to buy, as well as sell, shares in the company for which they "make a market."

Before You Tune In on the Web, You Need to Install a Video Player

Many sites offer video broadcasts of news or market reports on the Web. Many use a technique called streaming video, which enables you to view the video at the same time it is delivered to your computer (instead of requiring you to download the entire file first and then watch it). To take a peek at these video feeds, you need to have a video player installed in your browser. The most common programs are RealVideo, VivoActive, Videogram, VDOLive, Vxtreme, or Microsoft Media Player. When you encounter a site that requires a viewer that isn't installed on your machine, you will be provided with a link to the appropriate software. Just install it and tune in!

Companies are willing to be market makers because they earn a markup on every share they sell from its inventory. They sell shares at a higher price than other investors are willing to pay for that company, and buy shares at a lower price than other investors are willing to sell their shares. A market maker could buy one hundred shares of stock from an investor for $10, and immediately sell those hundred shares to you for $10-1/8. The broker keeps the difference; one-eighth of a dollar in this case, for his services. Although it might not sound like a lot of money, market makers handle thousands and thousands of trades a day, and all those little fees add up to lots! The NASDAQ Web site (http://www.NASDAQ.com) can tell you more about how its market works. Click About NASDAQ to learn more about the organization, and how trades are made in the NASDAQ market. Be sure to visit the NASDAQ Facts section here for its Ask the Economist feature, which answers common questions about the NASDAQ market. NASDAQ's Investor Resources includes tips and lessons about investing, and the Reference area offers links to other stock markets and investing sites. When you're learning about a new subject for the first time, there's nothing like actually doing it to really teach you what you need to know. Investing in the stock market is no different. To do that, however, you need a bundle of money, right? Wrong! A number of Web sites feature market simulators that can help you to understand how stock markets work.

These sites are not only educational, they can be fun to play, too! And you won't necessarily practise trading with stocks, either. Some sites allow users to buy and sell shares of celebrities, politicians, and sports stars!

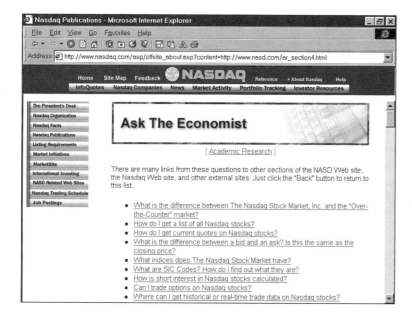

The NASDAQ Web site can answer many of your questions about how its stock market works.

One of the most popular and educational stock market simulations on the Web has nothing to do with the stock market at all! Do you think Leonardo DiCaprio's star is rising? On the Hollywood Stock Exchange (http://www.hsx.com), you can "buy" shares of hot stars like DiCaprio, while you "sell" the bonds of that just-cancelled television sitcom or movie bomb.

On the Hollywood Stock Exchange, you can try your hand at "investing" in your favourite movies and stars.

This simulated marketplace is based on the entertainment industry, and it's surprising how similar Hollywood and Wall Street can be—this year's hot actor might be tomorrow's has-been (the same thing that happens to stocks sometimes). After you register on the site, you will have $2,000,000 in play money to begin buying and selling your favourite movies and actors.

In no time at all, you will begin to get the hang of how the laws of supply and demand work (just like in the stock market). If you would prefer a more serious approach to learning about the stock market, try MarketPlayer (http://www.marketplayer.com). Each month, MarketPlayer hosts the HedgeHog Competition, a free contest that lets you build a portfolio of stocks and begin to understand how the market works.

When you arrive at the MarketPlayer Web site for the first time, click the Register Free button to open your account. You then receive $1,000,000 in "cash" to begin buying and selling stocks. But that's not all: Besides providing the capability to build a portfolio and test your skill, MarketPlayer has a host of tools for searching and studying stocks.

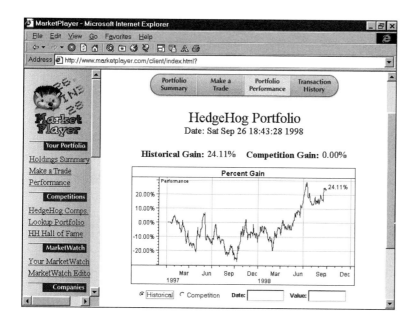

MarketPlayer allows you to build a stock portfolio, and then will provide a graph of the performance of your picks over time.

The Least You Need to Know

➤ Companies sell shares of stock to investors to raise capital to expand their businesses.

➤ The stocks of public companies trade on organized markets or exchanges. The major Canadian stock exchange for senior equities is the Toronto Stock Exchange. At the time of writing, most junior equity trading will be concentrated on the Canadian Venture Exchange. Each exchange has a Web site where you can learn more about how they operate.

➤ You can learn more about stock markets and how they work by trying your hand at a market-simulation Web site. These sites allow you to buy and sell shares in a fake portfolio, and track your performance. They teach you how the laws of supply and demand can affect the price of a stock.

Chapter 5

Principles of Investing for the Mathematically Challenged

In This Chapter

➤ Understand how risk and return go hand in hand

➤ Learn the importance of diversification and asset allocation

➤ Hear what the academic world has to say about investing

Does the mere mention of algebra bring painful memories to mind? Or did you have a bad run-in with calculus in high school or college? If so, you will be happy to know that even if you were never a math whiz in school, you can still be a successful independent investor. You need to master (or at least understand) just a few simple principles before you set foot on the investing trail. Being "mathematically challenged" is no obstacle!

The Riddle of Risk and Return

Sure, you would like to make a fortune in the markets—who wouldn't? The first thing you need to understand, before you commit even a dollar to a portfolio or begin surfing investment Web sites is that it is impossible to realize a return on any investment without facing some amount of risk.

No matter what you decide to do with your savings and investments, your money will always face some risk. You could stash your dollars under your mattress or in a cookie jar, but then you would face the risk of losing it all if your house burned down. You could keep your money in the bank, but the buying power of your dollars

You'd Better Understand Beta

One measure of investing risk is known by professionals as the *beta coefficient*, often referred to as simply *beta*. The beta of a stock or mutual fund is determined by comparing its returns to the overall market (usually that means the TSE 300 Index). Sound complicated? All it means is that a security with a beta of 1.0 rises and falls in perfect sync with the market. A security with a beta of greater than 1.0 will be more volatile than the market in general; a security with a beta below 1.0 is less volatile than the market. Is a higher beta better? Not necessarily, because it all depends on how much risk you can take—and beta gives you a way to measure that risk.

would barely keep up with inflation over the years, leaving you with little more dollars in real terms than when you started. So, you must face the fact that increased return from your investment portfolio comes from taking an increased amount of risk. And, although risk in your portfolio may be unavoidable, it is manageable. The riddle of controlling risk and return is that you need to maximize the returns and minimize the risk. When you do, you ensure that you will make enough on your investments, while facing an acceptable amount of risk.

So what constitutes acceptable risk? It's different for every person. A good rule of thumb followed by many investors is that you shouldn't wake up in the middle of the night worrying about your portfolio. If your investments are causing you too much anxiety, it's time to reconsider how you're investing, and bail out of those securities that are giving you insomnia in favour of some investments that are a little more calming. When you find your own comfort zone, you will know your personal *risk tolerance*—the amount of risk you are willing to take on to achieve your financial goals.

What's an Asset Class?

An *asset class* is a broad category of securities, such as stocks, bonds, or cash. These are often broken down into more specific categories, such as large-cap stocks and small-cap stocks, or corporate bonds and government bonds.

Every type of security carries a different amount of risk. In the following illustration, you can see how some different asset classes stack up against each other as far as risk is concerned.

When it comes to your long-term financial future, however, the biggest risk of all may be just to do nothing. If you *don't* invest for retirement, or for the post-secondary education of your children, or to help meet your personal financial goals, you are most likely guaranteed a future of just scraping by.

RISK PYRAMID

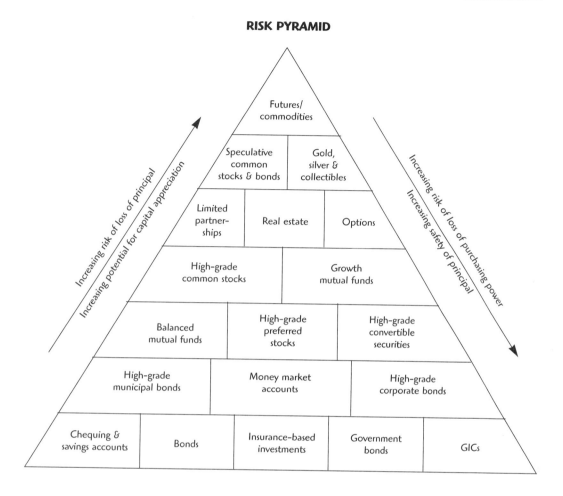

Not Putting All Your Eggs in One Basket (a.k.a. Diversification)

Before you commit to burying Mason jars of cash in the backyard, read on to learn some strategies you can use to manage risk in your portfolio. The first rule is a trite saying, but it's true. The advice "don't put all your eggs in one basket" is sound. The image of a basketful of eggs cracking in unison all over your kitchen floor is pretty vivid. The message for investors in this advice is that risk can be managed by diversifying your portfolio.

Diversification means building a portfolio that includes securities from different asset classes. Because bonds tend to do well when stocks don't, you could construct a portfolio that includes a certain percentage of stocks and bonds. When bonds are doing

Over-Diversification Can Cause Problems, Too

Make sure that your portfolio isn't over-diversified. Research shows that the benefits of diversification can be lost if your portfolio has too many holdings. The returns of your portfolio are likely to slide toward the average of the overall market, while your risk level remains the same.

What Is Noncorrelation?

Noncorrelation is a fancy way of saying that different types of securities, or stock markets in different countries, tend to move in different directions at the same time.

well, that part of your portfolio would do well. When stocks do well, the other part of your holdings would do well.

Another way to diversify is to buy securities in the same asset class but choose those that are affected by different variables. Entertainment companies, utilities, grocery stores, and airlines, for example, are completely different businesses. Depending on the country's economy, one or more of these industries might perform better than the other industries. If you built a portfolio that included securities from a number of sectors, chances are that one or more would always be doing better than average.

When you diversify, you try to ensure that at any given time, the value of some of your holdings might be down, and some might be up, but overall your portfolio is doing fine. The trick is to find securities that don't have tendencies to increase or decrease in price at the same time.

The trade-off for the balancing of risk and return in a diversified portfolio is that your overall return might be somewhat lower than you could get in an undiversified portfolio. Along the way, however, a diversified portfolio will have less volatility and steadier returns.

Allocating Your Assets

Asset allocation is the primary tool in the battle to build a diversified portfolio. This is the task of figuring out how much of your portfolio will be invested in different asset classes such as stocks, bonds, or cash.

Asset allocation has been recognized as a very important part of the process of building a portfolio. In fact, one study has found that your decision on how you will divide up your portfolio into several classes is more important than the process of choosing the actual stocks, bonds, and funds that you will own!

In developing your asset allocation strategy, you should remember that, generally, the younger you are, the more risk you can afford to take. As you get older and closer to retirement, you will probably be less interested in growth and more interested in the *capital preservation* of your portfolio—protecting it from any declines. One rule of thumb that many experts use is to subtract your age from one hundred to determine the

What's the Difference Between "Tactical" and "Strategic" Asset Allocation?

Tactical asset allocation is an attempt to shift the assets in your portfolio based on a prediction of where the market is headed in the short term, such as moving into bonds when you think a bear market is coming. This usually doesn't work. On the other hand, *strategic asset allocation* is a long-term approach to investing where you create a plan for the asset allocation of your portfolio, and rarely make changes to the percentages you initially established.

percentage of investments to invest in stocks. If you're 45, you might put together a portfolio that's 55 percent stocks and 45 percent bonds and cash.

Most full-service advisory firms maintain a suggested asset allocation for their customers. The firm's chief investment strategist determines the optimal percentage of a typical portfolio that should be invested in particular asset classes at any time, and then updates the asset allocation strategy on a regular basis. When it comes time to design your portfolio, resources on the Web can help you figure out the best asset allocation plan for you. You will learn more about these in chapter 17.

You Can't Completely Eliminate Risk

Even if you use the principles of modern portfolio theory to build a portfolio, you can't entirely eliminate risk from your portfolio. You can, however, manage to reduce the risk to an acceptable level—all any of us can hope to do!

Making the Most of a Buck— with Dollar Cost Averaging

The funny thing about investing is that, too often, investors react to the stock market quite differently than they react to other money decisions. If you went to the grocery store and found that some essential item was on sale for a terrific price, you wouldn't hesitate to stock up. But when you log on to your portfolio and see a good stock fall in price, you're likely to hesitate, or even sell your holdings—the complete opposite of how you would react to a sale in a grocery store!

Dollar cost averaging is the antidote to emotional investing. This method of investing involves two steps. First, select a good quality stock or mutual fund. Second, make a commitment to invest the same amount of money each month to purchase shares in that fund, say $50 or $100 a month. Now, whenever the price is low, your set investment will buy a lot of shares. When the price is high, that same amount will buy fewer shares. It may sound too easy, but the end result of regular investing in this fashion is that you're likely to end up with a greater number of shares at a lower average cost per share than if you had invested the same amount of your money all at once.

In fact, you may come out way ahead if you use dollar cost averaging. In 1998, *Money Magazine* commissioned Value Line to do a study of how investors would have fared if they had invested $100 a month in domestic stock mutual funds over the past five and ten years. The results? Investors would have received an average annual return of 25.7 percent over five years and 23.7 percent over ten years if they invested each month—compared to average annual returns of 17.4 percent and 13.3 percent for a lump sum invested in the same funds at the beginning of the periods. That's a big difference!

The Institute for Systematic Investing Research (ISIR) is a private, independent, not-for-profit research organization devoted entirely to research about dollar cost averaging. Its Web site (http://www.isir.com) is filled with educational articles, applications, and research about the topic. If you want to really dig in, or see some examples of how dollar cost averaging works in specific mutual funds, drop by this site.

The final word on dollar cost averaging is that it commits you to investing regularly, and not trying to guess the market's future direction. Sure, it's boring! But it works, and that's what's most important to remember.

What Is Standard Deviation?

In the context of investing, *standard deviation* is a term that's used to describe the level of risk that comes with investing in a particular security, usually a bond or mutual fund. To figure an investment's standard deviation, first you need to calculate the average returns of a security over a long period. Then you compare the actual returns during a short period to the long-term average, and measure the difference. In the past two years, for example, bond A has returned 15 percent in the first year and then 5 percent in the second year. Its average annual return is 10 percent. But bond B has returned 9 percent and then 11 percent in the same two years, and its average annual return is also 10 percent. Obviously, investors who invested in either bond in either the first year or the second year would see very different results in their portfolios! Bond A appears to be much more volatile in these two years than bond B; and bond A has a higher standard deviation than bond B. The higher the standard deviation of a particular security's returns, the greater the risk that comes with investing in that security.

It's Hip, It's Now, It's Mod: Modern Portfolio Theory

You can divide the history of investing into two periods: before and after 1952. That was the year that an economics student at the University of Chicago named Harry Markowitz published his doctoral thesis. His work was the beginning of what is now known as modern portfolio theory.

How important was Markowitz's paper? Well, he received a Nobel prize in economics in 1990 as a result of his research and its long-lasting effect on how investors approach investing today. In fact, the principles of asset allocation and diversification outlined in this chapter really derive from Markowitz's work.

So here's the crux of modern portfolio theory, and why it's important to you. Markowitz starts out with the assumption that all investors would like to avoid risk whenever possible. He defines risk as a standard deviation of expected returns (see the previous sidebar for more about standard deviation).

Rather than look at risk on an individual security level, Markowitz proposes that you measure the risk of an entire portfolio. When considering a security for your portfolio, don't base your decision on the amount of risk that it carries. Instead, consider how that security contributes to the overall risk of your portfolio.

Markowitz then considers how all the investments in a portfolio can be expected to move together in price under the same circumstances. This is called correlation, and it measures how much you can expect different securities or asset classes to change in price relative to each other.

High fuel prices might be good for oil companies, for example, but bad for airlines who need to buy the fuel. As a result, you might expect that the stocks of companies in these two industries would often move in opposite directions. These two industries have a negative (or low) correlation. You will get better diversification in your portfolio if you own one airline and one oil company rather than owning just two oil companies.

When you put all this together, it's entirely possible to build a portfolio that has a much higher average return than the level of risk it contains. When you build a diversified portfolio and spread out your investments by asset class, you're really just managing risk and return.

The Least You Need to Know

➤ You can't avoid risk in your portfolio if you want to earn a respectable return. You can balance risk and return, however, with some simple strategies.

➤ Diversifying the assets in your portfolio can help steady your overall return, and smooth out the bumps as you reach your goal. Diversification can cushion the inevitable bottoms.

➤ Dollar cost averaging can help increase your returns. By investing a regular amount of money according to a set schedule, you can smooth out the bumps in your portfolio holdings.

Chapter 6

Learning More About Investing

In This Chapter

➤ Investor organizations and educational Web sites you should know about

➤ News organizations can be a valuable storehouse of unbiased information you won't get anywhere else

➤ An investment club can be a great learning experience

It's easy to be overwhelmed by the sheer volume of financial sites you'll encounter on the Web. And it's not just the number. At some corporate sites, the message track seems to be relentless: "Buy our product and all your problems will be solved." And that's not too surprising. Is a mutual fund company going to tell you about cheaper alternatives to its products? Is an investment dealer going to show you how to buy stocks without a broker? You get the point. That's not to say those sites have nothing to offer. In fact, you'll see some particularly useful ones highlighted in this book (if they have a great retirement planning calculator, for instance). But deep down, corporate sites are designed to *sell*. They may help investors...even inform them...but always on the company's terms.

Investing Rules to Live By

The National Association of Investors Corporation has four basic principles for investing. Many investment clubs and individual investors share similar philosophies. The NAIC principles are:

1. Invest regular sums of money once a month in common stock.

2. Reinvest all earnings, dividends, and capital gains. Your money grows faster.

3. Buy growth stocks—companies whose sales and earnings are increasing at a rate faster than the industry in general. They should also have good prospects for long-term, continued growth.

4. Invest in different industries. Diversification helps spread both risk and opportunity.

Source: NAIC

Fortunately, there are many sites out there that put the average retail investor first—with no strings attached. Several organizations focus on helping individuals learn about investing, and some have been built with the sole aim of educating investors. With their focus on "newbies," these sites are worth visiting—and revisiting—as you expand your own understanding of investing.

Investor-Friendly Educational Web Sites

If you need help learning to manage your new portfolio, don't worry—you won't need to go back to school to get a degree in finance. But you will need to spend some time on your investment education. Fortunately, a number of organizations are devoted to just that. These groups also have Web sites that you can explore to help you learn much more.

One of the best sites around for independent investment information belongs to the Investor Learning Centre (http://www.investorlearning.ca). This not-for-profit organization provides a wealth of user-friendly detail on just about any aspect of investing you could think of. Its online Investments 101 course features useful primers on stocks, bonds, the capital markets, the market system, and investor protection. Wondering what your rights are as a shareholder? This is the place to find out. And once you've mastered the course, you can test your Investment IQ. The ILC has also commissioned some of the most respected financial writers in the business (Gail Vaz-Oxlade, Bruce Cohen, Hugh Anderson, Glorianne Stromberg) to tackle timely investing issues. And there's an online archive of recommended financial books that can be ordered directly from the ILC.

For information from the regulatory side, many of the country's provincial securities commissions have Web sites. Most provide the standard FAQs, structural detail, and information about investor protection, but some go a step further. For instance, the B.C. Securities Commission's site (http://www.bcsc.bc.ca) was the first to post insider trading data on companies trading in Vancouver. Look for it in the Weekly Summary section.

The Ontario Securities Commission site includes the Investor Information Kit put out by the Canadian Securities Administrators (http://www.osc.gov.on.ca/en/Investor/Csa/csa_info.html).

For Those Who Really Want to Learn More About Investing

The Investor Learning Centre offers seminars in almost one hundred Canadian towns and cities. Free extracts from Intelligent Investing: Part 1, and Intelligent Investing: Part 2, are available on the ILC's Web site.

The Financial Pipeline (http://www.finpipe.com) is another good source of impartial investment information. It's sponsored by a number of corporate organizations, but you won't find any hard sell here. Look for extensive sections dealing with stocks, mutual funds, bonds, derivatives, consumer finance, and investment strategies.

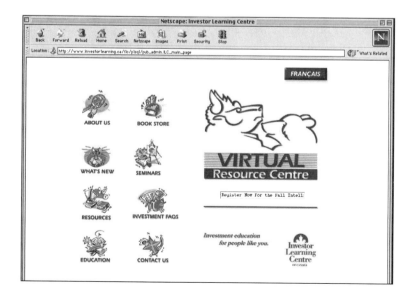

The Investor Learning Centre's Web site is an authoritative, yet down-to-earth source of independent investment information.

The Toronto Stock Exchange's Investor Centre can answer all kinds of market-related questions.

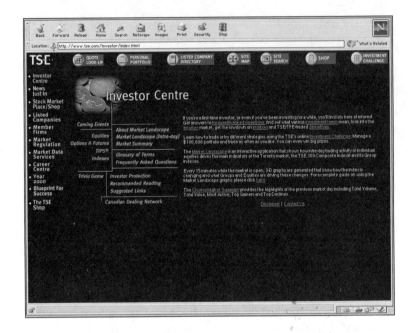

The Financial Supersites

The financial "supersites" try to be an investor's first and last stop for all their investment needs. Need a quote? They'll have it. Need company research? No problem. Need basic information about how something works? They can help there too.

I1money (http://www.imoney.com) has all the bells and whistles you'd expect from a site that bills itself as "Canada's Personal Finance Web Site." For the purposes of this chapter, though, it's the i1money Library that will catch your attention. This is a rich collection of primers on everything from investment basics to RRSPs. A definite stop on your learning tour.

Another financial supersite in Canada belongs to Quicken.ca (http://www.quicken.ca). Here, you'll find a useful archive of paragraph-long explanations on dozens of topics (Quicken.ca Advisor). There's also a Financial Focus feature that explains everything from index funds to universal life insurance in easy-to-follow language. And the Learning Centre has a Ten-Step Guide to Better Investing that's a must read for anyone starting out.

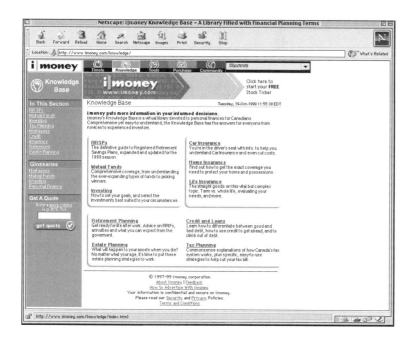

I\money is one of the main financial supersites with a great cache of information for investors.

The Media Sites

If there's a bigger growth industry in Canada than media that specializes in catering to investors—magazines, TV shows, news Web sites—we haven't found it yet. News organizations have heard from their readers and viewers that the world of investing is getting so complicated that they need impartial guides to help them navigate the waters. Many of the media sites mentioned here feature quote servers, portfolio trackers, or handy links to other sites. But it's the value-added features that are of interest to information-hungry investors, and often available nowhere else.

IE:Money (http://www.iemoney.com) calls itself "Canada's Personal Finance Magazine." And it posts a surprising amount of content on its Web site (even from the issue that's currently on the newsstands). The writing is timely, accurate, and entertaining. Even veteran investors will learn something.

MoneySense magazine (http://www.moneysense.ca) is Maclean Hunter Publishing's foray into the world of personal finance. *MoneySense* lets its online visitors in on some of the magazine's content, and the first few issues showed that it will give *IE:Money* a good run for, well, its money. The writing is sharp and accessible. *MoneySense* has also forged an alliance with Quicken.ca, so you can easily link to their online offerings too.

CBC News Online (http://cbc.ca) is the home of the CBC's online window on the world. Click on Business and then Personal Finance and you'll be able to see some of the country's best-known names in personal finance talking to you! Video clips on a variety of investment topics from mortgages to stocks and bonds can be downloaded in either

RealVideo or Quick Time so you can replay them on your own computer. You'll also be able to hear Gordon Pape's weekly CBC Radio commentaries. And you can link to the sites of such CBC programs as *Venture, Newsworld Business News*, and *The Money Show*.

GlobeInvestor.com (http://www.globeinvestor.com) allows people free access to a powerful search engine that can delve deep into *The Globe and Mail's* vast database of business and personal finance stories.

Canoe Money (http://www.canoe.ca/money) has got the depth of the *Financial Post's* columnists going for it. And here, you can access many of their columns that run the gamut of personal finance and investing issues.

Canadian MoneySaver magazine (http://www.canadianmoneysaver.ca) has posted a vast amount of material on its site for average investors. The do-it-yourselfers will be in Web heaven. Everything you'd want to learn about dividend reinvestment plans (see chapter 15), investment clubs (later in this chapter), and dozens of other topics can be found here.

Other Useful Sites

The YourMoney Network (http://www.yourmoney.cba.ca) is the work of such diverse groups as the Canadian Bankers Association, the Toronto Stock Exchange, the Bank of Canada, the Ontario Securities Commission, and the Investment Funds Institute of Canada (whew!). Its mission is to answer young people's financial questions that trouble their parents too—things like how to budget, use credit, make your money work for you, and get a good job. There are some good links too.

Want to know which of your financial accounts are covered by deposit insurance? For instance, did you know that mutual funds aren't covered at all? Or that GICs with terms over five years aren't insured either? The site of the Canada Deposit Insurance Corporation (http://www.cdic.ca) provides all the answers, along with an online calculator for you to figure out your coverage.

Want to know how the Bank of Canada works? The central bank has a good site that tells all (http://www.bank-banque-canada.ca). And while you're learning, you just might get a windfall. This site has a free search feature that lets you find out if you have any long-forgotten bank accounts. Click on Unclaimed Bank Accounts and start looking. There are more than 770,000 lost accounts with $132 million just waiting to be claimed. Talk about investor education paying off!

For a different slant on stocks (and no small amount of irreverence), you can visit the U.S. site operated by The Motley Fool (http://www.fool.com). The Fool's motto is "To Educate, Amuse, and Enrich," and its Web site is filled with ample selections of each. At the core of the Fool's philosophy is the premise that it's quite possible for individual investors to do better in the markets than the experts of Wall Street. Because the

The Fool's School on the Motley Fool site can teach you the basic principles of "foolish" investing.

so-called wise men of the financial world are so often wrong with their predictions and analyses, it's far better not to follow in their footsteps, and to be a "fool" instead! In the Motley Fool's world, there's no higher compliment than to be called "foolish."

Mutual Funds

If mutual funds are more your style, the Investment Funds Institute of Canada (http://www.ific.ca) is a good place to start. This is the association that represents the fund industry. Its Investor Education sections feature good fact sheets, information brochures, and investor checklists. Globefund (http://www.globefund.com) is *The Globe and Mail*'s entry into the mutual fund Web universe. Besides quotes and portfolio tracking, you can search the *Globe*'s database on fund articles, and read the articles from its monthly Report on Mutual Funds.

The Fundlibrary site (http://www.fundlibrary.com) has more than 10,000 pages of text, and it's all about mutual funds. Its Learning Centre has dozens of articles on all things mutual, including pieces by such writers as Evelyn Jacks, David Tafler, and Sandra Foster. And if you missed Garth Turner's *Investment Television* show, or Paul Bates' radio program, *Canada's Money Show*, you can listen to past editions here.

The Investment Funds Institute of Canada site has a particularly useful Investor Education section for people with questions about mutual funds.

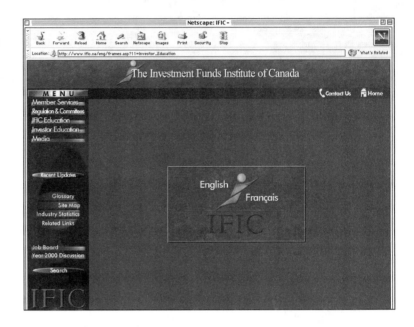

Investment Clubs

"There's strength in numbers," as the old saying goes, and that just might be the motto of thousands and thousands of investment clubs now in existence around the world. An investment club is a small group of individuals who pool their money and invest in a single portfolio. Most clubs are formed by groups of friends, neighbours, coworkers, church members, or relatives, who meet once a month and decide how the club will invest its money. Clubs have their own bank and/or brokerage accounts, and elect officers to run the meetings and handle the club's operations.

You don't need a lot of money to be a member of an investment club. Many clubs require their members to contribute just $20 to $50 a month. When you add up the contributions of a dozen or so members, however, you can see how clubs can quickly build up a sizable portfolio.

But the biggest advantage of investment clubs is that they provide a terrific educational opportunity for their members. Most successful clubs don't focus on "making a lot of money," but rather on contributing to the investment education of their members. Fortunately, these clubs usually find that profits will follow.

The First Canadian Investment Club

Canada's first investment club was formed in 1928, when a group of schoolteachers in Oshawa, Ontario formed the Old Canada Investment Company.

Source: Investors Association of Canada

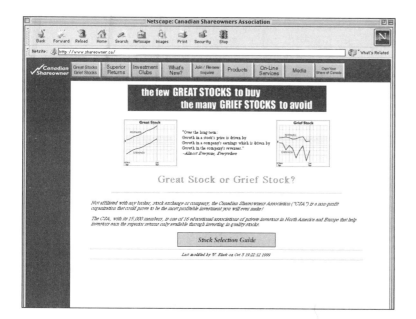

The Canadian Shareowners Association welcomes memberships from individuals and investment clubs.

In Canada, there are a couple of investor associations that can provide advice and guidance for prospective clubs and their members.

The biggest of these is the Canadian Shareowners Association (http://www.shareowner. ca). It's a non-profit group of more than 15,000 investors who are dedicated to learning about how to find quality stocks (or as the CSA puts it, how to separate "great stocks" from "grief stocks"). The benefits really come from membership. And at $89 a year, it's arguably one of the best investments you can make. For that, you get a subscription to its *Canadian Shareowner* magazine and the association's *Stock Selection Guide*. Membership also allows access to its Low-Cost Investing Program, which allows people to buy stocks without a broker, and pay fees that are a fraction of what a discount broker would charge (see chapter 15 for more on this whole issue.) The CSA offers a club starter kit for $79. That includes an investment club manual, an investors' basic training manual, a list of the sixty stocks and index funds that clubs can buy through the CSA's Low-Cost Investing Program, and a set of investment club forms.

The Investors Association of Canada (http://www.iac.ca) also offers an investment club kit. It costs $37 and includes partnership agreements, investment tracking forms, and sample minutes. Members and non-members of the IAC may buy it. Membership in the Investors Association of Canada costs $49 a year, and brings with it an online subscription to the *Money Digest*.

Staff of the Canadian Securities Institute have written a good guide to the world of investment clubs. *How to Start & Run an Investment Club for Fun & Learning* can be ordered online from the CSI's sister organization, the Investor Learning Centre (http://www.investorlearning.ca) for $25.95 plus tax.

You Can Communicate with Other Investors by Subscribing to a Mailing List

One of the popular methods of connecting people on the Internet is by means of a mailing list. A discussion mailing list is made up of a group of people who use e-mail to talk about a particular topic. The group could be two people or 2,000 people—it doesn't make a difference! To participate on a particular list, you just need to "subscribe."

In the United States, investment clubs are much more common and enjoy more support. The Web site of the U.S. National Association of Investors Corporation (http://www.better-investing.org) hosts a popular discussion mailing list, the I-Club-List, which is an ongoing and dynamic source of investor education. I-Club-List is short for Investment Club List, and it welcomes any investors who follow NAIC's approach to the market, regardless of whether they are club members.

As long as you have an e-mail account, you can subscribe to the list (for free) and join more than 2,500 other investors in discussions about growth stock investing. Each month, a moderator leads an online workshop: a study of a particular stock, an analysis of an industry, or a lesson on a related investing subject. Questions from beginners are welcome, which makes the I-Club-List a friendly online home for many investors. Just remember that some of what is discussed here will be of interest only to American investors (things like taxes and reporting requirements).

There is one cyberspace effort we know of where 300 Canadians gather from time to time. It's a well-moderated online forum, so it manages to avoid the kind of stock-hype atmosphere that invades so many online message boards. You can find it at http://clubs.yahoo.com/clubs/canadianstockclub.

Are You a Lurker?

If you read messages on message boards or mailing lists, but never send or post any messages of your own, you are a lurker! There's nothing wrong with being a lurker, but if all the people on a list or board were lurkers, it would be awfully quiet! An online community is only as strong as the interaction and participation of its members. Your thoughtful contributions (when appropriate) would only enhance the experience, both for you and for all other members of the community.

An Alternative to Investment Clubs

Several years ago, Dale Ennis, the publisher of *Canadian MoneySaver* magazine, started a new kind of investment club called a share club. These clubs get around the problem of having to keep complicated financial records. How? Well, in share clubs, people still meet once a month; they still listen to the research they've each done on a particular stock or sector; they just don't pool their money to invest together. They take the knowledge they get from each gathering and go home, where they invest on their own. There are now dozens of share clubs in Canada, and Dale's always looking for people to volunteer to start more. For a list of active ones still looking for members, you can link to http://www.canadianmoneysaver.ca/reg_shareclub.htm.

Good luck...and have fun!

The Least You Need to Know

➤ The Investor Learning Centre is an organization whose sole purpose is to help you learn more about investing. Its Web site includes plenty of information.

➤ You can also learn more about investing at a number of sites with investment education content that's often unique. You'll find tutorials, articles, audio and video clips, and message boards where you can add to your knowledge about stocks, bonds, mutual funds, and just about any other financial topic.

➤ Joining or forming an investment club is a great way to further your investment education. And it's fun.

Part 2

Investing in Mutual Funds

Okay, so you probably know that mutual funds are one type of investment, but do you know anything more about them? Wouldn't you want to? Mutual funds appear everywhere in the investment world and they make a lot of money for a lot of people, so it is time to learn all about these gems.

Chapter 7

The ABCs of Mutual Funds

In This Chapter

➤ Learn the ins and outs of mutual funds

➤ Understand how index funds work

➤ Find out how to get started with funds with just a small amount of money

---

What Mutual Funds Are (and What They're Not)

When individuals finally decide to start building an investment portfolio, they usually turn to mutual funds. After you have decided to invest in the stock market, you should consider mutual funds. Mutual funds are an easy way to own stocks without worrying about picking and choosing individual stocks. As an added bonus, you can find plenty of information on the Internet to help you learn about, study, select, and purchase funds.

What is a mutual fund? It sounds like an easy question to answer, and it's not so hard, really. A dictionary definition of a mutual fund might go something like this: a single portfolio of stocks, bonds, and/or cash managed by an investment company on behalf of many investors.

What Is an Investment Company?

Although the term *investment company* sounds official, it really refers to any bank or brokerage house that offers mutual funds for sale to the public. Some investment companies are firms whose sole business is to manage mutual funds. You might be surprised to learn that any individual or company could theoretically start a mutual fund and offer shares to the public—there is no particular expertise required. Fortunately, in the real world there are some pretty serious financial, legal, and logistical obstacles that make it a bit more complicated.

The investment company is responsible for the management of the fund, and it sells shares in the fund to individual investors. When you invest in a mutual fund, you become a part owner of a large investment portfolio, along with all the other shareholders of the fund.

Every day, the fund manager counts up the value of all the fund's holdings, figures out how many shares have been purchased by shareholders, and then calculates the *net asset value* (NAV) of the mutual fund, the price of a single share of the fund on that day. If you want to buy shares, you just send the manager your money, and new shares will be issued for you at the most recent price. This routine is repeated every day on a never-ending basis, which is why mutual funds are sometimes known as *open-end funds*.

If the fund manager is doing a good job, the NAV of the fund will usually get bigger. Your shares are worth more!

But exactly how does a mutual fund's NAV increase? Well, a mutual fund can make money in its portfolio in a couple of ways: the same ways that your own portfolio of stocks, bonds, and cash can make money!

A mutual fund can receive dividends from the stocks that it owns. *Dividends*, of course, are shares of corporate profits paid to the stockholders. The fund could also make money from bank interest, or on the interest payments that it receives from the bonds that it owns. Mutual funds are required to hand out (or distribute) this income to shareholders. Usually they do this twice a year, in a move that's called an *income distribution*.

Don't Be Alarmed If a Fund's NAV Goes Down Due to a Distribution

When a mutual fund makes a *distribution* to shareholders, the NAV of the fund is immediately reduced by the per-share amount of the distribution. It doesn't mean that your investment is worth less, because you would have received the difference in the price of the fund in cash!

Watch Out When You Buy Shares near the End of the Year

Mutual funds typically distribute capital gains to all shareholders at the end of the year. What happens, however, if you buy shares after the *record date* of the distribution (the day the fund determines all the owners of record of the fund) but before the *payable date* of the distribution (usually several days later)? You would not receive the distribution of gains and income, but the NAV of the fund would still be reduced, leaving you with a loss on your investment. If you buy shares at the end of June or December, you should make sure you don't hit the few days in between the record and payable dates of the fund's distribution.

At the end of the year, a fund makes another kind of distribution, this time from the profits they might make by selling stocks or bonds that have gone up in price. These profits are known as *capital gains*, and the act of passing them out is called a capital gains distribution.

These are all ways that a fund can share any profits from the sale of securities with all the fund's investors. Unfortunately, funds don't always make money—sometimes they lose money, too. These are *capital losses*. Everyone hates to have losses, and funds are no different. The good news is that these losses are subtracted from the fund's capital gains before the money is distributed to shareholders. If losses exceed gains, a fund manager can even pile up these losses and use them to offset future gains in the portfolio. That means that the fund won't pass out capital gains to shareholders until the fund has at least earned more in profits than it has lost (although you might want to reconsider your decision to remain invested in a fund that's losing money if the rest of the market is growing!).

Now that you understand the basics of mutual funds, it's time to dig in a bit deeper—particularly if you want to learn how to separate the winners from the losers!

All mutual funds share three basic characteristics:

➤ An investment objective

➤ An investment plan

➤ Professional management

A fund's investment objective is not merely to make money for shareholders (although that's certainly important). Each mutual fund has a specifically defined mission that tells you its overall approach to investing. A fund might have an objective to produce current income; another might strive to generate long-term growth. And some mix the two approaches.

Choosing the right one is important. If you were retired and were looking to supplement your company pension and Canada Pension Plan, it would be very important for you to buy an *income fund*. The manager of an income fund tries to generate gains, usually from dividends or interest, which are paid out to shareholders on a regular basis.

On the other hand, the manager of a *growth fund* doesn't care about producing income for shareholders. A growth fund manager will probably want to invest in fast-growing stocks. Shareholders hope to profit when they eventually sell their shares in the fund at a much higher price than the price they paid for them. If you have ten or twenty years until retirement, you will probably want to go for the growth! There's no need to be taking income from the fund right now.

You Can't Compare Apples and Oranges

When you compare two mutual funds, you should make sure you're comparing funds that have similar characteristics. It's not fair to compare a growth fund with an income fund, for instance. They have different objectives, and you might have different reasons for choosing to own one over the other.

Growth and income fund managers try to balance the two objectives, maybe by buying some bonds to provide current income and some stocks that are rapidly growing. The notion of *balance* is key to these funds, as the fund manager hopes to protect you from big bumps in the stock market.

Well, that's the investment objective. Now, what about the investment plan? This plan describes how the fund's manager will invest to meet the fund's objectives. Will the manager buy blue-chip stocks, small-cap stocks, municipal bonds, government bonds, or some combination of several different security types?

When you begin researching a mutual fund on the Web, you may not know these answers, but the investment plan will tell you. It describes all types of securities the fund will purchase in its portfolio and states the minimum and maximum percentages that the fund can invest in any particular type of security.

Finally, the main advantage of investing in a mutual fund is that your money has the attention of professional management. A fund can be managed by an individual or by a team of managers. In fact, when you buy shares in a mutual fund, you're really hiring a manager to invest your money in a portfolio of his or her design. Of course, your investment is immediately thrown into the pot with the investments of thousands of other shareholders, so you can't expect personalized attention from the manager. But it can be very helpful to think of investing in a fund as paying a professional to manage a part of your investment portfolio.

After professional management, the second most important benefit of a mutual fund is that it provides instant *diversification* to its shareholders. As you may recall from chapter 5, diversification is how you can spread out your eggs in different baskets. When you buy a fund, your new portfolio is likely to be made up of hundreds of eggs—or rather, stocks. Because the fund's portfolio contains so many stocks, the entire portfolio won't be dragged down if one or two stocks do poorly. You would certainly have your hands full trying to manage that many stocks in your own portfolio. But, be careful! The management style and the market also influence a fund's performance. For example, in a small-cap fund, the entire fund will be hurt by a slump in small caps.

Another benefit of investing in a mutual fund is that you can concentrate your investments in a particular area if you wish. This seems to contradict the advantages of diversification, and it does! But if you have a hunch that now is the time to invest in Japan, or healthcare stocks, or emerging markets, you could buy a fund that invests solely in those areas. (Not that you would ever invest on the basis of hunches, mind you.)

You've Got Plenty of Mutual Fund Choices

Canadian investors had 1,800 mutual funds to choose from at the end of 1997.

There's No Such Thing as a Free Fund

Mutual funds are businesses. Period. Fund companies are in business to make a profit, just like any other business. So how do fund companies make money? They don't necessarily make their income from wise investing, but more likely from the fees that they charge you and other investors.

It's important that you understand the many different types of fees that funds charge. These fees will be outlined in a fund's prospectus, on its Web site, or in reports from mutual fund research companies, such as FundMonitor.com Corp. You will learn more about the online sources where you can find information on a fund's fees in chapters 8 and 9.

To help you understand how fees work, you can separate a fund's expenses and fees into three categories: ongoing expenses of operating the fund, which are already accounted for by the return figures you see in newspapers and fund reports; loads, charged when you buy or sell shares, and which aren't included in return calculations; and miscellaneous fees and charges.

It costs money to operate a mutual fund! Ongoing expenses include the salaries and advisory fees paid to the investment managers, as well administrative expenses (such as preparing and mailing statements and confirmations, staff to answer the phones, office expenses, and so on). These costs are known as the fund's expense ratio. You will usually find that they range from 0.2 percent to more than 3.5 percent of a fund's net assets.

Some Fund Managers Increase Returns by Waiving Their Fees

One practice that is becoming more popular, particularly for new funds, is for a fund company to temporarily waive its management fee or absorb all operating expenses, and thereby inflate the fund's return. If a fund is waiving its fee, you might be in for a surprise when the fund starts paying its manager, and its returns decline by a percentage point or two.

The second category of fund expenses, the load, is the fee for buying, selling, or just owning shares in the fund. *Load* is certainly the right term, too, because there are light loads, heavy loads, and downright backbreaking loads that you might have to carry as a shareholder of these funds.

Loads are either front-end or back-end. The difference between the two comes down to whether the fee is charged when you buy a fund (front-end) or when you sell it (back-end). Front-end loads are paid by the investor directly to the fund company. Back-end loads are paid by the fund company to the advisor up front, but the fund company then passes that cost on to the investor in the form of a higher expense ratio.

Many investors don't like loads, for a number of reasons. First of all, mutual fund companies aren't required to include the impact of loads when calculating the total return of their funds. That makes it harder for investors to evaluate the true return of a load fund. You need to make sure that you consider any loads when you are comparing the returns of different funds.

This distaste for loads has spawned a new type of fund, the *no-load fund*. These are funds that don't charge sales charges at all, and they appeal to investors who are turned off by excessive sales charges.

Here's an imaginary example that demonstrates just how much of a problem a load can be. Let's say the Consolidated Conglomerate Sector Fund is a no-load fund, and its main competitor, the Occidental Oligopoly Specialty Fund, charges a 4.5 percent back-end load. The fund managers of both have done pretty well lately, turning in a five-year average 16 percent annual return on their portfolios.

If you had invested $10,000 five years ago in Consolidated's fund, you could sell your shares today for just over $21,000. If you had invested in the Occidental fund, however, the 4.5 percent back-end load would have cost you just under $1,000, lowering your actual annual return to about 14.95 percent after the load.

Not All Load Funds Are Bad

Load funds are not necessarily always the worst choice for your portfolio. Because you usually purchase these funds from a financial professional, you may be able to receive other financial services as a client of that advisor. But the bottom line is that the performance of any load fund should outperform comparable no-load funds, after the loads have been paid—and that can be a tall order to fill.

To keep up with its no-load competitor and give its investors the same return, the Occidental fund needed to generate an annual 17.1 percent rate of return over the period. It doesn't sound like much, but think of it this way: For every $100 that Consolidated made in profit, Occidental needed to earn $114.40, just to end up giving shareholders the same return in the end! Too many load funds just can't compete with their no-load brethren.

The third category of fees includes maintenance fees, transaction fees, and redemption fees. A typical account maintenance fee is $10 or $25 a year, and is usually applied to smaller accounts. If you don't have a large amount invested, these maintenance fees can add up, and that can lower your returns.

Transaction or redemption fees are different from loads, in that they generally go back into the pot (the fund's portfolio) rather than into the fund company's pockets. These fees are designed to discourage market timers and more active traders from moving in and out of the fund to the detriment of long-term shareholders.

What Funds Are Not

Now that you know what mutual funds are, let's go over what mutual funds are not.

Mutual funds are not securities, as are stocks and bonds. Funds invest in securities, however, and the share price of a fund is determined by the value of the securities it owns.

Mutual funds are not an asset class. Back in chapter 5, you learned how to divide up your portfolio among such assets as stocks, bonds, and cash (to name some of the more common classes). As part of your asset allocation decision, you can't decide to allocate 75 percent of your portfolio to mutual funds and 25 percent to stocks—you have to consider what the funds own. If all the funds you bought invested in stocks, your portfolio would be 100 percent invested in stocks. And that's not asset allocation!

When you choose to buy shares in mutual funds, you need to be aware of the asset classes of the securities they own. If you so desire, you can build a diversified portfolio by investing 100 percent of your money in mutual funds that each own different asset classes.

Mutual funds are usually not short-term investments. Fund companies put up all sorts of barriers to prevent shareholders from buying and selling funds too frequently—and it's for good reason. Frequent buying and selling wreaks havoc with a manager's portfolio plan, making it hard to figure out how much cash the company might need on hand to take care of withdrawals. It also generates extra activity that raises costs for all shareholders.

Growth, Balanced, Specialty, Bond, International, Yada-Yada-Yada

What Is an Equity Fund?

Stocks are known as equities; therefore an *equity fund* is a fund that primarily invests in stocks.

It's Easy to Figure Out a Stock's Market Cap

There's no big secret about how the market cap of a stock is determined. You can do it yourself! Just multiply the current price of a single share times the number of shares the company has issued.

So far, you have learned that there are funds that own stocks, bonds, or some combination of those two assets. Most mutual funds specialize in much more specific approaches to investing than just buying stocks or bonds, however. Before you begin your research about mutual funds on the Web, you will need to know what you're looking for, and how to identify the various kinds of funds.

Mutual funds are generally categorized by *what* they invest in, *where* they invest, and *how* they invest.

First, let's look at the kinds of investments that mutual funds make. Most mutual funds invest in stocks, and these are called *equity funds*.

Although mutual funds most often invest in the stock market, fund managers don't just buy any old stock they find attractive. Some funds specialize in investing in large-cap stocks, others in small-cap stocks, and still others invest in what's left, mid-cap stocks.

"Cap" has nothing to do with hat size or what your spouse left off the tube of toothpaste (again). On Bay Street, cap is shorthand for capitalization, and is one way of measuring the size of a company—how well it's capitalized. Large-cap stocks have market caps of billions of dollars, and are the best-known companies in North America. Small-cap stocks are worth several hundred million dollars, and are newer, up-and-coming firms. Mid-caps are somewhere in between.

How Big Is Large?

Mutual funds are often categorized by the market capitalization of the stocks that they hold in their portfolios. But how big is a large-cap stock? Formulas differ, but here are some guidelines:

Small-cap stocks   < $250 million

Mid-cap stocks $250 million to $2.5 billion

Large-cap stocks   > $2.5 billion

Other funds have a narrower focus and only invest in stocks in a particular sector, such as technology or healthcare companies. That Consolidated Conglomerate Sector Fund, mentioned earlier, would belong in this category.

Still, there are other funds out there, and not all of them are interested in stocks. *Money market funds*, for instance, typically invest in short-term government bonds and aim to provide a modest return to investors, comparable to a savings account in a bank. These are quite safe investments, but won't give you a big bang for your buck.

Bond funds, on the other hand, purchase and hold bonds issued by corporations, municipal governments, or federal government agencies.

The second way that funds are categorized is by geographic location—where in the world does a fund invest? Funds that invest specifically in Canada are known as *domestic* funds, and these include domestic equity funds and domestic bond funds.

Some funds specialize in securities outside Canada, as well. These are known as international funds or global funds. There is a subtle but important distinction between these two types of funds. The *international fund* invests only in companies outside Canada, but the *global fund* invests both internationally and domestically.

Your Global Fund Might Not Be as Global as You Think

Because global funds can invest in stocks from Canada, you need to be aware of how much the fund has invested in and out of Canada. If you bought a global fund to provide a little international diversification to your portfolio, you might be surprised to learn that the fund's major holdings are North American stocks.

International and global funds can specialize in bonds, stocks, or some mix of the two. An international fund can also specialize in a particular country or region of the world, such as the Pacific Rim, Latin America, or Germany.

Those are the *what* and *where* of mutual funds; next comes the *how*. Equity fund managers usually employ one of three particular styles of stock picking when they make investment decisions for their portfolios.

Some fund managers use a *value* approach to stocks, searching for stocks that are undervalued when compared with other, similar companies. Often, the share prices of these stocks have been beaten down by the market as investors have become pessimistic about the future potential of these companies.

Another approach to picking is to look primarily at *growth*, trying to find stocks that are growing faster than the market as a whole or than their competitors. These funds buy shares in companies that are growing rapidly, often well-known, established corporations.

Some managers buy both kinds of stocks, building a portfolio of both growth stocks and value stocks. This is known as the *blend* approach.

After you gather information about a fund from the Web, you will have a good idea of how that fund works. Put it all together, and you can identify whether a fund is a domestic small-cap growth fund, or an international large-cap value fund, or a mid-cap value fund, or a specific-country sector fund. And the combinations go on and on!

Strategies for Getting Started in Mutual Funds

If you are ready to buy shares in that Consolidated Conglomerate Sector Fund, or even an index fund that tracks the TSE 300, you have two choices:

➤ Buy shares through your advisor.

➤ Buy shares from the fund directly.

If you buy shares through an advisor, you will probably have to pay a commission. An advantage of buying fund shares through an advisor is that you can consolidate all your investments in one portfolio, and on one statement. Sometimes, the minimum initial investments are lower in these fund marketplaces than if you bought shares from the fund directly!

If you buy shares from the fund company directly, you won't have to pay a commission (although there may be an annual maintenance fee for your account). You will be able to easily make transfers between different funds in the same family. If you want to sell your shares of Consolidated Conglomerate and buy shares of Consolidated Growth instead, you just have to call the company or log on to your account. There probably won't be a charge for the transfer, either. One disadvantage of purchasing shares directly from a fund company is that you're usually limited to buying that company's funds.

It Can Be Tough to Get into a Hot Fund

The more popular and successful a mutual fund is, the more likely that it will require high minimum initial and subsequent investments. The demand for the fund means that the management can demand (and receive) a more substantial commitment from investors. Conversely, a fund that has been less successful or is just starting out may have low minimums to make it as easy as possible for investors to invest.

Some funds are only available through brokers or financial advisors. These are almost always load funds—the advisor's compensation comes from the sales charge. The downside of buying funds from an advisor is that the advisor has an incentive (to earn the sales fee) to sell you a fund that might not be the best choice for you.

Investing in Funds on the Cheap

One of the advantages of mutual funds is that you don't need thousands of dollars to begin investing. Do you have $250 or less to start your investing plan? Many funds will accept an initial investment as low as that. Another bunch will let you start with $500 or less.

The Quicken.ca Mutual Fund Finder (http://www.quicken.ca) enables you to search for funds with low minimum investments. Select the amount that you have to invest, and then you will see a list of all the funds that will sell you shares.

After you've established your account, most mutual funds have minimum amounts for additional purchases. Often these are as low as $50, or perhaps $100. This can be an important consideration when you select a fund—if minimum subsequent investments are too high, it may be difficult for you to invest on a regular basis.

Fundomatic Investing with Automatic Investing Plans

If it is a stretch for you to come up with $250 all at once, there is another way to get started in mutual funds. Many fund companies will allow you to invest in their funds with as little as $50, as long as you make a commitment to invest that amount each month for a year or so. This is called an *automatic investment plan* (AIP).

71

Get Acquainted with This Method of Regular Investing

Investing using an automatic investment plan *is* sometimes known as *systematic investing.*

How do fund companies make sure that you honour your commitment to invest each month? They require that your monthly investments be automatically deducted from your paycheque or chequing account. Each month, a preset amount is automatically transferred to the fund company and invested in the fund that you've selected, purchasing shares at whatever the price might be on the date of the investment.

Besides allowing you to start investing with small amounts, the beauty of AIPs is that they make it extremely easy to invest regularly. You don't have to worry about writing a cheque each month. When you "pay yourself first" automatically, you will make sure that your investment plan is being funded, before you've had a chance to buy that new outfit you have had your eye on or a new set of golf clubs.

As you work toward your goals, step by step, you will also put the power of dollar cost averaging to work for you. Remember that when you invest the same amount in a mutual fund on a regular basis, you buy more shares when the price is lower, and fewer shares when the price is higher. Over time, this can reduce your average cost per share. It can also make market fluctuations work *for* you, not *against* you.

To get started with an AIP, just ask your mutual fund company for an application, or download one from its Web site. If you're having money transferred from your bank account, you will probably need to send along a voided cheque with the application. Before you sign up, be sure that you understand how long you need to continue in the AIP before you can stop, and what the procedures are for stopping the plan altogether.

Dollar Cost Averaging Works Great with Stock Funds!

Dollar cost averaging works best with investments that fluctuate in price. Because stock market funds tend to be more volatile than other types of funds, an automatic investment plan can be a great way to invest in these funds.

In a Down Market, Dollar Cost Averaging Won't Protect You from Losses

In a declining market, not even dollar cost averaging or an automatic investment plan can protect you from losses on your investments. That's why it's best to implement your AIP with an eye to the long term, and invest an amount that you can continue to invest no matter what happens in the market.

The Least You Need to Know

➤ You can invest in your choice of thousands of mutual funds. There are funds that strive to meet many different investment objectives.

➤ You can buy mutual funds through an advisor or directly from most fund companies. Many advisors offer mutual fund supermarkets that allow you to invest in funds from many (but not all) families.

➤ You can get started in many funds with $100 or less, as long as you invest in the fund automatically each month for a year or so.

Chapter 8

Finding and Researching Mutual Funds on the Web

Now that you understand how mutual funds work, it is time to find out more about the funds that are out there. On the Web, you can learn plenty about mutual funds, from the fund companies' own Web sites to independent services that rate and review mutual funds.

It's a Family Affair

When you are ready to hit the Web to learn more about mutual funds, you will find that most fund families have Web sites that are a great source of information about their funds.

You probably recognize the names of some of the largest and best-known fund families, such as Fidelity and Trimark. Both firms have terrific sites on the Web that provide plenty of information to potential investors.

The Largest Fund Families Manage Billions and Billions of Dollars

The following are the top mutual fund groups in Canada, ranked by their total assets under management:

Fund Family	Assets ($Billions)
Investors Group	39.1
Royal Mutual Funds Inc.	30.8
Mackenzie Financial Corp.	28.6
Trimark Investment Management Inc.	25.1
Fidelity Investments Canada Ltd.	23.7
Templeton Management Ltd.	20.5
CIBC Securities Inc.	20.2
AGF Management Ltd.	18.1

Source: Investment Funds Institute of Canada, July 1999

Online Mutual Funds and Families

The first place to start your online search for a mutual fund on the Web is the listing of mutual fund Web sites on the Greenpage$ at http://www.magi.com/~mftrackr/grnintro.html.

Before you set off on an exploration of a fund's Web site, ask yourself what kind of information you hope to find about this fund. If you expect a revealing look at the fund itself, think again. Fund companies will gladly tell you all the good things about their fund, but what if the fund has performed poorly?

Do you really think that a mutual fund company's Web site will just "tell" you that their funds are weak performers? Securities and exchange commissions watch how funds present their track records to investors, even on the Web, so you will rarely find a fund that will come right out and shamelessly lie to you about its history.

And could it be possible that a bit of glitz and glamour on a Web site might distract you from uncovering the essential truths? Could your attention be easily diverted by flashy graphics to another section of a site—away from that page that describes a fund's lousy performance?

If you are the kind of person who is never fooled by a magician who tries to distract you

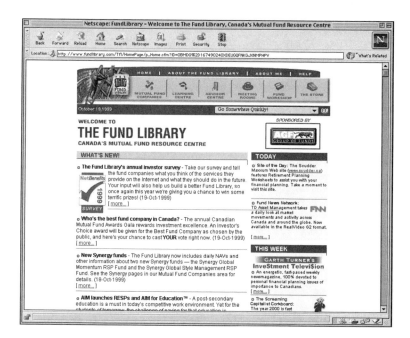

The Fundlibrary Web site offers educational articles, as well as information about funds.

with chatter while sliding the ace of spades up a sleeve, you are all set. For the rest of you, remember that a glossy brochure—or a snazzy Web site—doesn't mean that a mutual fund is a good investment.

Keep that thought in mind as you navigate mutual fund Web sites. On most sites, you can find a lot of good information that can be important in helping you make a decision to buy (or not to buy) a particular mutual fund. The key is that you have to know what to look for.

Here are the key items that you should search for on any mutual fund's Web site.

General information about the fund company and the fund managers. Here's where you can learn about the company and the people who are offering to manage your money. Some firms publish mission statements. These can be informative and illuminating articles that help you understand a fund company's character. On the other hand, you might find just a sentence or two of over-simplistic babbling, such as "Our mission is to serve our shareholders." Every fund company should have that mission!

Often, a fund Web site will publish a photograph of a fund's managers, just to let you know that fund managers are people too. Just don't be deceived by their smiling faces—remember that fund managers usually are paid a salary regardless of whether the fund performs well.

Specific information about the company's funds. Although this information may not seem like much more than spin, you can learn much about a specific fund by reading through the general information on its Web site.

Many sites, such as Trimark's (http://www.trimark.com), group their funds by categories: stock funds, bond funds, specialty funds, growth funds, international funds, and so on. You can browse through all the funds a family offers, or zero in on funds in which you are especially interested. This can be a quick way to compare the different funds offered by the same company.

Online fund profiles can be easier to read than the prospectus, but they are not nearly as complete. On Trimark's site, you can learn about a fund's performance, investment strategy, top holdings, expenses, and minimum investments, for instance. After you have reviewed a profile, you can then download the prospectus for further study.

Many families skip the fund profiles altogether and just reprint their prospectus on the site.

The fund prospectus. The most important thing to look for is the fund's prospectus. Investment companies are legally required to outline the fund's objectives and operating procedures in a formal document called a prospectus. (You will learn more about the kind of information that's in a prospectus a bit later.) Most fund companies now offer Web surfers the chance to download a copy of their prospectus right from their sites.

Most recent net asset value (NAV) of the funds. On the Web site of Fidelity Investments (http://www.fidelity.ca) and other fund families, you can also find the closing NAV of a fund posted after the market closes each day. Often, you can access an archive of historical NAV data, or the fund company will calculate performance figures for the funds on a daily, weekly, monthly, yearly, or multiyear basis.

Application to open an account. Most fund companies include an account application that you can download from their site. At the least, every fund Web site provides easy instructions for requesting an application. Other forms, such as those required to open an automatic investing plan, may also be provided. If the company doesn't sell its funds directly to investors, the site will direct you to advisors where you can purchase their fund.

Commentary from the fund managers. Many funds publish the current market outlook of their management or interviews with managers. Here, fund managers share their perceptions about the markets and how their funds will perform in the future. Some companies produce audio versions of market commentary so that you can listen to the fund manager describe his or her views. In these reports, you can often get a better understanding of a manager's approach to the stock market.

Annual, semiannual, and quarterly reports. Mutual funds are required to keep their shareholders informed about their activities in reports produced at least twice a year. This is helpful information for analyzing a fund's history and learning about where the fund's managers plan to take it.

Press releases and news stories. Mutual funds typically issue press releases that detail the fund's year-end or semiannual distributions of capital gains and dividends or describe changes in management and other news about the fund and its operations. You can often find archives of these stories on a fund company's site.

Calculators, quizzes, RRSP analyzers, educational articles. Many fund sites provide educational information and decision-making tools for investors. It is not uncommon to find calculators to help with developing a financial plan, such as determining how much you need to save to put your children through college or when you will likely be able to retire comfortably. Many sites have analyzers that can outline the best scenario for your personal investing situation. Interactive quizzes test your knowledge of the markets (and hopefully you will learn a thing or two!). These "added bonuses" can really contribute to your investment education.

Online account access (for shareholders). If you are a shareholder of a mutual fund, many sites offer access to your accounts. You can log on and check your account balances, review a history of your transactions, and even make transfers between funds. Although you probably shouldn't buy a fund just because it offers online access, this feature can be very convenient in keeping track of all your purchases and account balances.

Contact information. Nearly every fund company Web site provides (at the very least) a phone number that you can call to request a prospectus, application, or other information. If you have any questions, go ahead and send an e-mail message or telephone the fund company. And don't worry that your question may be too "basic" or "simple"—most funds have trained customer service representatives who can answer any questions you might have and will patiently walk you through the process of completing an account application or selecting a fund from within their family.

Getting Acquainted with a Fund's Prospectus

A mutual fund prospectus is your best decision-making tool. Securities commissions require that certain information be contained in a fund's prospectus, and that each prospectus be updated on a regular basis. Often, a fund company prospectus will include information about a company's entire family of funds, or a particular "portfolio" of funds in that family.

The Commissions consider the information in a prospectus to be so important that they won't allow a fund company or advisor to offer to sell you a mutual fund without giving you the prospectus first. If you place an order to buy a mutual fund with your advisor, you will get a copy of the prospectus in the mail along with or soon after you receive your order confirmation.

Be Patient! Acrobat Files Can Be Big

Adobe Acrobat files are large, so it can take a few minutes to download a prospectus or application from a fund Web site, especially if you have a slow connection to the Internet.

Companies like Trimark and Fidelity provide downloadable versions of their prospectuses in Adobe Acrobat format. You must have the Acrobat software installed on your computer to read the prospectus. But don't worry—the Acrobat reader is available for free from Adobe, and publishers who use Acrobat files provide a link to Adobe's Web site so you can download the reader program.

The advantage of publishing documents in Acrobat is that the prospectus you download to your computer looks exactly the same as the printed version a fund company might send you in the mail, including any charts, graphics, and fonts used in the publication.

Adobe Acrobat Is a Graceful Way of Delivering Information over the Internet

If you have ever tried to open a file that was created on someone else's computer, you might be familiar with the problems that this seemingly simple task can create. If you want to open a spreadsheet file, for instance, you need to have the same application installed on your computer as the one that was used originally to create the spreadsheet. Even then, new wrinkles can pop up if different versions of software or different operating systems (Macintosh versus Windows) are involved, making a file unusable on some computers. And if specific fonts are used in the file, those have to be installed on both computers; otherwise, it won't look the same. Printing adds another level of complication, because not all printers work within the same margins. All in all, if can be tough to share information with others—at least so that it looks exactly the same no matter what kind of computer is used.

Adobe Acrobat tackles this problem by letting information publishers convert any document into an Acrobat file. Acrobat files are created in something called a "portable document format." This means that these files can be viewed on any type of computer by any user, regardless of the fonts or printers that might be installed on a machine—and the document will look almost exactly the same on screen and in print. Brochures, application forms, and legal documents are often converted to Acrobat files so that they can be distributed online and ensure that all users get exactly the same information. The best news is that the Adobe Acrobat reader program is free to users (the program that creates Acrobat files must be purchased if you plan to create Acrobat files). Just go to the Adobe Web site at http://www. adobe.com and download the correct version for your computer.

Just the Facts, Jack: Understanding a Fund Prospectus

No matter where or how you access a fund prospectus (by downloading it from a company's Web site, for example, or receiving it in the mail), the same information will be included in the document. Getting your hands on a fund prospectus is the easy part—interpreting all the facts and figures in a prospectus is another story, however.

All mutual fund prospectuses follow the same general format. If you can get through the following information in a prospectus (and understand it), you will be well on your way to making better decisions about your fund purchases.

Expense summary. It costs money for a company to run a mutual fund, but those costs are passed right along to shareholders in the form of "expenses." Some funds directly charge shareholders certain fees for services and transactions, or just for managing the fund.

All prospectuses include a summary of these fees and expenses near the beginning of the document. Fees can be divided into several categories:

➤ All funds have an annual management fee. This fee typically varies from under 1 percent to more than 3 percent of the fund's assets. These are the costs of administrating the fund, and they are passed along to shareholders.

➤ Distribution fees are used to cover the expenses of marketing and advertising the fund to new investors.

➤ A sales load is a charge you pay when you buy a fund.

➤ A deferred sales load is a charge you pay when you sell a fund. Often, this charge disappears if you hold a fund longer than a specific period, such as five years.

➤ Redemption fees (also known as back-end loads) are assessed when shares are sold. These fees are sometimes used to discourage frequent trading of a fund.

The total of these fees can range anywhere from a low of 0.2 percent (for no-load bond funds and index funds) up to 8.5 percent (for an international stock fund with a load) of the fund's assets.

The key point to remember is that fees reduce your profits (or increase your losses). If the managers of two mutual funds can both generate returns of 10 percent on the investments in their portfolios, but one fund has a 1.5 percent expense ratio and the other charges 4 percent, you will be better off with the fund that has lower expenses. The actual return

Get a Load of This!

A *load* is a charge that you pay to the fund when you purchase or sell shares in it. Loads come in two varieties: front-end loads, charged when you buy a fund; and back-end loads, charged when you sell a fund. These charges are usually a percentage of the total amount you are investing in the fund.

of the fund with lower expenses is 8.5 percent, compared to a 6 percent return of the more expensive fund. The best thing to do is compare the fees and expenses of several similar funds and see how they stack up. You can also compare a fund's expenses to the averages for that type of fund).

Fees aren't included in total return calculations, so you will have to figure out for yourself what investing in a specific fund really costs you. Comparing the prospectuses of all the funds you are considering is a way to figure out which fund may be better for you.

Financial highlights. Each prospectus includes a table of the fund's results over the last ten years (or for the life of the fund, if it is been around for less than ten years). The table shows the fund's total return in each fiscal year, as well as each year's expense ratio, distributions, dividends, and portfolio turnover rate (this is how frequently the fund manager buys and shares securities in the portfolio).

Investment objectives and policies. The next section that you will encounter in a prospectus is an outline of the fund's basic investment objectives. You will also hear how the managers expect to meet those objectives.

A fund's objectives are usually very broad. A fund might seek "long-term growth" or "capital appreciation" or "the highest rate of current return on its investments." You need to make sure that your personal objectives and the fund manager's are in sync.

The prospectus also details the policy that governs the kinds of securities that the fund expects to own, often with minimum or maximum percentages for different classes or categories. An intermediate-term bond fund might invest in "securities issued or guaranteed by the U.S. Treasury and maintaining a weighted average portfolio maturity, which ranges from three to ten years." A growth stock fund might invest in "small- and mid-cap companies, to create a portfolio of investments broadly diversified over industry sectors and companies."

Other investment practices and risk considerations. If the fund manager is permitted to own speculative investments such as derivatives, or to use "hedging strategies" to manage the portfolio's risk, those points will be covered here.

Management of the funds/portfolio managers. What is the company and who are the people who would be managing your money in this fund? This section provides information on the fund manager, his or her experience and length of service, and details of the firm behind the fund. Remember that when you buy a mutual fund, it is like you are paying the fund manager to handle your investment decisions. Read through this section as if you were interviewing a job candidate!

Investment methods. Now it is time to get down to the nitty-gritty of investing in a fund. This section of the prospectus explains how to buy and sell shares in the fund, the minimums for initial and subsequent investments in the fund, and whether the fund offers services such as cheque writing. Other details may be stated here as well, such as whether exchanges within the fund family are free, whether an automatic investing plan is available, and how to redeem shares. If you are investing on a shoestring budget, it is important to know whether you can manage the minimum investment amounts. This is where you can get the scoop.

Dividends, distributions, and taxes. The prospectus will explain the tax consequences of the investment for the shareholder, and the fund's policies regarding distributions of gains, income, and dividends.

The Least You Need to Know

➤ Check out a mutual fund company's Web site for important information about a fund—before you invest.

➤ Several Web sites provide important details about a fund and its performance.

➤ You can use the Web to find the prospectus for nearly every mutual fund. The prospectus is the single most important document you should review before investing in a fund.

Chapter 9

Getting Cyber-Advice About Funds

In This Chapter

➤ Research particular funds on the Web

➤ Get advice and information to help you build a portfolio of mutual funds

➤ Talk with other investors about mutual funds

➤ How to find mutual funds that meet your objectives

Although the information on a fund company's Web site may help you to learn about one of their mutual funds, let's face it: Before you invest any of your hard-earned dollars, you will probably want to check out some information provided by an unbiased third party. Fortunately, a number of Web sites are happy to oblige your quest for more information. And plenty of the fund research on the Web is free!

Mutual Fund Reports

Start your fund research at FundMonitor.com (http://www.fundmonitor.com). FundMonitor.com Corp. is an independent analysis firm that reviews and rates mutual funds. They produce printed reports of funds, and their star rating system is widely regarded as one of the best overall measures of a fund's potential future performance.

FundMonitor.com provides ratings and reviews of mutual funds.

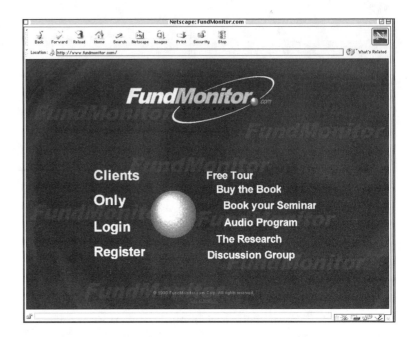

Commentary and tutorials from FundMonitor analysts can help you to learn more about fund investing, or you can ask your questions on the site's message boards and get responses from Duff Young (CFA), one of Canada's top mutual fund analysts. You can track your own customized portfolio of funds on the site, too. Most of the good services the site has to offer are for members only though, and because they don't let any of the fund companies advertise on their site (to keep their independence), there is a membership fee.

Quicken

Millions of people are familiar with the Quicken line of financial software, programs that help balance a personal or business chequebook or keep investing records. The Quicken.ca (http://www.quicken.ca) online financial network is a robust Web site featuring articles, message boards, and data, available for free.

One handy feature of Quicken.ca's fund charts is that they can be customized by date to plot the NAVs of up to nine separate funds on a single chart.

Quicken.ca's Fund Finder is the best way to zero in on the right funds for your portfolio. The combination of reports from major fund analyzers, as well as quotes and charts, makes Quicken.ca a convenient, informative, and essential resource for fund investors.

Quicken.ca's Fund Finder enables you to search using a dozen different criteria.

Yakking About Funds

If you have questions, chances are that someone has answers. At least that's the philosophy behind the numerous message boards and chat rooms on the Internet. Online discussion groups are often referred to as bulletin boards because users post messages on a site and wait for other users to post responses (think of a cork board with notes on index cards hanging by thumbtacks).

If you are a fund investor, you can choose from several sites where you can talk to others who are fond of funds. You can ask for recommendations from other investors, or eavesdrop on the conversations and try to soak up the knowledge. Online discussion groups provide a good place to ask your questions about mutual fund investing, and meet other people who have been in your shoes as a beginning investor—and who are willing to share what they have learned with others.

The Armchair Millionaire (http://www.armchair millionaire.com), for example, hosts message boards that are particularly useful for beginning mutual fund investors. In fact, one of the first message boards you will see when you arrive on the site is titled There Are No Dumb Questions. The mutual

Who Is FundGenius1234, Anyway?

Although you can never be sure who exactly is behind a particular nickname, the best message boards are truly virtual communities, with members who know each other, know whom to avoid, and know whom to listen to. If you hang around long enough, you can usually figure out who is the loudmouth (and who is the quiet genius).

Most Message Boards Require Registration

Nearly all these message boards on the Web require that you register before you can post a message on their boards. That's to make users more accountable for the messages they post on the board, and to make it difficult for anyone to post messages anonymously.

fund boards feature a lot of beginner questions and lively responses from more experienced fund investors. The site also features an asset allocation strategy using stock market funds (often called index funds) to build a long-term portfolio.

Searching for Funds in All the Right Places

If you have decided to do it all yourself and design your own portfolio of mutual funds, you need to start picking some funds. Although it is relatively easy to find information about mutual funds on the Web, you must first understand your own goals. Among the questions that you must ask yourself are the following:

➤ How much risk can I stand?

➤ What are the objectives of my entire portfolio?

➤ When do I need the money that I'm investing?

➤ What's my asset allocation strategy?

➤ How will my portfolio be diversified?

Answering those questions can guide you toward the right funds for you.

The Charles Schwab Guide to Investing (http://www.schwab.com/invest/invest index. html) features an Investor Profile questionnaire, with seven simple questions about your approach to the markets and your risk tolerance. The program analyzes your responses and then determines the type of investor you are—aggressive, moderate, or conservative—and how much you should consider investing in stocks, bonds, and/or cash.

Online Mutual Fund Screening

After you have determined your strategy, you need to find the funds that complete the puzzle. Fortunately, computers and the Internet make one particular investing task

Don't Forget the Importance of Proper Asset Allocation When Choosing Funds

Don't get too caught up in picking the perfect mutual fund. Academic studies have shown that the most important part of building a successful portfolio is your asset allocation strategy—not your stock- or fund-picking prowess. Particular stock or fund selections determine only about 5 percent of your long-term return. The remaining 95 percent is determined by the way you allocate your assets among stocks, bonds, and cash.

much, much easier—the job of sifting through the 2,500 available mutual funds to find the handful of funds right for you.

Screening is the process of determining the particular qualities that you want in your funds, thus enabling you to spend your time studying a handful of funds most likely to meet your criteria, instead of the thousands of funds that are wrong for you.

On the Web, you can screen mutual funds at a number of different Web sites. The big advantage of online screening is that you don't have to worry about maintaining or updating an enormous database on your own computer. The site that offers the screening tool will keep its database up to date, which means that you will be accessing current information.

The Globe Fund mutual fund screener (http://www.globefund.com) is one of the easiest screening tools to use on the Web.

You Still Have More Work to Do

After you have run a screen, the funds in your search results are not immediate candidates for purchase. You still need to do your research on the funds, because some other factors may make some funds unsuitable for your portfolio.

Globe Fund makes searching for funds a snap.

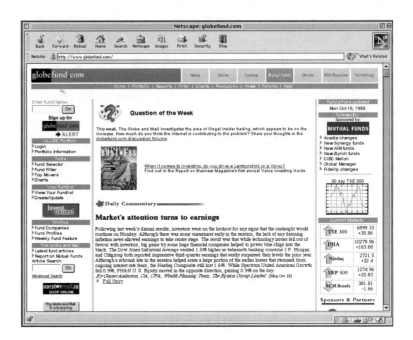

Sometimes, You Just Can't Seem to Go Back!

You may occasionally try to use the Back button on your Web browser to return to a page you have already visited, only to be greeted with an ominous-sounding message such as "Warning: Page Has Expired" or "Data Missing." Although they sound grim, these messages mean only that the page you are trying to view was created on-the-fly just for you. You may have entered some information on a form on the site, or made some selections in a search tool, for instance. The next page that you viewed was built by a program on the Web site using your input. As a security precaution, and to keep Web servers from needlessly re-creating the same page time after time, your browser may not save these pages in its cache. If you want to view the page again, you need to click the Reload button on your Web browser, and the customizing information will be sent from your browser back to the Web server to create the page again.

Remember these two rules of thumb about screening. First, it is always a good idea to start your search with broad criteria, then whittle your search down to become more restrictive.

Second, don't use search criteria that cancel each other out or aren't even possible. You could build a search that looks for a bond fund with a one-year 40 percent return, for example, but it would be exceptionally uncommon for a bond fund to have that kind of return.

The Least You Need to Know

➤ You can learn more about particular mutual funds by visiting sites that offer research reports, many for free.

➤ Message boards and chat rooms on the Internet are a good place to ask other investors your basic questions about investing in funds.

➤ You can use the Web to search for mutual funds using several screening tools. These screening sites are quick and convenient ways to find the funds that warrant further research.

Part 3

Investing in Stocks

Ever wished that you were lucky enough to have bought stock years ago in the little company with the big idea that made everyone rich? Then, this section is just for you. Remember, clever investing isn't always about buying stock in that one, magical company with the exploding profits. Sure, picking good stock is important, but the reward is in investing in a variety of stocks to create a portfolio with stamina. On the Internet you can find sources to help you make those money decisions that really matter.

Chapter 10

Strategies for Investing in Stocks

In This Chapter

➤ Understanding fundamental and technical analysis of stocks

➤ The dangers of penny stocks

➤ Investing in the "Dogs of the Dow"

Ah, the allure of the stock market! For the hardcore, do-it-yourself investor, there's nothing more satisfying than picking a stock that turns out to be a winner.

But a successful portfolio takes more than merely trying to buy stocks that you hope will go up in price. If you want to consistently beat the market, you need to choose a methodology of investing, and then stick with it. The most successful stock investors are the ones who never waiver from their selected approach.

You can use a number of different approaches to select stocks. You can look for stocks that are growing faster than the market in general, or stocks that are undervalued compared to other similar stocks. You can look for stocks with prices that are moving up really fast, or stocks that are being publicly sold to investors for the first time. Investors use dozens of methods and techniques when deciding which stocks to buy.

The approach to the stock market that you ultimately select will be determined by a couple of factors. For instance, do you want to spend hours a day on your portfolio? Or would you rather spend a few hours a month researching and following the stocks you own or would like to own? Do you want to build a solid blue-chip portfolio? Are you a computer buff who really wants to maximize the capability of that expensive piece of hardware on your desktop to analyze stocks?

To help you figure out the best approach to use, here's an overview of the most common methods that investors use in building a portfolio of stocks.

Fundamentally Speaking

One of the most popular ways of studying stocks is called *fundamental analysis*. Investors who use this approach like to learn as much as possible about a company and its management. They read annual reports and study financial statements and the industry in an effort to figure out what they think is the true or "fair" value of that company's stock. By comparing the current stock price to that fair value you can determine whether it might be a good time to buy that stock—or if it's a stock to avoid like the Black Plague!

The Internet can deliver just about all the information that you need to make a decision to buy or sell a stock based on fundamental analysis. In the rest of Part 3, you will learn more about these sites. Some of the best-known investors in history have been fundamental analysts, including Peter Lynch, the legendary manager of the Fidelity Magellan mutual fund in the U.S. Under his management, Magellan was the best performing mutual fund in history. Another famous American fundamentalist is Warren Buffet, the brilliant investor behind Berkshire Hathaway. Berkshire Hathaway was once a textile company, but Buffet turned it into a vehicle in which he could invest in other stocks, with phenomenal success. A single share of Berkshire Hathaway now trades for more than US$65,000!

Most individual investors use fundamental analysis in some way to pick stocks for their portfolios. If you are looking for a way to build a buy-and-hold portfolio of stocks, made up of companies that you can purchase and then own for years and years without losing too much sleep at night, you will probably use the methods of fundamental analysis.

Investors who use fundamental analysis usually focus on two separate approaches to picking stocks: *growth* or *value* (or sometimes a combination of both). On the Internet, you can learn more about both varieties of fundamental analysis, and determine which is best for you.

Going for Growth or Seeking Out Value?

When you gaze into your crystal ball, what future do you see for the stock market? Investors who focus on growth try to predict which companies will grow faster in the future—faster than the rest of the stocks in the market, or faster than other stocks in the same industry. If you're successful in buying a company that does grow faster than other companies, it's likely that the price of that company's stock will increase as well, and you can make a profit!

Peter Lynch primarily used a growth stock approach in managing the Magellan mutual fund. Individuals who invest in growth stocks often prefer this approach because their portfolio will be made up of stocks in established, well-managed companies that can be held for many, many years. Companies such as Coca-Cola, IBM, and Microsoft have demonstrated great growth over the years, and are the cornerstones of many portfolios. Investment Club Central features a tutorial about how you can use the growth approach to evaluate and select growth stocks for your portfolio. Just surf on over to http://www.iclubcentral.com/ssg to check out this free lesson in fundamental stock analysis.

What's a Growth Stock?

The stock of a company that grows its earnings and revenues faster than average is known as a *growth stock*. These companies usually pay little or no dividends, because they prefer to reinvest their profits in their business.

Value investors, on the other hand, look for stocks that have been overlooked by other investors and that may have a "hidden value." These companies may have been beaten down in price because of some bad event, or may be in an industry that's looked down on by most investors. However, even a company that has seen its stock price decline still has assets to its name—buildings, real estate, inventories, subsidiaries, and so on. Many of these assets still have value, yet that value may not be reflected in the stock's price.

Value investors look to buy stocks that are undervalued, and then hold those stocks until the rest of the market (hopefully!) realizes the real value of the company's assets.

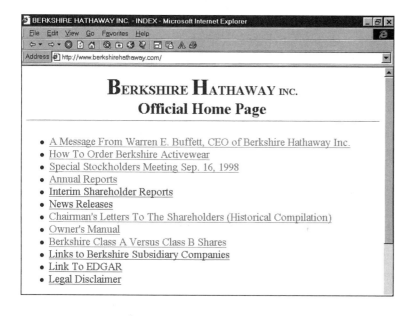

The Berkshire Hathaway Web site isn't flashy, but the Chairman's Letters to the Shareholders are required reading.

Warren Buffet is usually recognized as one of the greatest investors of all time, and his approach to buying stocks is grounded in the value approach. As Chairman of Berkshire Hathaway, Inc., headquartered in Omaha, Nebraska, Buffet has managed to increase the book value (the total net worth of the company on its books) at a compounded annual growth of 24.1 percent.

Even if you're not a shareholder of Berkshire Hathaway stock, you can still benefit from his expertise. Each year, Buffet pens a Letter to the Shareholders for the company's annual report, and these missives have become legendary for their wit, insight, and education. The Berkshire Hathaway Web site (http://www.berkshirehathaway.com) is low on pizzazz—at least the visual kind—but high on substance, featuring all the letters to shareholders for the past twenty years. The site also features the Owners Manual, outlining Buffet's philosophy and rules for running the business. Every investor should spend some time here to learn from the master.

Although some investors stick closely to either the value or growth approach, many investors look at characteristics from each side, and look to buy growth companies that they think are temporarily undervalued by the market.

Getting Technical

If you're a "numbers person," or a heavy-duty computer geek, you might be more interested in a method of picking stocks known as *technical analysis*. Technical analysis looks at the relationships that exist between a stock's price, its volume (the number of shares that trade hands during a single day), and other factors. When they plot all these numbers on a chart, or do some other calculations, technical analysts hope to be able to predict future changes in the price of a particular stock.

By looking for particular patterns on a price chart of a stock, for instance, technical analysts try to figure out the direction that the stock's price is likely to move in the future. These patterns often have unusual names such as "cup and handle," "head and shoulders," or "double top." If you can identify any of several dozen different established patterns in a stock's price, you might have a good chance of knowing whether a stock is about to "break out" (that's technical analysis talk for rise in price) or "retreat" (fall in price).

This Kind of Technician Can't Fix Your Stereo

A *technician* or *market technician* is someone who practises technical analysis.

To learn more about this method of investing, check out the online book *Technical Analysis from A to Z* by Steve Achelis, available free on the Web site of Equis International (http://www.equis.com/free/taaz). Equis is a maker of MetaStock, a popular software program for technical analysis. Company president Achelis's tutorial

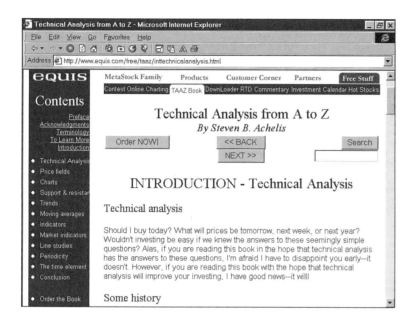

Equis International's online book, Technical Analysis from A to Z, *can help you learn all about this method of analyzing stocks.*

will explain the details of technical analysis, along with illustrations of all the various chart patterns and other indicators.

After you have the basics of technical analysis under your belt, you will need a couple of things before you start investing. You need access to charting software, access to price data, and plenty of time!

A stock's price chart is the primary tool of technical analysis. There are many technical analysis software programs to choose from if you want to study stocks using these methods. Besides MetaStock, you can use Windows on Wall Street, Omega TradeStation, and many others. You can subscribe to your pick of many services on the Web that provide daily price updates that can be imported into these programs. (You will learn more about downloading price data from the Internet in chapter 18.)

To use technical analysis successfully, you need to be able to spend time on your portfolio on a regular basis. You need to be able to consistently sit down and analyze charts, or perform the calculations necessary to update the indicators you use. And

Does Technical Analysis Work?

Opponents of technical analysis point out that there is little likelihood that this method even works! Debate rages about whether it's possible to predict future price movements on the basis of a stock's past performance, or if patterns on a chart are indicative of anything other than pretty designs.

You can try your hand at technical analysis using ProphetCharts.

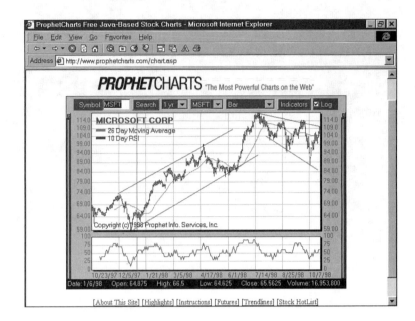

after you've bought a stock, you need to be vigilant in watching that stock's chart to know when to sell. There's no time to relax if you're a technician.

What a Difference a Day Makes

A recent phenomenon that has surfaced in the stock market is a method called *day trading.* Day traders buy and sell dozens (or even hundreds) of different stocks in a single day, usually never owning any of those stocks for more than a few seconds or minutes. Traders make their profits by locking in very small profits—pennies per share—on, say, $50,000 worth of stock at a time. Some day traders make tens of thousands of dollars in a single week, a few dollars at a time. Before you jump onboard this train, however, better take a closer look. Trades can go down as well, leaving you thousands of dollars in the hole when the week ends.

If you're still interested and have a bundle to start out with (you will need about $25,000), pay a visit to the Day Traders of Orange County (http://www.worldwide traders.com). Although the group is headquartered in California, they provide plenty of resources about day trading, as well as links to similar groups elsewhere. In day trading, you can look forward to sitting behind a special computer trading terminal in a high-pressured, noisy, windowless office that's been set up to service a roomful of day traders, and you will pay for the privilege of being there. You will rarely have a chance to sneak a bite to eat or run to the bathroom while the market is open. You've got to be able to think fast, and react even faster with nerves of steel (and a cast iron stomach!).

The Day Traders of Orange County provides support for people who are trying to make sense of the hectic world of day trading.

Common Cents or Nonsense

Does this sound like a bargain to you? You discover that shares of Fabulous New Products, Inc. are selling for just 32 cents per share. You try to do a little research to find out more about this company, but there's not much available on the Internet. So you go ahead and buy 2,000 shares, at a cost of $640 plus commission. How much could you lose, you figure?

Well, you could lose $640, that's how much! And in the world of "penny stocks," chances are good that you will lose out on your investment! Penny stocks are those companies whose share prices are below a dollar. Although many investors are attracted to them because of their low prices, they are actually some of the riskiest investments you can purchase.

In nearly ever case, penny stocks are penny stocks because they've had a miserable life as a public company. These stocks had to fall long and hard to get from their initial offering price of $10 or more a share. Penny stocks are the remnants of the stock market, and although some of these companies may claw their way back to the top, many will languish and ultimately die.

Some investors specialize in penny stocks. Typically, these are aggressive individuals who are willing to speculate, and can tolerate huge losses. Most sensible investors will stay away from penny stocks altogether.

Warning: Penny Stocks Can Be Manipulated!

Because they have lower share prices and fewer actively traded shares, it's not too difficult for someone to use a variety of techniques to stir up interest (and the price) of a penny stock. The Internet is fertile territory for manipulators who try to get investors excited about a particular company and drive up the share price. When the stock's price peaks, the manipulators dump their shares and make a tidy profit. But they also stop promoting the stock, and the lack of interest now causes the share price to fall, leaving the investors who bought at the high with nothing but a hefty loss. (You will learn more about protecting yourself from these schemes in chapter 20.)

Investing on Auto-Pilot

If all of this stock-picking business sounds like it might be way over your head, don't worry! There is a way that you can build a portfolio of stocks without worrying about doing research on individual stocks. As a bonus, you will only need to spend less than an hour a year on your portfolio, and you will never own more than ten stocks. And the end result of this "auto-pilot" investment approach is a portfolio that will provide excellent returns, beating the market averages year in and year out.

Does this sound like your idea of investing nirvana? This approach goes by the lowly sounding name of "the Dogs of the Dow." And you can learn more about it at a Web site devoted just to this investment strategy.

Running with the Dogs of the Dow

Visit the Dogs of the Dow Web site (http://www.dogsofthedow.com) and you will get some quick training about this popular and low-maintenance method of investing.

The "Dow" part of this strategy refers to the Dow Jones Industrial Average, an index of thirty companies that is used to measure the performance of the overall market. These companies represent some of the biggest companies in America, including Sears, Hewlett-Packard, General Motors, Exxon, and AT&T.

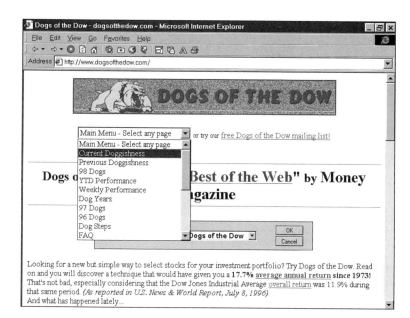

The Dogs of the Dow Web site lays out this popular and easy approach to building an investment portfolio.

The "dogs" part of this approach refers to the ten companies (out of the thirty in the Dow) that you must invest in once a year. You see, the idea here is to invest in the ten recently worst performing stocks out of the thirty in the Dow—the "dogs" of the Dow.

Invest in worst, you ask? Why would any investor do that, you wonder? Well, the answer is fairly simple. Because these thirty companies are among the best-known companies in the country, even the ten worst of the bunch have proven to be exceptional recovery acts, year after year. Although a handful of the Dow might be beaten down at any point in time, they usually rebound quite handily.

On the Dogs of the Dow site, click on Dog Steps and you will be presented with an explanation of how you can invest in the dogs. Once a year, you need to review the dividend yields of all thirty stocks in the Dow. The dividend yield of a stock is figured by taking the total annual dividend that's paid per share of stock, and then dividing it by the current share price. You can find this figure in any newspaper's stock listings, or many Internet quote servers (or on the Dogs of the Dow Web site—just click Current Doggishness for an update).

Next, identify the ten Dow stocks with the highest dividend yields. These are the stocks that have had their prices knocked down (that's why the dividend yield is so high).

Finally, buy an equal dollar amount of all ten of these stocks. Hold them for one year, and then repeat the process. That's all there is to the Dogs of the Dow approach!

So, does it work? From 1973 to 1996, the dogs approach would have earned an annual return of 17.7 percent, compared to a return of 11.9 percent for the entire Dow Jones Industrial Average during the same period. That's quite a difference! And with no worries about deciding when to sell, the Dogs of the Dow method is truly a couch-potato investor's dream come true! The same practice can be followed with the dogs of the TSE or any other exchange.

The Least You Need to Know

➤ Fundamental analysis is a common method used by individual investors to evaluate stocks, and to identify companies with strong growth and/or that are undervalued in the market-place.

➤ Technical analysis is more of a by-the-numbers approach to investing. By using charts and statistics, technicians hope to pinpoint the right times to buy and sell stocks.

➤ Stay away from penny stocks!

➤ The Dogs of the Dow can be an easy way to invest in the stock market, and can help you achieve better-than-average returns.

Chapter 11

Building a Portfolio of Stocks

In This Chapter

➤ What is a portfolio of stocks?

➤ The importance of a diversified stock

➤ How to evaluate your portfolio's balance

A stock is a stock—but a portfolio is where the real money is! Even the name *portfolio* suggests the idea of power and wealth. Your grandfather may have had a portfolio of genuine, thick, well-worn leather, stuffed with ledgers and account statements and other important documents. Within this portfolio would have been meticulous records of all the investments he had made, row after row of numbers and calculations.

Today, a portfolio refers to any group of investments that you can make. You can consider all your stocks as one big portfolio, or you can group your investments by the different goals you're trying to achieve. If you've decided to invest in the stock market, it's a good idea to pay attention to all the stocks you own and what happens to your risk and return when they all come together.

Diversify, Diversify, Diversify

When you build a portfolio of stocks, it's very important to consider the diversification of your holdings. Remember the discussion about diversification back in chapter 5? Diversification is the process of spreading out your investments so that

Don't Forget the Importance of Asset Allocation

While many investors are comfortable with a portfolio that's made up solely of stocks, other investors will be more comfortable with a portfolio that includes bonds as well.

you decrease risk as much as you can while still maintaining an acceptable rate of return.

One of the fundamental truths about stocks is that their share prices will fluctuate. Even if you're right about a particular stock you've picked, you might not be right at the right time!

Stock prices rise and decline for lots of reasons, often through no fault of the company at all! The overall status of the economy, the condition of a company's industry group, and a thousand other factors can influence share prices, turning a stock you've just bought into a loser, at least on paper.

There's nothing worse than seeing your entire portfolio decline all at once. If you diversify your portfolio, you will be more likely to have at least one or two winners in your portfolio whenever the rest of your holdings falls in price.

You can look at the diversification of a portfolio of stocks in several ways. The first way is to buy stocks from several different sectors or industries. If the entire tech sector is in a slump, transportation stocks might be doing very well. If you own one technology stock and one airline, your portfolio could experience less "bouncing around" as stocks in one sector fall and those in another rise.

The second way you can look at the diversification of your holdings is by buying companies of differing sizes. Remember the concept of noncorrelating markets that was explained back in chapter 5? Well, studies have shown that the stocks of small companies tend to increase in price at completely different times than those of large companies. When large company stocks are rising in price, small company stocks tend to stagnate, and vice versa.

Also, small company stocks are generally more volatile than large company stocks. You can expect a portfolio that's made up of nothing but small stocks to experience big swings in price. But a portfolio that includes large, small, and medium-sized companies can have less overall risk and still provide a good return.

You can determine a company's size in two different ways. The first is to determine its *market capitalization*. Market cap (as it's known) is calculated by multiplying a company's current price per share by the number of shares of that company's stock that are outstanding. Although there are no hard-and-fast rules for how to categorize companies after you know their market cap, here are some general guidelines:

Small-cap	Less than $250 million
Mid-cap	Between $250 million and $2.5 billion
Large-cap	Greater than $2.5 billion

What's the Difference Between a Sector and an Industry?

A *sector* is a broad classification used to group companies that share common characteristics. For instance, companies are classified into the following sectors:

Basic Materials	Financial
Capital Goods	Healthcare
Conglomerates	Services
Consumer/Cyclical	Technology
Consumer/Non–Cyclical	Transportation
Energy	Utilities

Each of these sectors is made up of several different *industry* groups that further define the operations of companies. Be aware, however, that different data providers use different classification systems when it comes to industries and sectors.

Although investors commonly use this method, sometimes it provides a distorted picture of a company's size. A company that has just gone public may see its share price climb to the sky as investors are optimistic about the company's future prospects, for example. And although that same company may not yet have any profits, it could still be considered a large-cap stock if you do the math.

For this reason, some investors like to use a company's revenues (sales) rather than market cap to determine its size. A mid-sized company has revenues between $250 million and $2.5 billion—anything smaller is small, and anything larger is large!

Finding the Right Balance

Now that you know how to diversify your portfolio of stocks, what's the right percentage you should allocate to each category? The key is to find the right balance.

It's possible to build a well-diversified portfolio with just seven to twelve stocks, spread out among a half dozen or so sectors. A portfolio of growth stocks should ideally be made up of 25 percent small companies, 25 percent large companies, and 50 percent mid-sized companies.

A portfolio with this general makeup will provide an optimal rate of return.

Everybody's Got a Different Definition of Big and Small

Investors use a lot of different breakpoints when categorizing companies by market cap. Some analysts consider small companies to have market caps of less than $250 million; others might push that figure to $1 billion. Some investors consider a stock a large-cap if it's bigger than $1 billion, and others think $10 billion is closer to the mark. You should know the definitions that a particular data service or analyst uses.

So how do you figure out how your portfolio measures up? One way is to use the portfolio tracking tool available at Quicken.ca (http://www.quicken.ca). After you have entered the stocks that you own into its online portfolio program, you can view charts and tables of your holdings, arranged by company size and by sector. Click the Portfolio Analysis link and you will be presented with a pie chart of your portfolio.

Even though Quicken.ca doesn't include mid-cap stocks in its analysis, you can still get a good idea of how your portfolio is balanced.

Then, click the Sector Diversification link to view a chart of your portfolio's holdings by sector. Below the chart is a table of the percentages of your stocks that fall into different sectors. You can tell in an instant whether your portfolio is out of balance!

As you build your portfolio, it's important to keep the balance of your holdings firmly in mind. If you own a few stocks that have performed well and increased in price significantly, you might see that you have become overweighted in a particular part of the market. Likewise, a stock that has fallen in price may cause your portfolio to be underweighted in one sector.

Quicken.ca's Portfolio Analysis tool provides a quick way to calculate your portfolio's balance.

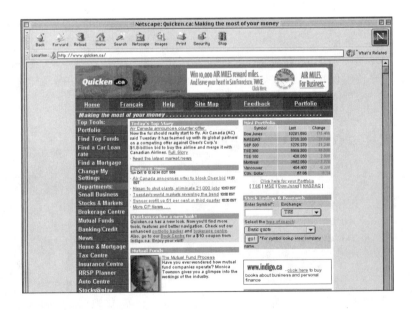

Don't Sweat Your Portfolio's Diversification If You're Just Getting Started

When you first start investing in stocks, your portfolio is likely to be way out of balance. Gradually, however, as you purchase more stocks, you will want to buy stocks that fit into your plan, and eventually you will have a well-balanced portfolio. Don't feel like you have to buy a bunch of stocks all at once just to have a diversified portfolio. It's probably better to take your time, do your homework, and make wise stock choices. In time, you will achieve the optimum balance.

How Do Mutual Funds Fit into a Diversified Portfolio?

The same principles of balance and diversification also apply to portfolios that include mutual funds. Funds already have the diversification element taken care of, because they own hundreds of different stocks. You should still consider the holdings of each fund you own as part of your overall diversification plan, however. A single small-cap mutual fund might take care of all the small company stocks that you need to own in your portfolio. But if you own a mutual fund that primarily owns large companies, and your stocks are also all large companies, your portfolio could be dangerously out of balance.

To correct the imbalance, you could sell some of your holdings in the overweighted sector. What's probably more appropriate, however, is to designate future investments to purchases of stocks in underrepresented sectors.

The Least You Need to Know

➤ A diversified portfolio can help smooth out the bumps in the overall market.

➤ You should aim to build a balanced portfolio of stocks, one that includes companies of different sizes and from different sectors.

➤ You can evaluate your portfolio's balance and diversification by using the tools available on the Web.

Chapter 12

Finding the Right Stocks on the Web

In This Chapter

➤ Getting advice from pros and newsletters

➤ Using stock-screening tools on the Web

➤ Sharing tips with other investors on the Internet

If you're ready to start building a portfolio of stocks, your next step is to find some stocks to buy! The Internet can help you in your search by providing tools, tips, and advice about stocks.

Getting Tips from the Pros

Many money managers, financial planners, and investment advisors use the Web as a platform to reach clients and potential clients. Sometimes, these pros maintain a model portfolio of stock picks, or publish e-mail newsletters that allow individual investors to follow along—and hopefully profit from the wisdom of the pros!

One financial professional who has established an informative and educational Web site is Bob Bose. Bose follows the value-investing principles of Warren Buffet for clients of his Green Mountain Asset Management.

The Green Mountain Asset Management Web site (http://www.stockresearch.com) includes a weekly economic update, current buy recommendations for a portfolio of stocks that Bose tracks, and an Investor Education Center. What's more, you can sign up for Bose's free weekly e-mail newsletter, too!

Hot Tips and Chilly Dogs

If you're searching for hot stock tips, you might consider subscribing to a stock market newsletter. In fact, you might even get offers in your mailbox that tout the success of a market pundit and urge you to subscribe to a printed newsletter.

Plenty of advisory services and newsletter publishers have turned to the Internet, however, to distribute their advice to investors. Now you can get instant recommendations via e-mail or on the Web from market experts of all sorts—for a price, of course.

The good news is that many stock market letters publish free editions to help promote their paid services. Often these newsletters contain only excerpts from the full edition, or they may be published on a delayed basis. But these free newsletters give you a chance to sample the wares of a particular service before you shell out big bucks for a subscription.

Tip Sheets and Advisory Services

For a sampling of the market commentary you can find online, surf over to Invest-O-Rama!'s market commentary section (http://www.investorama.com/commentary.html). Here you will find an assortment of opinions, news, and perspectives on American stocks. Besides offering advice about individual stocks, many of these experts also provide an overview of the entire market.

You Might Not Get the Same Rates of Return as Those Listed in a Newsletter

Most stock market newsletters will provide statistics about their past performance. Although the old adage holds true—"past performance is not indicative of future results"—there are other reasons why you might not get the same return in your own portfolio even if you follow the newsletter's recommendations. First of all, a newsletter's track record includes all its investments. Because no expert can boast a 100 percent accuracy rate in picking stocks, if you pick and choose particular stocks from among all the recommendations you may end up missing out on some of the biggest winners. Second, even if you follow a particular service's picks to the letter, you may not be able to make purchases at the same price as the recommended price in the newsletter.

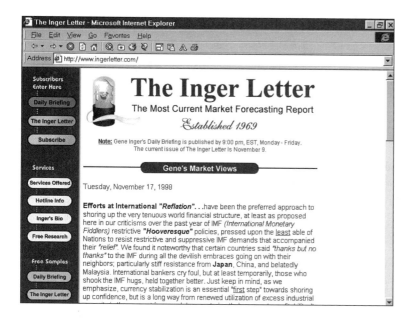

The Inger Letter is a stock market newsletter published daily, and available to subscribers on the Internet.

Some financial newsletter publishers provide samples of their products for free on Invest-O-Rama! so that you can get a taste of their advice. After you have reviewed a particular offering, you can also check out each publisher's own Web site.

Separating the Wheat from the Chaff: Online Stock Screening

Another way of finding stocks that might be worthy of consideration for your portfolio is to use a stock-screening tool. Screening is the process of looking at the whole universe of stocks and then "screening out" those stocks that most likely do not meet your criteria.

More than 10,000 different stocks trade on the stock exchanges in Canada and the U.S., so where do you begin when you're trying to find stocks for your portfolio?

Basics of Stock Screening

The first thing you need to know about stock screening is what kind of stocks you're looking for. Are you looking for stocks that pay a high dividend, or ones that have had good earnings growth in the past? Are you looking for large or small companies? Would you like to invest in stocks in a particular sector or industry?

Some Stocks That Pass a Screen
May Not Be Suitable for Your Portfolio

Stock screening is the process of eliminating companies that are unlikely to be sound candidates for purchase. But some of the stocks that pass the screen may have other qualities that make them undesirable for your portfolio. You need to do your homework before you make any investment decision, and that includes analyzing the stocks that pass your screening.

After you've identified the characteristics of the stocks that you would like to own in your portfolio, you can proceed to the process of building a stock screen.

You can find a few Canadian—and a lot of American—stock-screening programs on the Web. The big advantage of these online tools is that you will always know that the database you're using is current. Before the Internet, if you wanted to use a stock-screening program, you had to maintain your own database of thousands of stocks, an often expensive and time-consuming task. Today you can just connect to a stock-screening Web site!

One stock-screening site that is easy to use is Directions (http://www.ndir.com). It isn't flashy, but it's loaded with great stuff. Another is *The Globe and Mail*'s Stock Filter (www.globeinvestor.com). This screener allows you to build a screen for both Canadian and American stocks. It screens by industry, performance, type of security, and price.

StockScreener, which screens only for U.S. stocks, provides twenty variables for you to choose from, including financial ratios, growth rates, rates of return, and margins. All you need to do is fill in the maximum and/or minimum parameters for the criteria you select, and you will get a list of stocks that fit the bill.

Here's how you can build a stock screen using StockScreener. Let's say you are looking for established companies that have had good growth of sales and earnings in the past, have low debt, and are selling for Price/Earnings (P/E) ratios that are low relative to the expected growth of the company's earnings. It might be a good idea to get rid of very small companies, because micro-cap stocks tend to be dangerous territory. This basic screen could present you with some stocks that currently are undervalued but have good growth potential for the future.

In StockScreener, you would enter the following criteria:

Price/Growth Rate, Maximum 1.0

Debt/Equity Ratio, Maximum 0.5

1-Yr. Revenue Growth Rate, Minimum 15

1-Yr. Earnings Growth Rate, Minimum 15

5-Yr. Revenue Growth Rate, Minimum 15

5-Yr. Earnings Growth Rate, Minimum 15

Latest 12 Mos. Revenue, Minimum $100 (million)

After you have entered those values, click the Search button and see how many companies pass muster. In this example, 108 companies passed the screen—you've eliminated more than 9,000 companies from consideration! Even though it's a lot easier to look through a list of a hundred companies, that's still a lot of stocks. You can adjust your screening parameters still further, however, just by clicking the Refine Search button at the top of the page. This will give you a chance to refine your screen, perhaps by increasing the growth rates or requiring a lower debt/equity ratio.

A particularly useful feature of StockScreener is the capability to sort your results by criteria. Click on the arrow beneath a column header to sort by that criterion, either in descending or ascending order.

Getting Social About Stocks

One common way that many investors get ideas about possible investments is through the advice of friends, family, and coworkers. It is also possible to talk about stocks on the Internet, and even find people whose opinions you trust when it comes to investing!

You can find thousands of investing communities on the Internet—investors who use mailing lists, newsgroups, and message boards to talk to other like-minded investors. The key to the success of these groups is the concept of community. Groups of anonymous people who "mouth off" on a message board with a lot of bluster but few facts are not a community.

Groups of individuals who respect the opinions of others and engage in thoughtful, meaningful dialogues together can find that sharing ideas and information can be profitable to many. But these communities are most successful when they are focused on a particular subject or their members share a common approach to the market.

You can find online communities around just about every corner on the Internet! One top spot to talk stocks is at Yahoo! Finance (http://messages.yahoo.com/yahoo/Business_and_Finance). Here you can find more than 8,000 message boards, each one devoted to

What's the Difference Between a Moderated and an Unmoderated Community?

Some online communities are moderated. This means that someone is responsible for approving and reviewing each message that's posted in an online forum, either before or after it appears publicly. Other forums are unmoderated, which means that anyone can say anything, and no one is responsible for overseeing the contents of messages posted in that forum. It is important that you recognize whether a particular form is moderated or unmoderated. Unmoderated communities can be much "noisier." With no one to keep participants on track, discussions can stray off into other areas, or users can behave in a nasty manner, or messages can contain blatant lies.

Discuss any stock on the Yahoo! Finance message boards.

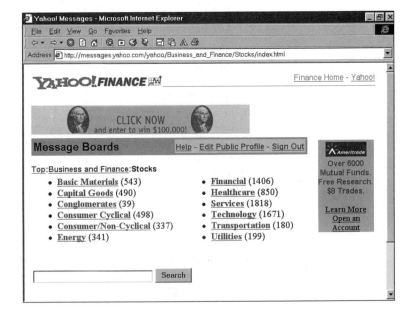

a particular stock. You will either have to know the sector and industry group of your stock to navigate to the board where discussions take place, or you can use the search engine to find the right board.

Another useful site to know about when you want to talk stocks is The Silicon Investor (http://www. techstocks.com). Tapping into the very heart of the tech sector, The Silicon Investor is the largest financial discussion site on the Web, and it is the place to talk about tech stocks. (Anyone can read messages that have been posted on the site, but a subscription is required if you would like to create your own messages on its boards.)

The Silicon Investor also features research tools and articles, but the real strength is the collective wisdom of its membership. Tune in to the talk here, and you can learn to evaluate stocks in the volatile technology sector.

How Can You Tell Whether a Message Is True?

Often, you can't! There will always be people with ulterior motives who post deceiving messages on public discussion boards. The best way to make sure that you've got the facts is to independently verify all online information that you find before you choose to invest in that stock. Assume that nothing is true, and then prove it or disprove it to yourself. Remember, just because someone said it online, doesn't make it true. Be sure to review chapter 19 for ways to protect yourself from online hype.

The Least You Need to Know

➤ You can find many financial advisors on the Internet. Even if you aren't a client, you may be able to take advantage of their expertise by reviewing the stock tips they provide online. Stock market newsletter publishers are taking advantage of the Internet to offer immediate delivery of their publications. No more waiting for the letter carrier to bring you stock recommendations—now you can get them in real time as soon as your favourite newsletter publisher issues them!

➤ Take the time to learn how to use the stock-screening tools available on the Web. These are a powerful way to find stocks that meet your criteria.

➤ Message boards can provide communities of investors the chance to swap ideas and trade barbs (before trading stocks).

Chapter 13

Researching Stocks on the Web

> **In This Chapter**
>
> ➤ Access company data online to find out about its performance
>
> ➤ Annual reports can be real page-turners
>
> ➤ News sources provide clues you can use
>
> ➤ Price charts give you a picture of past performance
>
> ➤ Analyst earnings estimates offer a glimpse of the future

There's an old saying among investors who prefer stocks: "You should always do your homework before you buy." That doesn't mean you have to go back to elementary school, but it does mean that research is the core of good stock selection. It doesn't matter what method of stock analysis you use, you'll still need the right information—and the know-how—to interpret that information and to make sure you're buying the right stocks.

One of the biggest strengths of the Internet is its capability to deliver information about publicly traded companies. No matter what you want to know about a stock, you can probably learn it on the Web.

The Data, Just the Data, and Nothing But the Data

If you base your stock purchase decisions on technical analysis, then you'll only need to get your hands on data about the stock's daily trading volume and share prices for the past several months. There are many subscription services that you can use to maintain this data, which you'll then plug into your charting software. But that's all you'll need—many chartists couldn't tell you any more about the stocks in their portfolio other than the name and ticker symbol!

When you use fundamental analysis to examine a stock, whether from a growth or value perspective, you'll want to become intimately familiar with a company. For that, you'll need access to all kinds of financial information about the company. One of the quickest ways to access stock research on the Web is to use the Research a Stock tool on Invest-O-Rama! (http://www.investorama.com/research.html). Although it deals only with U.S. stocks, it is a great tool. Just enter a stock's ticker symbol and you'll get links to more than seventy-five Web sites with news, quotes, charts, and more about that company. The information you'll find here can keep you busy for hours—but more importantly, it will help you learn as much as possible about any stock.

Getting Acquainted with EDGAR

Fortunately for investors, public companies prepare financial statements on a regular basis so that their owners (the shareholders) can be kept informed about the companies' activities and their financial condition.

In fact, the U.S. Securities and Exchange Commission (SEC) maintains a Web site where you can find reports about nearly any publicly traded American company (http://www.sec.gov/edgarhp.htm). EDGAR (Electronic Data Gathering, Analysis, and Retrieval) is the system devised by the SEC that enables companies to send required reports to the Commission by modem. Within twenty-four hours after the SEC receives these reports, they are made available on the Web site for investors to download.

You can learn a lot about a stock by studying the information in these reports. And because you can get these reports online, and at no cost, they are a rich source of research for investors. Some of the reports that you'll find on the EDGAR system are the following:

➤ 10-Q: This is a company's quarterly report, filed three times a year (the fourth quarter report is included in the company's annual report).

➤ 10-K: Companies must file this report after the end of each fiscal year.

➤ Schedule 14A: Better known as a "proxy statement," companies must send this report to shareholders whenever a vote is required, usually before an annual meeting. These reports are identified as DEF 14A (definitive) or PRE 14A (preliminary) in the EDGAR system.

➤ 8-K: Companies sometimes file Form 8-K to provide an update of important events and financial changes that affect shareholders.

To find a company's filings in the EDGAR system, just enter part of the company's name in the search box on the EDGAR main page. You'll get a list of EDGAR reports that concern your company. (If you see the names of other companies in the list, it's probably because your search term appeared in those reports, too.)

To read a report, click on the company name. The first part of the report includes some codes and data fields, but then the actual report begins. A company's 10-K and 10-Q reports follow the same basic format, so you can learn to navigate through them with ease once you get the hang of it!

Companies Don't Always Celebrate New Year's Eve on December 31st!

Many businesses don't operate on a calendar-year basis, but according to their own fiscal year. A *fiscal year* is twelve months long, just like a calendar year, but it can start and end in any 365-day period. Companies have fiscal years that end June 30th, September 30th, January 31st, or any other day of the year.

The first part of the report includes financial statements: the income statement, the balance sheet, and the cash flow statement.

Quarterly and annual reports also include a section called Management's Discussion of Operations, where a company is obliged to detail any problems that affect its profitability. These reports also include a statement from the company's auditors.

While a single current 10-Q or 10-K report can provide important information about a company's operations, you also might want to consider how a company fared in the past. FreeEDGAR (http://www.freeedgar.com) provides a company's financial statements for several years, and in an easier-to-read format, too. FreeEDGAR collects a company's EDGAR filings, and then lists a company's financial statements for many quarters or years in a single table. This enables you to see changes in profits, sales, and other figures over time.

You can also retrieve complete EDGAR reports from FreeEDGAR, or you can sign up for a free e-mail service that notifies you when a company makes a required filing with the SEC. One last thing to note is that FreeEDGAR publishes EDGAR reports as soon as they are filed, even before they are available from the SEC's own site! The SEC delays the publication of reports on its site for twenty-four hours, selling a real-time feed to commercial publishers (like FreeEDGAR) who want to get their hands on the material sooner.

Annual Reports

A terrific source for information about a company is its annual report. Often, this document is printed on glossy paper in full colour, and serves as more of a publicity vehicle than an information source. However, annual reports must present a company's financial statements, and they usually include plenty of material that can help you understand the company.

If you're a shareholder of a company, you should receive its annual report in the mail each year. If you're not a shareholder, you can contact the company and request a copy to be sent to you free of charge. Usually, the company sends other information as well, including recent press releases, quarterly reports, and brochures.

If you can't wait a couple of weeks for an annual report to arrive in the mail, there's another option. Many corporations are using the Internet as a tool to distribute information for investors and shareholders, and often this means that they'll publish their annual reports on their Web sites.

Glossy Four-Colour Annual Reports Have Their Downside

Many companies go all out in creating their annual reports, filling the pages with colour photographs, printed elegantly on expensive paper. While you might find a photograph of the board of directors interesting to look at, remember that all of the money that's gone into creating a costly annual report comes straight from the profits that rightfully belong to investors. And what's the purpose of these fanciful reports, anyway? Is it to provide important information to investors? Or is it to sell investors on the idea that this company is well established and worthy of your investment (in other words, an extended advertisement)? Many companies today are taking a more frugal route, by publishing a simple annual report or not publishing an annual report at all. For instance, in 1997, Apple Computer chose not to publish a glossy annual report, instead sending all shareholders a copy of their 10-K form filed with the Securities and Exchange Commission.

All the News (and How to Use It)

While you can learn plenty from a company's annual report, you should remember that sometimes things change over time. That goes for public companies, too. Any number of factors about a company's business can change and affect its bottom line. These factors include plant closings, increases in raw material costs, decreases in sales, changes in management, acquisitions of other companies, mergers, or any other unexpected events. Any of these could change your outlook about investing in a particular stock—as long as you know what's going on!

For that, you'll need to keep abreast of the news. One of the best places to find company-specific news (for both Canadian and American stocks) on the Web is on the Yahoo! Finance site (http://quote.yahoo.com). Yahoo! Finance maintains an archive of news stories from various sources as well as press releases for publicly traded companies, going back at least ninety days for most companies.

To search for news at Yahoo! Finance, first get a quote for the stock by entering the ticker symbol on the main page of the site. Then click the News link from the quotes display screen, and you'll see a list of available stories.

The news items are listed by date, and each headline is followed by the source of the news and the time it became available. Just click on the headline to read the article.

When you're researching a stock, these news articles and press releases can tip you off to important recent developments about a company. It might be an announcement of a new product, or a report from a financial analyst about the stock. It could be a

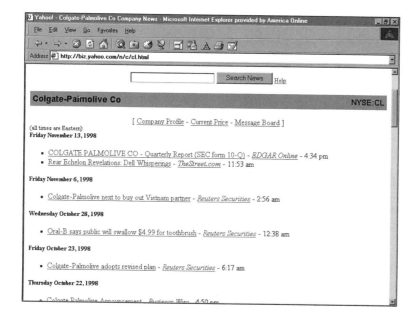

Yahoo! Finance provides an archive of news stories and press releases for any publicly traded company.

statement about a lawsuit that's been filed against or by the company, or a pundit's commentary about a stock's future prospects. All this information can assist you in better understanding a stock's suitability for your own portfolio.

Bear in mind that there are two types of "news" that you'll find on the Web: press releases and news stories. There's a world of difference between them.

Press releases are issued by companies themselves. They are distributed to newspapers and other publications, and are intended to provide information that stimulates editors to assign the story to a reporter or summarize the release in their publication. Press releases are sometimes sent to shareholders, too, or are published on a company's Web site. They often make their way onto many online news services where investors can find them. PR Newswire (http://www.prnewswire.com) and Business Wire (http://www.businesswire.com) are two of the biggest services that distribute company press releases, and you can search their sites for news about many public companies.

News stories are the actual articles that appear in a publication or newspaper. A news story can take many different forms. It might be a straight news story: a short reporting of a particular event, for instance. Or it could be a feature story: a more in-depth look at a company, individual, market trend, particular sector, or some other topic. Or it might be a commentary about a particular subject or company, infused with the opinion of the writer.

Whatever form a story might take, and regardless of whether the story is a more objective news item or a subjective commentary, it is written from the perspective of an outsider looking in at a company and its business. A press release, on the other hand, is written by a company's public relations staff, and is intended to cast the company's

Press Release Information

A company's press release can give you the details of a company's quarterly or annual report before you read it in the newspapers.

Many companies issue press releases that outline their performance in their most recently completed quarter or year, before they make the required filings with their securities commission. These releases can give you timely information about the company's operations. Just remember that the financial figures cited in the release may be labelled "preliminary" and be subject to change before the company files its official report.

business in the best possible light. No matter how awful the news may be that's included in a press release, the company's executives will always be "optimistic about the future" or "disappointed, but taking positive steps." Press releases to a company's operations sound their rosiest, even when bad news is being announced.

That's not to say that press releases can't sometimes be helpful. You can learn a lot by reading what a company has to say about itself, or how it explains a particularly bad bit of news.

Top of the Charts

As the old saying goes, a picture is worth a thousand words. And a chart of a stock's prices over time can give you an indication of how a stock has performed during the period.

BigCharts (http://www.bigcharts.com) is a provider of fast, easy-to-read charts of American stocks and indexes. Type in a ticker symbol or part of a company's name on the main page and choose to display a Quick Chart or Interactive Chart. The Quick Chart gives you the choice of time periods, from one day to a decade (or longer). The Interactive Chart gives you the capability to customize the time frame, style, or indicators that are also plotted on the chart. You can also compare two stocks on the same chart!

Once you've built the chart that's perfect for you, you can choose to have it automatically e-mailed to you on any schedule you set, from once a day to once a week (click the

How to Send and Receive Pictures and Formatted Text in an E-mail Message

E-mail is usually plain text. You type some words into your e-mail software, click Send, and those words are delivered to the recipient with no formatting (no bold, italic, or underlined words), no coloured text, and no fancy fonts. However, there is a way to dress up your e-mail, as long as you have the right e-mail software. Many e-mail services require the use of an e-mail program that can handle HTML-formatted messages. HTML is the language of the Web, but it can also be used in e-mail, as long as your software can interpret the codes. The advantage of HTML-enabled e-mail is that you can send and receive graphics (such as a stock chart) and text that doesn't look like it was created on a typewriter. The most recent versions of Eudora Pro, Microsoft Outlook, and Netscape Messenger all support HTML mail.

E-mail Services link below the graph to enter your preferences). Or you can add the chart to your list of favourites that will appear whenever you arrive at the BigCharts site.

What's a Whisper Estimate?

Today there's another number that's even more important than analysts' published estimates. It's the *whisper estimate*, which, as its name suggests, is an unpublished earnings estimate that investors are discussing before the release of the actual earnings. It's often higher than the more conservative published figures. If a company beats its consensus estimates, but doesn't beat the whisper numbers, the stock may fall dramatically in price.

Estimates and Guesstimates

One of the biggest games on Bay Street is the effort to predict a company's future earnings. Investment banks and full-service brokerage firms employ teams of financial analysts whose jobs are to follow particular companies and make recommendations to their clients. Much of the work of these analysts revolves around the practice of making regular estimates of a company's earnings for each of the upcoming quarters and years.

Based on these earnings estimates, an analyst can make a recommendation that an investor buy, sell, or hold a specific stock. These analyst recommendations are also the basis of the endless stream of "upgrades" and "downgrades" you'll hear or read about a stock, as these experts determine that it's the right time or wrong time to buy that stock.

There may be dozens of analysts who follow a company's stock, so how do you know whom to believe? One way is to look at what are known as the *consensus estimates*. There are services that track the recommendations of all of the analysts who follow a stock, and then determine the average earnings estimate made by the group. Every

You'll Always Be Last in Line to Know About an Analyst's Recommendations

Typically, an analyst's recommendation about a stock is made available to the firm's institutional clients—the large pension funds, mutual funds, and other companies that buy and sell large blocks of stock at a time—and to its full-service clients before it's made available in other channels. If you're not a customer of that firm, you'll only get a crack at buying that stock after all the VIPs get theirs, at which point the price may have already gone up significantly.

quarter, investors look at a company's earnings report, and see how it compared to the consensus figure. If the company's actual earnings were higher than the estimate, the company is said to have "beat its estimate."

While it's easy enough to get consensus analyst estimates, it's much harder to get your hands on copies of an analyst's actual report about a stock. These reports and updates are between one and twenty pages long, with a careful examination of a company's business and operations, and explanation of the analyst's projections for the future. If you're a client of a full-service brokerage firm, you can get that firm's research from your broker.

If you don't have a relationship with a full-service firm, then you can still get these reports on the Web—for a fee. Multex Investor Network (http://www.multexinvestor) is a service that distributes analyst research reports for public companies. You can search for all available reports from the main page of its site, and then you'll have access to a list of reports available for purchase at costs ranging

The Truth Behind Analyst Ratings

While one site may categorize broker ratings into five categories (strong buy, moderate buy, hold, moderate sell, or strong sell), each firm has its own system of appraising stocks. Some firms use the term *outperform* when they're most optimistic about a stock—this stock is set to outperform the overall market. Some firms say *neutral* when others say *hold*. And *attractive* can mean *buy*, but so can *accumulate*. It can be confusing, and there's no universal system in place for stock ratings.

When Is a Hold Really a Sell?

Many investment banks have two types of clients—the customers of the full-service brokerage side of the business, and the publicly traded companies who are clients on the investment banking side. Analysts may have more than the interest of individual investors in mind when they evaluate companies, because they may not want to offend a potential investment banking client. Or an investment bank might be a market maker and profit from sales of a specific stock. And because analysts are dependent on getting information directly from a company, they may refrain from being overly harsh in writing their evaluation. Taking all these factors into account, you'll rarely see a sell rating issued by an analyst, except in the direst of circumstances. That means that many hold ratings really mean that an analyst is recommending that investors sell. Of course, there's no way to read the mind of an analyst, but you should consider this tendency to optimism whenever you look at analyst ratings.

from a few dollars each up to $50 (for one report!). Occasionally, you'll find some free reports. All of these reports require the Adobe Acrobat reader.

The Price Is Right: Stock Quotes

There's one last thing you need to know about a stock before you make the decision to buy: its share price! Fortunately, you can find stock quotes at countless Web sites. And with the results of your stock study in hand, you can determine if a stock's current price represents a good value for your portfolio, or if it might be more sensible to look elsewhere.

You'll learn more about current price quotes and historical price data in chapter 18. For now, however, it's time to learn about how you can buy and sell stocks online.

The Least You Need to Know

➤ Access online data to keep you informed of a company's performance.

➤ News stories and press releases can inform you of recent developments in a particular company, though you should be wary of overly optimistic press releases written by the company itself.

➤ Price charts can tell you where a stock has been. Many online chart services can be customized, offering additional insights and comparisons.

➤ Analyst earnings estimates can shine the light on a company's future potential. Analyst ratings can also tell you if a stock is a buy, sell, or hold.

Chapter 14

Buy, Sell, or Hold Begins with Buy

> **In This Chapter**
>
> ➤ The difference between full-service and discount brokers
>
> ➤ How to select the best broker for you
>
> ➤ The ins and outs of online trading

After you've decided which stocks to buy, it's time to actually make the purchase. Unfortunately, you just can't walk into a McDonald's and order a Big Mac, fries, and ten shares of stock! You also can't log on to a company's Web site and buy shares directly with a credit card. (At least not yet, anyway!)

If you want to be a shareholder of a company, you will need to use the services of a brokerage firm to buy shares of stock. This is where the Internet comes in—you can buy and sell stocks at an online brokerage firm after you've established an account. But how do you choose an online broker? And how do you know whether the firm is reputable?

Cost Versus Service: The Battle Between Full-Service and Discount Brokers

The brokerage business breaks down into two basic categories: full-service (sometimes known as full-commission) and discount-commission brokers. As you can imagine, the battle lines are drawn around the level of service and the costs of the two types of brokerages.

Customers of Discount Brokerage Firms Can't Count on Personalized Service

If you open an account at a discount brokerage, you probably won't be assigned a particular representative at that firm.

When you think of a stockbroker, you probably think of someone who works for one of the big-name, traditional brokerage firms. These companies have worked hard to build up an aura of authority and respectability about their businesses, usually with a lot of marble and granite logos and advertisements featuring attractive, older, successful-looking people who are meant to represent their clients.

Full-service brokers are the traditional way that Canadians have invested in the stock market. Brokers have access to all sorts of information about the markets, and are trained and licensed to be able to give investment advice to the public. The companies have teams of analysts who research stocks, bonds, and mutual funds, and make recommendations for customers of the firm.

Of course, you will pay some fairly steep commissions whenever you buy a stock, bond, or mutual fund from a full-service broker. That's the price you pay for expert advice and for the privilege of working with a broker (at least, that's the theory).

Discount brokerage firms, on the other hand, charge commissions that are a fraction of what the full-service firms charge. However, the employees at a discount brokerage firm are not allowed to provide investment advice to customers. When you have an account at a discount firm, you get cut-rate commissions (especially on the Internet), but you won't get any handholding or recommendations from the company. That's the trade-off of saving on commissions.

So how do you know which is right for you? Are you better off with a full-service broker, or should you go it alone and work with a discounter?

Is a Full-Service Broker for You?

Full-service firms take pride in their ability to provide "full service" for all your financial needs. Besides helping you build an investment portfolio, most firms offer you the chance to meet with a planner to review your complete financial situation. Full-service firms can provide help or referrals to accountants and lawyers to deal with some of the more complicated components of personal finance.

You can get help with estate planning issues such as how to make sure your heirs are taken care of in the manner you desire after you pass away, for example. Your full-service firm can help you decide whether you need to set up some sort of trust or may suggest some other strategy to manage your estate. If you need assistance setting up your will, the firm can refer you to a lawyer, and can even work with you to make sure your will covers all the right financial concerns. If you would like to minimize your tax liabilities, your broker can offer you an array of government bonds for your portfolio.

You Can Get "Full Service" from a Smaller Brokerage

Although "full service" is often used to describe the major, national investment banks and brokerage firms that charge full commissions, plenty of other, smaller firms provide full service, and at much lower rates. Often, these firms are regional or local businesses that serve a community or part of the country, but their brokers can be just as knowledgeable as those at larger firms.

If you decide that you just don't have the time to manage your own portfolio, you can give your broker the power to take over your accounts for you. Then, he or she can make sales and purchases on your behalf without getting your approval each time. If you travel abroad frequently, for instance, it might be a good idea to give your broker the ability to move quickly if something changes drastically with an investment you own, without making him or her track you down in the outback of Australia!

On top of all that, full-service brokers have the research of his firm's analysts at their fingertips. Brokers can give you the best picks of the firm and their own ideas about which stocks might be good for your portfolio.

The bottom line is that full-service brokers should emphasize service. If you think these services are helpful, you might want to consider working with a full-service broker.

Full-Service Brokerage Firms on the Web

If you decide that a full-service broker is for you, next you will need to find one! Because you will be working with your broker on a one-on-one basis, you will probably want to find someone who is near where you work or live. That way you can sit down with your broker periodically and review your portfolio.

One of the best ways to find a broker is to ask for referrals from people you know. Chances are that some of your friends, coworkers, and family members use a full-service broker, and they can offer a recommendation.

When you check out full-service brokerage sites on the Web, you will see, by and large, that full-service firms don't provide online trading functions or a lot of interactive tools. In fact, full-service firms have been downright slow to embrace the Web. That's because they have concerns about how to maintain the personal relationships between brokers and their clients in an online atmosphere. If these firms allow customers to enter their own orders, how long will it take before they realize that they might be able to do without a full-service broker altogether (and then switch to a discounter)? Some brokerage firms do allow their representatives to communicate with clients using e-mail, another step in the right direction.

What you may find on the sites of many full-service firms is market news and commentary from their analysts and strategists, calculators, and educational materials, and maybe even some reports from their analysts about individual stocks, bonds, or mutual funds (although they may reserve the good stuff for clients only).

Some firms are even beginning to offer online account access for customers. Although you can't place orders, you can get your account balance and check the recent activity in your account. Merrill Lynch has just announced an online service for an annual fee. This service will debut in Canada soon.

Checking Out a Broker

After you've found a broker, you need to figure out whether he or she is right for you! Just like there are doctors who specialize in different ailments, brokers have expertise in some areas and know less about others.

Before you sign the paperwork to open an account, schedule a personal interview with the broker. Use this appointment to try to get to know the broker, and be prepared to ask about the broker's background, licences, work history, and approach to working with clients. Find out what kind of investments the broker is knowledgeable about, and what fees and commissions you will be charged. It can be helpful to bring along a notepad with some of these questions already jotted down so that you don't forget anything as the broker rattles off the advantages of working with his or her firm!

You should be prepared to meet with several brokers. Remember that you will be putting your financial future into the hands of your broker, so you need to find someone you trust, and someone who will answer your questions, no matter how "dumb" they might seem to you.

Cheap, Easy, Convenient: Online Brokerage Firms

The allure of online trading is one of the biggest reasons that investors have flocked to the Web in the past few years. And why not? Now you can buy shares in any company in less than sixty seconds, and at a fraction of the cost of a full-commission firm.

You can buy and sell Canadian and U.S. stocks over the Internet at twelve Canadian online discount brokerage firms. Some are well-established discount firms, like TD Waterhouse (http://www.tdwaterhouse.com), that have launched online trading services. Others, such as E*TRADE (http://www.canada.etrade.com), are companies launched as Internet brokers.

How do you figure out which broker to choose? The key is to know which services and features you require from your broker. After you understand your own needs, you can whittle the list of candidates right down to a more manageable size.

Choosing the Online Broker That Is Right for You

Not all online brokers are created equal. Some brokers cater to frequent traders, and some brokers offer a wide array of mutual funds that you can purchase with no transaction fees. No matter what your approach to investing, you can find a broker that can provide services that save you money.

The first thing you need to do is figure out what's important to you. All online brokers can buy and sell shares of stock for you, but here are some points to consider beyond that:

1. **How much money do you need to open an account?** Some firms have no minimum requirement to open an account. Others can require a deposit of $1,000 or more before they will let you open an account. If you don't have enough to meet the minimum requirement, you can strike that firm off your list.

2. **Do you want to include mutual funds in your portfolio?** Many online brokerages offer mutual fund "supermarkets," where you can buy and sell funds from many different fund families. The selection of funds varies from firm to firm, so make sure that a company offers the funds that you're interested in before you sign up. If you're not interested in funds, you don't need a brokerage that offers a large selection.

The Lowdown on Minimum Initial Balances

Many brokers require a certain amount, typically ranging from $1,000 to $10,000, to open an account. You may not be required to maintain a minimum balance after the account is opened, however. If you would like to open an account at a firm that demands a high mini-mum, but you don't necessarily want to keep all that money in the account indefinitely, just scrape together the cash and then withdraw part of it after the account is opened. Just watch for maintenance fees that some brokers charge if your balance falls below a certain amount.

Can Your Broker Handle Days When the Market Is Very Busy?

In the past, when the market has experienced very heavy trading volume, the customers at some online brokerage firms found that they could not log on to place orders. The online firms were simply unprepared for the number of customers who were trying to place orders! Some online brokerage firms will automatically give you their online commission rate (when it's lower) anytime you are prevented from logging on to their site. Check out a firm's policies, or you might be left out in the cold on the market's hottest days.

3. **Do you want to buy or sell options, foreign stocks, or penny stocks?** Not all online brokers offer these services.

4. **Is it important to be able to talk to an actual person on the phone?** Some brokerages charge a higher commission if you place an order by telephone instead of using their Web site (for example, E*TRADE charges $15 per trade). If you think you might need some help, or don't always have access to your computer when you might like to make a trade, make sure you won't be penalized for it.

5. **Will you be able to make use of the research that the company provides?** Many online brokerages advertise the "research" that's available for their customers, but the truth is that much of this information is already available elsewhere for free. It may be more convenient to access research, quotes, and your account balance all in one place, but you shouldn't have to pay for the convenience!

6. **Would you like to buy stocks on margin?** Margin accounts enable you to buy stocks on credit, borrowing against the value of the securities already in your account. Of course, you will have to pay interest on the money you borrow, and you will find big differences in the interest rates that different firms charge. Also, some firms require a higher minimum to establish a margin account than a cash account.

Low Commission Brokers Aren't Always the Cheapest

It's easy to compare brokers solely on the basis of their advertised lowest commissions. After you read the fine print, however, you will see that comparing commissions from firm to firm can be like comparing apples and oranges. To effectively compare the

Margin Can Be Dangerous in the Wrong Hands

If you have a margin account, you can borrow up to 50 percent of your total account value to buy other shares. If the value of your account falls, however, the amount you can borrow on margin also falls! If that happens, you will get a *margin call* from your brokerage, and you will have to deposit more cash to bring you up to the required amount. That means that in a falling market, your account will drop in value but you will have to keep coming up with money—or sell shares—just to cover your margin loans. At the same time, you will be paying interest on the loan, so it's possible that buying on margin could drain you dry.

commission rates at different brokers, you need to consider two things: first, whether you will be placing a "market" or a "limit" order; and second, how many shares you will be buying and selling at a time.

A *market order* is when you ask your broker to buy or sell shares at the best price available in the market at the time you place the order. A *limit order*, on the other hand, lets you specify the maximum price per share for a sale or purchase. Some online brokers charge significantly higher rates for limit orders—and they will probably advertise the lower rate for market orders most prominently!

If you like to specify your order price for all trades, or you frequently buy and sell fast-moving stocks, you will want to know how much a market order will cost you.

Secondly, many firms tout their low commissions, but those rates often change depending on the number of shares you're buying or selling. E*TRADE's flat-rate $27 commission is only good on orders of 1,000 shares or less. After that, you pay 3 cents extra per share. It might not sound like much, but for an order of 10,000 shares, the commission rate would be $297.

The Advantage of Market Orders Over Limit Orders

When you place a market order, you are almost certainly guaranteed that your order will be filled. With limit orders, on the other hand, your order price may or may not ever be met, so it's possible that your purchase or sale will never be made. If you really want to buy or sell a stock, use a market order.

The Advantage of Limit Orders Over Market Orders

When you place a market order, your sale or purchase will be made at whatever price shares are trading for at that moment. That could be many dollars per share more or less than the price when you placed the order, even if it was just a few minutes earlier! With limit orders, you will know exactly the maximum amount a trade could cost you—as long as the trade is executed. So if you want to know exactly how much a trade could cost you, use a limit order.

All online brokerage firms publish their commission schedules on their Web sites. Before you sign up, take a close look at the rates for various sizes of trades. Make sure that your brokerage fits the types and sizes of trades you're most likely to make.

Hidden Fees Can Cost You Big Bucks

Unfortunately, commissions aren't the only costs involved with online trading. Some brokers charge dozens of other fees.

Some firms charge a fee of $15 to $25 for issuing and delivering a stock certificate, for example. Although you will probably want to hold most of your stocks in your account, there may be times when you want to have a certificate issued (for instance, to enroll in a dividend reinvestment plan—more on that in chapter 15). Other firms may slam the door on your way out, and charge a fee of $50 if you close your account. You may be charged a fee if you request a copy of a statement, or if you wire funds into or out of your account.

The bottom line is that you should check out the fees, as well as the commissions, before you open an account at an online brokerage.

Online Trading Is Safe and Secure—Or Is It?

Many people are concerned about the security of the Internet. Before they put their personal financial information online somewhere, they worry about whether it's safe— or whether there's a risk that some hacker could find out their most personal financial secrets.

Never fear. All online brokers require the use of a secure Web browser, one that uses encryption to put your information into a secret code before it's sent out over the

Internet. At the other end, the broker uses a special Web server that decodes the information. Although your data is out on the Internet, it's virtually impossible that anyone could crack the code and get access to the protected information. You will learn more about Internet security in chapter 19.

Opening an Account

After you have decided to open an account with a particular firm, the procedure is easy—and at some firms, it's even easier!

Nearly every firm provides an account application on its site that you can download. (Look for the big, bold link that says something like "OPEN AN ACCOUNT NOW" on the main page of the site.)

Some firms walk you through the application process right on their site, enabling you to complete the application while you're on the site by filling in the blanks, and then letting you print out the form. All you have to do then is sign the form, and send it back—along with your cheque, of course!

A few online brokerage firms have taken the process a step further. At some, you fill out the required information, read the account agreement, click a few buttons, and your account is opened for you almost immediately! You will have an account number and a password, and you can start trading right away.

Of course, you will have to send a cheque within three days of your first trade. Some firms who offer online applications also require a signed form to be sent to them to finalize the process and grant you online access to your account.

You can always open your account the old-fashioned way, by asking the firm to send you an application in the mail. Most firms have an e-mail address or form on their site that you can use to request the paperwork. Then you will complete the entire form by hand and send it back to the brokerage with your cheque.

Why Do Brokerage Firms Ask So Many Personal Questions on Their Applications?

It's true, you can expect a brokerage firm's application form to require you to provide bank and credit card references, information about your salary and your employer, and other personal details. Much of this information is required by industry regulations, but they also want to try to find out whether you're likely to be a problem customer! Just answer truthfully and completely, and you won't have any problem.

The Least You Need to Know

➤ Full-service brokers offer customized investment advice and financial services to account holders, but at a price. If you work with a full-service firm, you will work with a broker who will be your partner in building a portfolio.

➤ Discount brokers can't offer personalized investment advice, but their commissions are much lower than the full-service firms.

➤ Some discount brokers offer online trading services. Choosing the right online broker depends on whether you're most interested in research, low commissions, other services, or a combination of these.

Chapter 15

Skipping the Broker Altogether

In This Chapter

➤ How to invest in stocks without using a broker

➤ Where to learn about DRIPs and SPPs

➤ How to find companies that offer these plans

If you've decided that the stock market is for you, but don't have thousands of dollars to open a brokerage account, there is a lower-cost alternative that will let you start building a portfolio of stocks without using the services of a broker. Did you know that you can buy stock in companies like TransCanada PipeLines, Canadian Pacific, Dofasco, and MacMillan Bloedel without paying commissions to a broker, as long as you own at least one share? In fact, you can start building a portfolio of stocks with as little as $25!

What's the secret to becoming a shareholder without using a broker? It's buying shares of a stock directly from the company through its *Dividend Reinvestment Plan* and *Share Purchase Plan* (commonly known as DRIPs and SPPs). DRIPs are a great way to invest, and it takes as little as $25 to buy shares in some of the best companies in Canada. If this sounds appealing to you, you can get started as a DRIP investor with the help of a few sites on the Web.

Successful Investing, DRIP by DRIP

The first key to understanding how DRIP investing works is to know about dividends. *Dividends* are payments of a company's profit to its owners—the stockholders. Most

Reinvested Dividends Are Taxable, Just Like Cash Dividends

Any dividends you receive from stocks you own are taxable. It doesn't matter if those dividends were reinvested in additional shares, or if you received them in cash—they still must be reported on your tax return each year. The bright side of this wrinkle is that reinvested dividends increase your cost base for tax purposes. So each time your dividends are reinvested, your taxable capital gains will be lessened.

blue-chip companies pay dividends to shareholders on a quarterly basis, sending a cheque to each owner of the company four times a year. If your shares are held in a brokerage account, your broker will credit your account each time a dividend is paid.

Some companies would rather not have to make these cash dividend payments each quarter. Instead, they give current shareholders the option to enroll in a special program and then receive their dividends in the form of additional shares of the company's stock—the dividends are automatically reinvested in purchases of additional shares. That's why these plans are known as Dividend Reinvestment Plans (DRIPs).

Once you enroll in a DRIP, you no longer receive quarterly dividend cheques. Instead, you receive a statement once a quarter showing the amount of the dividend and how many additional shares were purchased with those funds in your account. If your dividends didn't add up to an entire share, you would receive a fractional share (another nice touch—brokers usually only allow you to purchase whole shares). What's more, DRIPs charge little or no commissions on purchases made with these reinvested dividends. And in a few cases, the shares you buy with reinvested dividends are sold at a 5 percent discount to their current trading price on the market!

But the best part of DRIPs is still to come. Yes, it is great that your dividends are reinvested (it certainly can add up to a lot over the course of many years). But the real advantages of DRIPs are that most allow you to make additional purchases of stock free of commissions, and you can invest as little as $25 at a time. These are called *optional cash payments* (OCPs). And as the name suggests, you are under no obligation at all to buy more shares. It simply means that once you're a registered holder of at least one share in these companies, you can send money and buy more shares without paying any commission at all. These are Share Purchase Plans (SPPs), and they're what make the whole DRIP exercise really pay off. If you tried to buy $25 worth of stocks at even the

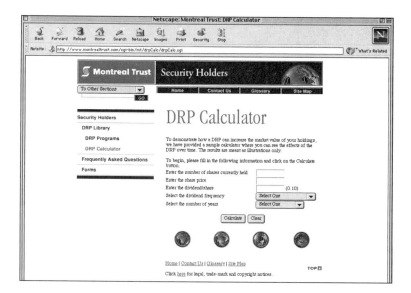

Montreal Trust offers a DRIP calculator that shows the value of a Dividend Reinvestment Plan as it builds over time.

cheapest online broker, the broker would eat up most, if not all, of your total investment. Now you don't need hundreds or thousands of dollars to get started investing in stocks, and you don't have to worry about high commissions eating into your profits. You can build a portfolio of stock, DRIP by DRIP!

Because you can get started in DRIPs without a large amount of money, they are a great way to learn about investing. Instead of sticking your head in an investment book, you can buy a few shares and actually be a stockholder. As you gain knowledge, you can continue to invest, bit by bit, and eventually you'll find that you're the owner of a portfolio of blue-chip stocks. And because these are usually high-quality companies, your portfolio may well end up outperforming the average mutual fund!

To learn more about DRIPs, a good first stop on the Web is *Canadian MoneySaver* magazine

The DRIP-SPP Connection

Canadian companies that offer Share Purchase Plans all offer Dividend Reinvestment Plans too. But it doesn't work the other way around. Many companies that offer DRIPs do not offer SPPs. And it's the Share Purchase Plans that allow large, commission-free accumulations of stock. Just remember to sign up for *both* plans, because they are separate programs.

(http://www.candianmoneysaver.ca/reg_drip.htm). This site features a series of articles of interest to DRIP investors, including a list of the more than thirty TSE-listed companies that offer DRIPs and SPPs. You'll also find links to U.S. DRIP sites (more about this later). One of the magazine's feature writers on DRIPs is Cemil Otar, and you'll find several of

Canadian MoneySaver *magazine is a good first-stop resource for DRIP education and research.*

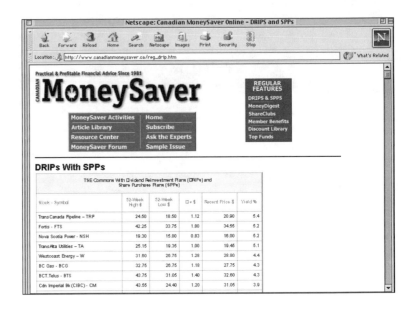

The following is from the Netscape browser window showing Canadian MoneySaver Online - DRIPS and SPPs at http://www.canadianmoneysaver.ca/reg_drip.htm

Practical & Profitable Financial Advice Since 1981

MoneySaver

MoneySaver Activities	Home
Article Library	Subscribe
Resource Center	Ask the Experts
MoneySaver Forum	Sample Issue

REGULAR FEATURES
DRIPS & SPPS
MoneyDigest
ShareClubs
Member Benefits
Discount Library
Top Funds

DRIPs With SPPs

TSE Commons With Dividend Reinvestment Plans (DRIPs) and Share Purchase Plans (SPPs)

Stock - Symbol	52-Week High $	52-Week Low $	□ × $	Recent Price $	Yield %
TransCanada Pipeline – TRP	24.50	18.50	1.12	20.90	5.4
Fortis – FTS	42.25	33.75	1.80	34.55	5.2
Nova Scotia Power – NSH	19.30	15.80	0.83	16.00	5.2
TransAlta Utilities – TA	25.15	19.35	1.00	19.45	5.1
Westcoast Energy – W	31.60	26.75	1.28	28.80	4.4
BC Gas - BCG	32.75	26.75	1.18	27.75	4.3
BCT.Telus – BTS	43.75	31.05	1.40	32.60	4.3
Cdn Imperial Bk (CIBC) - CM	43.55	24.40	1.20	31.05	3.9

DRIPs Can Be a Record-Keeping Challenge

One of the downsides of DRIP investing is that each reinvested dividend and optional cash payment must be carefully tracked to determine the cost basis of your investment for tax purposes. If you're doing everything on your own, a good record-keeping software program would be a wise purchase.

his articles here too. He's a Toronto-based financial advisor who's written an authoritative guide to these plans, *Commission Free Investing: A Handbook of Canadian DRIPs and SPPs*, that can be ordered online from the magazine.

The Basics of DRIPs and SPPs

The first thing you have to do is buy at least one share of the company you're interested in, and then have it registered in your name. Let's deal with the first share requirement first.

You can contact a discount broker, open up an account, and ask to buy one share. The online trading commission will range from $20 to $30, depending on the broker you choose. You must then tell the broker to register the share in your name (shares are normally registered in "street name"). This costs from $25 to $35. Once you've done that, you're ready to participate in the company's Share Purchase Plan and buy more shares without ever paying any more commissions. One potential problem here: Not all brokers will sell you a single share, especially if they think that's the only business you're ever going to give them.

There are other options. Let's say you're already a stockholder in the company. You can ask your broker to take one of the shares you already own and register it in your name.

Or you can arrange to buy a share from an existing shareholder. Let's assume a friend owns one hundred shares of TransCanada PipeLines. You can ask your friend to tell the trustee of TransCanada PipeLines to register one of your friend's shares in your name. This transfer of ownership doesn't cost any money. But you may want to take your friend out to dinner. And be patient. The paperwork may take two or three months to complete.

Investment clubs or share clubs (see chapter 6) are also an ideal place to find fellow investors who might want to help you out. Some investors looking to swap single shares find what they're looking for in the *Canadian MoneySaver* magazine's online Forum section (http://www.candianmoneysaver.ca).

The Transfer Agents

When you deal with the thirty+ Canadian companies and trusts that offer DRIPs and SPPs, you'll actually be dealing with their *transfer agents* (also called *trustees*). You can usually find out who the company's transfer agent is by looking up the company's Web site. There's often a section for shareholders or investors that lists that information. Or, you can do a company search with SEDAR (http://www.sedar.com) That's the System for Electronic Document Analysis and Retrieval. Just look up the company you're interested in and you'll find the transfer agent listed in the profile.

Globeinvestor.com (http://www.globeinvestor.com) is another great source of company information.

You can also go to the sites of two of the biggest transfer agents in Canada: CIBC Mellon Trust (http://www.cibcmellon.com) and Montreal Trust (http://www.montrealtrust.com).

SEDAR (the System for Electronic Document Analysis and Retrieval) can help you find the transfer agent for every Canadian company.

CIBC Mellon Trust is one of the main transfer agents for Canadian companies with DRIPs and SPPs.

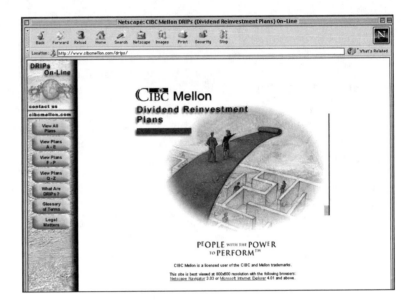

Beware "Synthetic DRIPs" Offered by Brokers

Many brokers offer their clients free "dividend reinvestment." But a broker's Dividend Reinvestment Plan is missing the crucial ingredient that's so appealing to stingy investors: the Share Purchase Plan (the ability to make additional purchases of stock free of commissions). Broker DRIPs also never give investors the 5 percent discount on shares purchased with reinvested dividends.

Both sites provide information on dozens of Canadian companies that offer DRIPs. But remember: you want companies that offer both DRIPs *and* SPPs. So be sure to check that the company listed offers the optional cash payment (OCP) feature. Only then can you send extra cash payments and take advantage of the Share Purchase Plans.

Both sites provide the key features of each company's plan. For instance, they'll indicate the minimum and maximum investment you can make in the SPP. As we've said, the minimums start as low as $25 and the maximum you can invest is usually very generous (many companies allow you to buy $20,000, $40,000, or even $80,000 a year worth of shares from them, without a penny in commission, as long as you own that first share and enroll in their plan.)

As an example, let's go to the CIBC Mellon site and find "MDS Inc." A look at the DRIP chart for this company shows that it does indeed offer the key optional cash payment feature. But here's an extra bonus. On the next line down in that chart, you'll find that MDS is one of the few companies that gives a 5 percent discount on new shares purchased with the dividends reinvested through its DRIP plan! The chart also reveals the specifics of its Optional Cash Payment Plan: that any payment must be at least $50 semi-annually, and no more than $3,000 semi-annually.

You can download information on many DRIPs directly from the Montreal Trust and CIBC Mellon Web sites. Enrollment and authorization forms will be forwarded to you for your signature. And both sites also feature general information sections on DRIPs and SPPs that make for valuable reading.

For a summary chart of Canadian DRIPs and SPPs, you can also link to Directions (http://www. ndir.com/stocks.drips.html). This is an ambitious site set up by avid investor Norman Rothery. He tries to keep it as up to date as possible, but as always, you should verify the information directly with the company or transfer agent.

Canadian MoneySaver magazine also publishes a complete list of Canadian DRIPs and SPPs at least twice a year, in the spring and fall. *Investor's Digest* newsletter also regularly updates its complete list of DRIPs offered by Canadian companies. Again, verify the information from the companies or transfer agents.

Don't Invest in a Stock Just Because It Offers a DRIP

A company that doesn't perform for its shareholders is a bad investment, even if it has a DRIP. Make sure you base your decision to invest in a company on sound, fundamental qualities—not simply because it happens to offer a DRIP.

Alternatives to Company-Sponsored DRIPs

If you've read this far, you're probably thinking this sounds too good to be true. Well, rest assured...it's all true. But it also involves a bit of paperwork. So if you like the idea of having some of that paperwork done for you, and paying a small commission (less than what a discount broker would charge), there's an easier alternative. It's called the Low-Cost Investing Program (LCIP), and it's offered by the Canadian Shareowners Association (http://www.shareowner.ca). Click on Investment Clubs and then Low-Cost Investing.

More than 2,500 of the CSA's 15,000 members take advantage of its LCIP. At last count, the CSA allowed people to invest in fifty-five companies (twenty-seven Canadian, twenty-eight American), as well as four index-based products (such as Toronto 35 Index Participation Units, and Standard & Poor's Depositary Receipts).

To take part, you must be a member of the CSA. That costs $89 a year, a fee that includes a subscription to the magazine *Canadian Shareowner*, and its *Stock Selection Guide*. There's also a one-time setup fee of $8 and a transaction fee of $4 for each sale or purchase. Not free, but less than what your online broker would charge. Still, the CSA plan has several advantages over the do-it-yourself route. For one thing, there's the convenience of one-stop shopping. For another, you can put all the shares you acquire through the CSA's plan into an RRSP account. That's difficult with the company-sponsored DRIPs/SPPs. The CSA program also allows people to accumulate shares in

The Canadian Shareowners Association offers a Low-Cost Investing Program, a convenient alternative to company-sponsored DRIPs and SPPs.

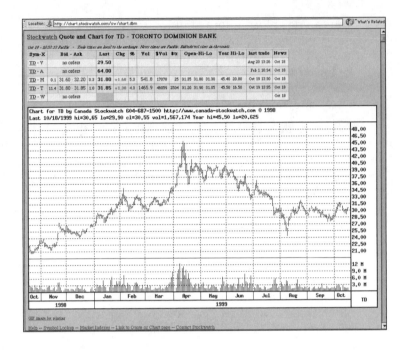

some companies that don't have their own DRIPs. And lastly, you can buy some American companies. The CSA is registered with provincial securities commissions to sell U.S. company shares to Canadian residents.

There are other ways of buying American DRIPs. But here, you enter a bit of a grey area. You can try setting up an account at a U.S discount broker. Or you can use the services of a company like The Moneypaper (http://www.moneypaper.com). This provides a service that will sell you the necessary first share and will charge a setup fee. More than 900 companies are available, and most will sell to Canadians. Remember, though, that The Moneypaper and similar services are not registered to sell shares in Canada. You may want to seek some advice from your provincial securities commission.

Direct Purchase Plans (and Direct Stock Plans)

There are ways of buying shares directly from companies themselves, even the first share.

That's the good news. The bad news is that you can't do that with Canadian companies. Securities regulations in this country require that Canadians buy their first share through a broker, or some other organization licensed to sell securities (like the Canadian Shareowners Association). There is, however, a strong likelihood that this policy will soon change. The Ontario Securities Commission is drafting proposed regulations for Direct Purchase Plans that would give Canadians clearance to buy shares directly from companies, bypassing brokers altogether. After all, Americans have been allowed to do this for years. In the United States, hundreds of companies allow investors to buy shares directly. Dozens of these companies (like Texaco, and Procter & Gamble) will sell shares directly to Canadians through their Direct Stock Plans. Do keep in mind, though, that for the time being, you're in this regulatory dark zone. Be aware, too, that many of the U.S. companies that offer Direct Stock Plans charge small setup fees as well as commissions.

NetStock Direct (http://www.netstockdirect.com) is one of many American Web sites that offers a searchable directory of U.S. DRIPs and DSPs.

More and More U.S. Companies Offer Direct Stock Plans

Nearly 500 U.S. companies now offer American investors the chance to buy shares directly, a tenfold increase since 1995.

One final note: All Canadians wishing to buy directly from an American company must file a W-8 form (Certificate of Foreign Status). You can download this form at the EquiServe site (http://www.equiserve.com). Go to Printable Forms and click through to get the W-8. Tax will likely be withheld at source, but will end up as a credit for your Canadian income tax return. Dividends from U.S. companies, by the way, do not qualify for the Dividend Tax Credit. That means that you'll pay the same tax on U.S. dividends as you would on interest income—at your highest marginal tax rate.

Still, all things considered, there's no doubt about it—DRIPs and SPPs are a powerful way for the beginner to start on the path toward becoming a Bay Street tycoon. And with the eventual arrival of Canadian company Direct Purchase Plans, the do-it-yourself investor will have even more opportunity to get a piece of the market action without having to pay a fortune in brokerage fees.

The Least You Need to Know

➤ Dividend Reinvestment Plans (DRIPs) and Share Purchase Plans (SPPs) are ways that you can invest in stocks without going through a broker. In addition, you can often invest without paying any commissions.

➤ There are low-cost investment plans that make it more convenient to take part in DRIPs and SPPs, with fees that are less than what a discount broker would charge.

➤ You can research company DRIPs and SPPs on the Web, and compare the features of their plans.

Part 4
Managing a Portfolio

Good job. You've built a market-savvy portfolio, but while you are patting yourself on the back and waiting for your ship to come in, don't let your investments just sit there! When you work hard at managing your portfolio, you will be able to anticipate changes in the financial climate and to adjust your investments for maximum growth. There are many online tools to make successful portfolio management achievable even for the novice investor.

Chapter 16

Record Keeping Versus Portfolio Management

In This Chapter

➤ Learn how the Internet can help you maintain your investment records

➤ Understand how your investment decisions can affect your taxes

➤ Calculate the return of your portfolio

Sure, it is a snap to get updated prices for your stocks and mutual funds from the Web. But is looking at the quotes for your portfolio six times a day the same thing as managing your portfolio? Absolutely not!

In fact, you need to manage two completely different tasks if you really want to be a successful online investor.

The first is to keep track of all the important records related to the stocks and funds you buy and sell, and all the other activity in your portfolio. This is called *record keeping*.

The second is to make sure that your portfolio is performing well and meeting all of your objectives. This is called *portfolio management*.

The problem is that too many people confuse these two responsibilities. You should make sure that you don't. Although checking on the prices of the stocks that you own is part of the process of both record keeping and portfolio management, being a good portfolio manager requires much more than just looking at quotes on a computer screen.

Good Record Keeping Is a Good Thing

After you start down the path to investing, one thing that you will notice is that the paperwork sure piles up fast! You will get a confirmation form every time you buy or sell a stock or mutual fund, and every time you move money into or out of an account. Each of your investment accounts will send you a statement every month, or at least every quarter. And each of those account statements will probably include a couple of transactions, such as dividends you have received or interest that has been credited to your account.

If you invest using Dividend Reinvestment Plans, you will have another set of statements to deal with for each DRIP and for each transaction. Every time you buy a mutual fund, you will receive a prospectus in the mail. Companies from stocks you own will send you quarterly and annual reports and proxy statements.

You Can't Avoid the Paperwork

One reason for the vast amounts of paperwork involved with investing is that regulatory agencies in the securities industry still require that certain information be sent to investors in printed format. Some of these regulations are slowly changing in the face of the cyber revolution to allow electronic communication, but for now, you can still expect to receive stacks of documents and statements in the mail from your investment accounts.

The bottom line is that you will be swimming in paper if you don't get organized! Besides the advantage of keeping your desk or dining room table clutter-free, being organized provides two other important benefits:

➤ You will be better equipped to know how much of your investing profits you will owe to Revenue Canada, and you can make better decisions regarding the tax implications of any investment.

➤ You will be better equipped to figure out how well your portfolio has been performing and what problem areas you might need to address.

Nothing Is Certain but Taxes and More Taxes

You probably won't be surprised to hear that someone is interested in how well your portfolio is doing (besides your spouse, children, and any other potential heirs!). If you are making money in the stock market, you can bet that Revenue Canada wants its fair share, too.

That's where good record keeping comes in. If you have kept good records and can document all your transactions, you will protect yourself from one day overpaying any taxes due to the government. As a general rule, Revenue Canada doesn't accept statements such as, "Well, I think I bought those shares for about $8 or $9, but then it split once or twice, so I guess I owe you about $1,000 or so in capital gains taxes."

On the other hand, won't your accountant be ecstatic when you waltz into her office next February or March with a neatly printed report of all your transactions for the year, with summaries of all your income from dividends and interest, capital gains, and losses in your portfolio?

It's time to briefly review how investing affects your taxes in the first place. First, your investment accounts come under two categories: taxable and nontaxable.

Nontaxable accounts are retirement plans, called Registered Retirement Savings Plans (RRSPs). The taxes in these accounts are postponed (or *deferred*) until you start taking your money out of the accounts (probably after you retire). In the meantime, you don't have to worry about paying any taxes on the money you make in these accounts. *Taxable accounts* are any investments that aren't part of an official retirement plan. This could include a brokerage account, mutual fund account, or a Dividend Reinvestment Plan. If you make money on these investments, Revenue Canada wants to know about it so that they can collect the appropriate taxes.

Let's say you bought one hundred shares of stock in Associated Worldwide at $10 per share. You paid a $10 commission to buy the shares, which you added to your initial investment of $1,000, making your total investment $1,010. This is the *cost basis* or *tax basis* or just plain *basis* of your investment, and it includes the cost of the investment plus any commissions or fees.

If the shares increase in price from $10 to $15 for the year, you have earned $490, and your portfolio

Commissions and Fees Are Not Investment Expenses

Any commissions or fees that you have to pay to buy (or sell) a security are added to the cost (or subtracted from the proceeds) of those investments. They are not considered "investment expenses."

Keep Track of the Costs of Your Investments

Your brokerage will send you a form at the end of the year, noting whether you sold any securities. Because your brokerage may not know the price you paid, however, you need to supply the original cost of those shares yourself.

An Annual Portfolio Checkup Can Save You Taxes

As the end of the year comes around, many investors review their portfolio to see how many capital gains they have received throughout the year. They also check to see whether any of their holdings have turned out to be dogs and whether they might be a candidate for selling in order to take the tax loss and wipe out some of the capital gains. It is important to do this before the end of the year—you can't sell a holding at a loss and apply it to the preceding year's gains.

is a bit richer for your investing skill! But do you owe any taxes on that increase? No, because these are unrealized gains.

Sure, your shares are worth a lot more, but no tax consequences come from having unrealized gains in your portfolio—that is, until you realize the gains. How do you do that? Just sell those shares. If you sell your shares at $15, paying another $10 commission, you will realize a $480 capital gain. Capital gains, you will be sorry to hear, are taxable. A set of special capital gains taxes exists just so that you can share your good fortune with the federal government.

Unless you are a superhuman investor, there's a good chance that some of your investing decisions won't work out quite as planned. You may end up selling some shares at a loss. Maybe those hundred shares of North American National, Inc. didn't do so well, falling from $10 to $8 after you bought them. The future of North American National doesn't look so good, you think, so you sell the shares. You end up with $780—$220 less than your original investment of $1,000.

This $220 is a *capital loss*. The good news is that you don't have to pay taxes on a loss— not even Revenue Canada has figured out how to do that! Also, you can apply the amount of any capital losses toward any capital gains, and reduce the amount of capital gains taxes you have to pay.

In your case, you had a $220 loss from North American National and a $480 gain from Associated Worldwide, leaving you with a net capital gain of $260. Your tax bill drops to compensate for your loss.

When it comes to taxes, dividends are another matter. Associated National pays a regular quarterly dividend of five cents a share, and you are liable for paying taxes on that money. Dividends, as well as interest, are taxable as ordinary income at the same rate as your weekly paycheque.

The previous examples are pretty simple, but what happens when you own a stock for twenty-five years? Chances are the shares have split along the way, or it may have spun off another company and issued new shares to you, or you may have made additional purchases of the same stock. All of these factors can make it a bit harder to figure out the cost basis of your shares and, therefore, what you will owe to the government if you need to sell.

In olden days (anytime before the 1980s), investors recorded all their investment transactions in big ledger books, using devices called pencils. Today, this is a job that computers are much better equipped to handle. It is far simpler to use your computer and a software program that keeps track

You Can't Get Rich Selling at a Loss

At the end of each year, you are likely to hear news reports about "tax selling" as investors dump their losers so that they can write off the losses against their gains. But don't get too excited about building up capital losses. After all, you will never get rich selling at a loss.

of all your investment records than to resort to the old-fashioned ways. You still need to file away the paperwork, of course, but once you enter all your investment transactions into your computer as you make them, you can easily figure out the cost basis of any shares, as well as the overall return of your portfolio—with just a few keystrokes.

How Are You Doing? Calculating Your Portfolio's Return

Not so long ago, New York City had a colourful mayor named Ed Koch, better known by some by his nickname, "Hizzoner." One of Hizzoner's particular habits as he travelled throughout his expansive domain was to greet a crowd of citizens with the question, "How'm I doin'?" The question almost always elicited enthusiastic cheers from the gathered crowds—at least until a block of voters decided that the real answer to the question was "not so good" and booted him out of office. You should be able to ask the same question—"How am I doing?"—of your portfolio at any time and have a pretty good idea of the answer. This is one of the reasons that record keeping is essential to successful investing.

On the surface, it is not too hard to figure out the return that you have made on any investment. An investment's return is expressed as a percentage. If your hundred shares of Associated Worldwide increased in price to $15 per share from $10, what is your return? (Go ahead and leave the commissions out just to keep the math simple.) You can figure it out pretty easily with a calculator or a spreadsheet:

100 shares × $10 per share = $1,000 (the beginning value of your investment)

100 shares × $15 per share = $1,500 (the current value of your investment)

$1,500 (the current value) – $1,000 (the beginning value) = $500 (your unrealized gain)

$500 (your gain) ÷ $1,000 (the beginning value) = 0.50 (which is another way of saying 50%; this is your return)

You might be impressed to find out that your shares of North American National increased 50 percent, but there's another very important variable that's missing: time.

It is one thing if your investment increased 50 percent in a month (yowza, that stock is moving!), but it is quite another thing if your shares took ten years to grow by that amount (um, a bank savings account might be a better investment than that!).

Can you tell which mutual fund is growing faster: the one that's increased in price by 30 percent in two years, or one that's increased by 22 percent in thirty months?

To get around that problem, returns are usually expressed on an annualized basis. An annualized rate of return is a percentage adjusted to a yearly figure. A 5 percent return on a stock in three months is equal to a 20 percent annualized return, for instance (if we temporarily forget about the effects of compounding), as follows:

12 months ÷ 3 months × 5% = 20%

A 20 percent return over two years is equal to 10 percent on an annualized basis:

12 months ÷ 24 months × 20% = 10%

These examples work fine—until you consider that many stocks pay dividends, and that the income from these dividends must also be considered when you want to figure out how well a stock is performing. When you include dividends, interest, or other income along with the changes in price when calculating the returns of any security or an entire portfolio, it is called the *total return* of the investment.

If your North American National stock pays a dividend of $0.10 each quarter, you would receive $0.40 a year per share in dividends. (By the way, because you purchased the shares for $10, your dividend yield is 4 percent.)

$0.40 annual dividend / $10 cost per share = 0.040 (or 4%, the dividend yield)

If your North American National stock jumps to $15 a share, your total return in a year is 54 percent:

50% change in price + 4% dividend yield = 54%

Total return is usually expressed as an annualized figure.

Things are beginning to get a little more complicated, aren't they?

How Does Your Portfolio Stack Up?

If you know the total return of your portfolio since inception, you can then compare how well you are doing with the major market indexes.

Here's another twist: How do you figure out the total return of a stock or bond or mutual fund when you have made several purchases of that same security over a period of months or years? Maybe you are using dollar cost averaging, making monthly purchases of a mutual fund. Or maybe you have enrolled in a Dividend Reinvestment Plan, and your dividends are used to buy new shares each quarter.

And what if you want to determine the total return of your entire portfolio? You probably own more than one security—are you going to do these calculations for every holding? Remember, you won't have invested equal amounts in each of the different holdings in your portfolio, or have owned each for the same amount of time.

If you are a glutton for punishment, you can figure out the return of your entire portfolio by weighting the total returns of the various holdings by time, like this: Multiply the return percentage of each investment by the length of time you have owned it, in years or months. Then multiply that figure by the percentage of your entire portfolio made up of that holding. Repeat for each investment, and then add all the figures together. This will give you a good idea of your portfolio's total return. But there's a much easier way, so keep reading. As you can see, you would need to perform dozens and dozens of calculations just to get to the magic total return number for a single investment or your complete portfolio. As long as you try to do these calculations by hand, this isn't going to get any easier.

Fortunately, this is exactly why computers were invented many years ago: to prevent mere mortals from having to agonize over mathematical calculations. It's time to become familiar with some record-keeping software.

Software Is Your Friend

Although no place on the Web currently enables you to keep track of your investment transactions, a number of software programs can help you with record keeping, and many of these can interact with online services to help make the chores even easier. Check out these more popular programs:

➤ Capital Gainz (http://localweb.com/alleycatsw)

➤ Captool for Windows (http://www.captools.com)

➤ Microsoft Money (http://www.microsoft.com/money)

➤ Quicken (http://www.quicken.ca)

➤ Portfolio Logic (http://www.blogicnyc.com/portfolio.shtml)

Microsoft Money and Quicken are full-feature personal finance programs, and they can balance your chequebook, track your mortgage, and keep your investment records. Either of these programs can help you keep accurate investment records.

Entering investment transactions is easy in Quicken.

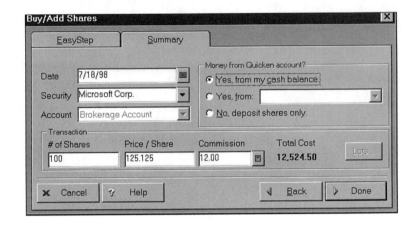

The other programs are specifically designed for investment tasks. That means they probably won't be much use with your chequing account, but they have additional features that will make your investing job a bit easier.

You can download free trial versions of all these programs from their Web sites, so the best thing to do is to check the descriptions and other information on their Web sites. Then, try out one or two of them and see how you like them!

All these programs feature wizards or interactive screens to walk you through the process of entering a transaction. If you buy shares, for instance, the program will prompt you to enter the number of shares, the commission, and the price per share. The same goes for sales, reinvestments, dividend payments, and any other type of transaction.

Every time you sell or purchase a security, you should enter the transaction in your software program. Some people prefer to enter the transactions as they occur; others will enter all of a month's transactions at the end of the month when a printed statement arrives in the mail. Either way, make it a habit to keep your records up to date.

To make record keeping even easier, Money and Quicken have established partnerships with banks and brokers to enable you to download account information directly to your computer. The only catch (and a big catch it is) is that your bank or broker must support the software that you use. Some firms support Quicken; others support Money.

Software Can't Replace All Your Record-Keeping Needs

Although software can help you to be organized, you still need to keep the paper versions of your account statements around. A good, old-fashioned filing system will help—but if your record-keeping software is good, you will never need to consult the paper copies!

After you have determined that your bank or broker or credit card supports the software you use, you will have to get on the phone with them to sign up for the service. The institution will assign you a username, a PIN, and any other identification numbers that you will need to get started.

Next, you need to tell your Quicken or Money software that you want to use electronic services. This is as easy as editing the account name and checking a box that says you want the account to be linked online, and then entering your account number and user information (the same numbers that your bank or broker gave you).

Now you are ready to go online! Go to the online centre in your software and connect! The first time you connect to your institution, you will have to change your trial PIN to a permanent one of your choice. Log on again, and then your transactions and balance will be downloaded to your computer.

Every week or so, you can download your transactions. You will always know exactly how much you have (or don't have) in the bank!

Besides tracking your transactions, good record keeping means that you will also need to update the prices of all your holdings on a regular basis. This is where the Internet can really make your life a lot easier. All of these software programs interact with the

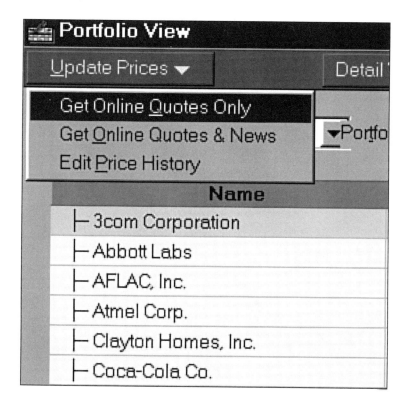

A click of a button in Quicken will automatically update your portfolio quotes from the Internet.

159

online world, although in different ways. They can import quotes that you have downloaded either from the Web or from an online service. Some will even log on to the Web for you and update the prices of all your holdings automatically. These save you time, particularly if you own a lot of stocks and funds. Instead of updating your prices manually, security by security, you can update them all simultaneously!

The Least You Need to Know

➤ You need to keep records of all your investment transactions, primarily to determine how much you might owe in taxes. Software makes the job easier.

➤ To determine how successful you are with your portfolio, you need to be able to calculate the returns you earn on your investment dollars. Computers can handle these complex calculations in seconds.

➤ Many banks, brokers, and credit card companies now offer online access to make the task of record keeping even easier. You may be able to download transactions and account information for your accounts directly to your computer.

Chapter 17

Keeping Tabs on Your Portfolio

> **In This Chapter**
>
> ➤ Discover services that help you keep up to date on your investments
>
> ➤ Track your investment portfolio using the Web and e-mail

You might be surprised to learn that the biggest part of investing is not figuring out what stocks or funds to buy. After you have built up your portfolio, the most important job is still ahead of you.

Now you need to manage your portfolio to make sure that all your investments are performing about as you expected when you first purchased them. Here is the point where most investors fail to follow through.

By far the biggest mistake investors make is confusing "stockwatching" (or its close cousin "fundwatching") with portfolio management. Stockwatching and fundwatching become addictive habits. The primary symptom is logging on and checking the prices of a portfolio several times a day. "Nortel is up $2!" "IBM is down 2 percent!"

These hapless investors love the Internet because it keeps them in touch with their investments (or so they believe). They also think that by just looking at the prices of their holdings, they are being successful portfolio managers.

It's your choice: You can be a real portfolio manager, or you can just look like one. Checking your quotes every twenty minutes might make you feel like a pro, but portfolio management is a lot more than that. Although the changes in price of your stocks are a sign that something may be amiss in your portfolio, you may be able to uncover the warning signals before a stock falls 15 percent in price in one day. How?

To keep tabs on your holdings, do these two things:

1. Keep a watchful eye on the news. If one of the companies you own makes an announcement about its operations, or if its business makes it into the newspaper, you should know about it.

2. Pay attention to the filings the company makes with the provincial securities commissions and the U.S. Securities and Exchange Commission. After all, if it's important enough to report to the government, shouldn't you know about it too?

Getting the Right Info

The Internet can help you with both of these jobs, of course. Many portfolio trackers on the Web include news stories and press releases about companies. And there are e-mail services that will send you a short announcement whenever a company files a report with the SEC.

There's plenty of information on the Web, but how much of it is really meaningful?

"Noise" is all the completely useless information about a topic that's floating around in cyberspace. One of the disadvantages of using the Internet is that you can quickly be the victim of information overload, as you are bombarded with information from all kinds of sources.

A Press Release Usually Tries to Portray the Company in a Good Light

There can be a world of difference between a company press release and a news story. Remember that a press release is written and issued by a company, and can be less than totally objective. A press release may put a positive spin on a problem, for instance. On the other hand, news stories, although aiming to be fair, often can't tell you the whole picture because of space constraints. In other cases, a company release may have more data, such as a complete financial statement. The bottom line is that you should be able to identify the source of the information in any "news" that you come across.

Here's the key to avoiding this problem. You have to learn to figure out what information is useful, and what information is next to worthless.

When you hear bad news about a company, you need to figure out the impact on your investment. Here are some questions you should ask about any information that you come across, good or bad:

➤ How is this news likely to affect the profitability of the stock in the future, both in the short term and the long term? Even great companies occasionally stumble, but many often recover quickly.

➤ Is this a problem that's specific to this company, or does it affect the entire industry? A company could be the subject of "bad news," but still be a standout among its competitors.

➤ How is this news likely to affect the performance of this investment in your time frame? Is the worst already over? In many cases, "bad" news is temporary and may have little impact on a long-term investment.

➤ If the company has announced changes in management, such as the resignation of the CEO or retirement of the Chair of the Board, are these unexpected events? Or has the company properly prepared for the succession of management, with a seamless transition period as the new executives take over control of the company? A sudden management change can be a bad sign that a company is desperately seeking solutions for its floundering business.

Another way that a company might make the news is when an analyst has "downgraded" or "upgraded" its stock. Before you decide to take action based on an analyst's recommendation, consider this: Do you know the time frame that the analyst used in making the recommendation? Many analysts are only interested in stocks that increase in price in a relatively short period. If you have a long-term goal, this action may be only a tiny ripple in the stock's otherwise steady performance.

Is the First Sign of Bad News a Sign of Impending Doom?

On Bay Street, there's a saying that "the first bad news is often the tip of the iceberg." Many times, investors sell at the first sign of trouble so that they don't have to worry about being sunk by larger problems later on. But often there is no iceberg—just a chunk of ice that floated on by with very little impact.

Think First!

If you hear bad news about your portfolio, above all else, don't panic! It's likely that by the time you hear any news, the price has already dropped significantly. So waiting until you can figure out the real impact of the news on your holdings won't result in too much further damage.

Remember that institutional traders and other professionals who have real-time newsfeeds can act much more quickly than you ever could. Don't try to beat them at their game. Take your time, and make a careful analysis of the situation before you take action.

Maintaining the Right Balance

If you build a portfolio of stocks according to the principles laid out in chapter 11, you will invest pretty equal amounts in ten or so companies, all from different industries and spread out in small, mid-sized, and large companies.

Some of the stocks you buy will go up in price, and some will go down in price. As they rise and fall, the percentage of each stock in your portfolio changes. After holding those stocks for a while, however, you will probably find that what was initially a nice, neat basket of stocks, with each holding making up about the same percentage, is now wildly out of whack!

Ironically, one of the problems that comes with being a successful investor is that the big winners in your portfolio usually end up turning your asset allocation plan upside down and making your diversification scheme completely lopsided! Remember this: If a stock you own outpaces the rest of your portfolio, perhaps by tripling or quadrupling in price, that stock may become a dominant part of your portfolio. That's great if the stock is rising in price. If the price falls, however, your portfolio could take a big hit. That's one of the big reasons you will need to rebalance your portfolio.

As your portfolio grows, you need to keep a watchful eye to ensure that your plans remain consistently on track. Good portfolio management is a perpetual rebalancing job.

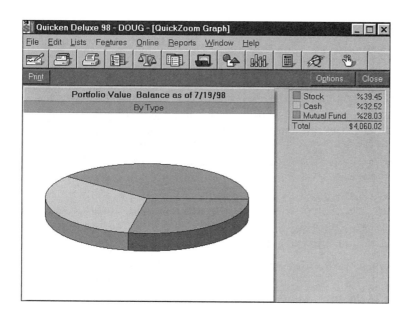

Quicken provides graphs to give you an instant visual picture of your portfolio's balance, growth, or performance.

Your record-keeping software, such as Quicken or Microsoft Investor, can help with the task of watching the balance of your portfolio. With a few clicks of your mouse, you can see graphs and charts of your portfolio holdings that indicate whether some of your holdings make up too much of your portfolio. You should periodically review the balance of your portfolio, perhaps twice a year or once a quarter.

If you see that your portfolio has fallen out of balance, you have two choices: You can direct future investments into those areas where your portfolio is underrepresented; or, you can sell some of your current holdings in the overweighted part of your portfolio, and reinvest those funds in other areas that you have targeted. In either case, good record keeping or portfolio management tools can provide the information you need to make an informed decision.

Tracking Your Portfolio Online

Lots of investors hang out on the Web at their favourite portfolio trackers. You probably will, too! It's easy to see the attraction of these online tools. Just enter the tickers once for all the stocks and funds you own, and then you can see the updated prices of those securities every time you visit the portfolio tracker. You can check up on your portfolio once a week, once a day, or once every twenty minutes. It's fast, easy, and convenient.

Some trackers go beyond the basics, and enable you to enter the date of your first purchase, price per share, number of shares you own, and other details. Then they will add up the value of your entire portfolio every time you visit.

With most trackers, you can create more than one portfolio. You can separate your RRSP from your regular brokerage account, or set up a portfolio just for your investment club, or organize your holdings in whatever other way works best for you.

Some trackers enable you to enter other assets, such as real estate or automobiles. Of course, they don't have a clue how much the assets are worth, so the trackers won't update their values for you! But this can be a convenient way of keeping track of other possessions. One important point to remember as you begin exploring portfolio trackers on the Web is that they are not designed for use as record keeping systems. You can enter only individual purchases for a particular stock or fund, and the tracker then displays the total number of shares of that holding. You can't enter individual purchases of a stock or fund and have them automatically "roll it up" each time you buy more shares of that particular holding. (The only exception to this rule is Microsoft Investor, although you can expect to see other sites adding this capability in the future.)

As you begin using these online portfolio trackers, you should be protective of the personal information you provide. Because trackers provide information customized just for you, all these services require registration. You have to provide a bit of personal information and create a username and password. Besides the details of your portfolios, you probably need to tell them your name and e-mail address, at the very least.

Fortunately, many quality portfolio trackers provided by reputable firms take steps to protect the personal information they do collect, and they don't use it for any disreputable purpose. An example of a tracking site is covered later in this chapter.

Some of the trackers offer you the ability to save your log-on information on your computer. If you are the only person who uses (or has access to) your computer, this can be a useful feature. If you work in an office where others occasionally sit down at your

Be Careful If You Check Your Portfolio on a Computer That's Not Your Own

If you check your portfolio in a public place, such as a public library, shared office terminal, or Internet cafe, you should take some extra steps to keep your information private. If the tracker has the option, log off after you finish checking your information. Then shut down the browser and restart it. In most cases, this ought to keep others from seeing your information.

desk and borrow your computer (even for just a few minutes), however, another user could pull up your portfolio just by surfing to one of the sites in your hotlist. You might soon learn that your personal net worth is the subject of office gossip! If you access the Web in this type of environment, you had better avoid this timesaver.

On a practical level, the information that will likely make its way to an online portfolio tracker is not the type of information that would be most useful to someone bent on fiscal tomfoolery. (You should never use account numbers or even the names of the brokerage firms and mutual fund companies where you hold your accounts, for example, when setting up your portfolios online.) The number of shares of Microsoft that you own, or even the total value of your portfolio, just isn't that interesting to a hacker bent on destruction. There are much bigger fish to catch!

Finally, no one can verify that the information you enter in a portfolio tracker is accurate. You could sign up with a phony name and build a portfolio that consists of a million shares of Microsoft, a million shares of BCE, and 10,000 shares of Chrysler Canada. According to the portfolio tracker, you would sure be one wealthy investor! But that doesn't make it true. That's one reason why few online portfolio trackers are set up on Web servers that would require the use of a secure browser.

The bottom line is that you really don't have much choice in the matter: If you want the convenience of using an online tracker, you have to put up with the minimal risks of providing some personal information.

To use any of these portfolio trackers, you need to follow these steps:

1. Register to use the service, usually by giving your name and e-mail address, and creating a password. (As always, remember your user-name and password!)

2. Create a portfolio, giving it a name that helps you identify it at a glance.

3. Enter the ticker symbols of the stocks and funds in your portfolio. If you don't know the ticker symbol, the tracker will help you look it up.

4. Optionally, enter the number of shares, cost per share, purchase date, and other informa-tion. You can always enter this information later.

That's it!

Don't Use the Exact Same Password for Every Site or Service

When registering for services on the Web, don't use the same password as the one you use for your account with your Internet service provider or online broker. If someone learned the password that you use at a low-security site, like a portfolio tracker, they might then be able to gain access to your brokerage account or run up charges with your ISP.

Build a Stock Watch List of Your Very Own

Some portfolio trackers come with a built-in watch list. With it, you can watch stocks that you might be thinking about buying. If the tracker you are using doesn't provide a special watch list, just create a portfolio called Watch List and enter the symbols of the stocks you are following.

An example of an online tracker that will handle Canadian and U.S. stocks is Pointcast (www.popintcast.ca). It utilizes a pretty cool function called *push technology* to update your portfolio whenever you're on the Web. You don't need to search out the stock and mutual fund prices for your portfolio, or even enter in the command to update your portfolio; instead, the tracker will push the information to you and you're portfolio will be updated automatically.

Stock Quotes

The push technology is offered by many sites (Pointcast is a favourite), and it also allows you to receive stock quotes within fifteen minutes. All you have to do is enter the names of the stocks that you want to follow and you'll see a scrolling ticker across the bottom of your screen with the current prices of your holdings. The only catch is that you have to be connected to the Internet to receive constant updates.

As mentioned earlier, real-time stock quotes are available all over the Internet. Most online brokerages offer the service to their customers, so if you're looking to make trades and get quotes often, your brokerage is a convenient place to do this. Most don't offer the streaming push technology though.

More About Trackers

The portfolio tracker provided by Quicken (http://www.quicken.ca) works nicely, and provides the option to enter the details of your holdings or just the ticker symbols.

The real bonus, however, is its Portfolio Analysis tool. Quicken looks at the holdings in your portfolio, and then displays a chart of your portfolio's asset allocation, dividing your stocks and funds (and the holdings of your funds) into categories such as large-cap stocks, small-cap stocks, international stocks, bonds, and cash. Quicken then calculates the returns that a portfolio with the same asset allocation would have earned historically and can even suggest a new asset allocation model that might improve your return. This tool is especially useful in X-raying a portfolio of mutual funds to see whether you hold too many funds that invest in the same asset classes.

The Least You Need to Know

➤ Software makes the job of tracking your investments easier.

➤ Portfolio management is more than just checking the prices of your investments. You need to watch for signs that your investments may be headed in the wrong direction. Portfolio trackers and e-mail services that can help you keep tabs on your portfolio are available.

➤ Online portfolio trackers provide an easy and convenient way to check up on your portfolio. Besides providing prices, these services also provide easy access to news, charts, and research about your investments.

Chapter 18

Getting Price Quotes Online

In This Chapter

➤ Get price quotes on the Internet for the stocks and mutual funds you own or are studying

➤ Find historical prices and charts for thousands of Canadian and American stocks

➤ Discover Web sites that offer free real-time stock quotes

Serving Up a Slew of Quotes

One of the easiest things to find on the World Wide Web is a price quote for a stock or mutual fund. In fact, if you haven't yet found a place to get these quotes on the Web, you're just not looking!

They're available from investment dealers, media organizations, stock exchanges, and companies that do nothing but provide quotes.

On the Web, sites that maintain databases of the prices of stocks, funds, and other securities are called *quote servers*. The busiest of them serve up quotes to interested investors millions of times each day. Quote servers get their prices directly from the stock exchanges (or from other quote servers). The stock exchanges charge for these continuous data feeds, and the quote servers package up the prices to display on Web sites for individual investors.

Canada Stockwatch provides a detailed chart that gives a good guide to a stock's historical prices for the previous year.

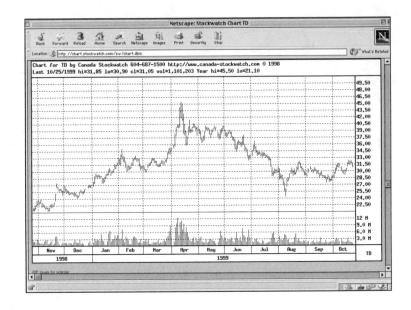

Canada Stockwatch (http://www.canada-stockwatch.com) is one of the main Canadian providers of this data. Many Canadian investors also rely on the financial supersites ilmoney (http://www.imoney.com) and Quicken.ca (http://www.quicken.ca). Others have gone to Canoe Money (http://www.canoe.ca/money) or Globeinvestor.com (http://www.globeinvestor.com). And still others use the Toronto Stock Exchange's site (http://www.tse.com) for their TSE-listed stocks. And since many of the American quote servers provide Canadian quotes, they each have many Canadian clients too. Popular U.S. sites include Yahoo! (http://www.yahoo.com), Quote.com (http://www.quote.com), and BigCharts (http://www.bigcharts.com). Each has its strengths, and as we go through this chapter, we'll highlight some of their special features.

Besides the current price of a stock, online quote servers often provide a lot of other information. Here's how you can retrieve and interpret the quotes and all the related data.

Let's start our look at the quote-gathering process by looking at the Globeinvestor.com site (http://www.globeinvestor.com). Once you're on the homepage, click on Quotes. A page called Stock Today will appear, along with a box asking you to enter a stock symbol. This is the single most important bit of information you need to know when you're looking up a stock quote. The ticker symbol is made up of one to five characters that represent a particular stock, or sometimes a particular class of stock.

If you don't know the symbol, just click on Symbol Lookup. All quote servers provide a lookup feature where you can search for ticker symbols. You may be able enter a part of

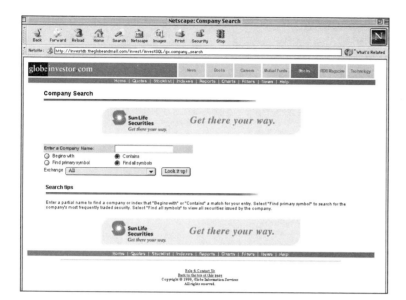

You can search for ticker symbols on the Globeinvestor.com Web site.

the company's name into a search box, or you can look through an alphabetical list of stocks.

For our purposes, let's assume that we know that "TD" is the symbol for TD Bank. We enter "TD" in the quote box, and we'll receive multiple quotes. That's because TD is traded on more than one stock exchange. "TD-T" refers to the Toronto Stock Exchange, while "TD-N" refers to New York.

Each quote server has its own method of distinguishing between identical securities trading on different exchanges. Some, like Globeinvestor.com, attach a dash and a suffix to the trading symbol (as in "TD-T" or "TD-N"). Others use a prefix and a colon (Quote.com requires "TSE:TD," and with BigCharts, you ask for "CA:TD"). Canada Stockwatch doesn't require any prefixes or suffixes—it will return every stock from every North American exchange that has the same trading symbol. The only rule of thumb you can count on here is that all American-based quote servers require some kind of appended prefix or suffix. If there is none, the server will assume you're looking for a security that's traded in the U.S.

Let's assume we're interested in the quote for TD stock on the Toronto Stock Exchange. Click on TD-T under the symbol heading, and you'll be presented with a box filled with trading data.

The most prominent figures are listed beside *last, net change*, and *% change*. *Last* is just what it sounds like: the price of the last trade of that stock. Stocks in Canada are bought and sold in prices based on dollars and cents. But decimalization has been slower to

173

catch on in the United States. Shares there have listed for 1/8ths and 1/16ths of a dollar. On the NASDAQ bulletin board market, some shares are actually priced in 1/256ths of a dollar! But that will end soon. U.S. exchanges are planning to decimalize, starting in the year 2000.

Net change is the amount that the security's price has changed from the previous day's closing price to the latest price. This is sometimes expressed as a percentage, as well. On

A Stock's Opening Price Doesn't Have to Be the Same as the Prior Day's Closing Price

Usually, the opening price of a stock is close to the preceding day's closing price. However, if important news is announced before the market opens, the opening price could be much higher or lower than the prior day's closing price. Remember that a stock is only worth what someone is willing to pay for it. Therefore the first price of Tuesday is not necessarily the last price from Monday!

The Toronto Stock Exchange offers a quote server that gives details of the previous five trades

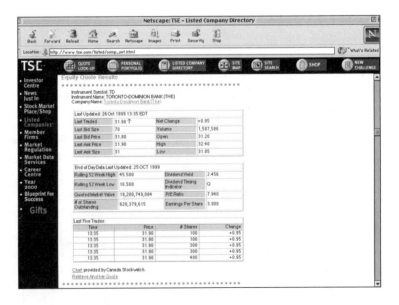

Bay Street you would say, "TD is down 15 cents today," which is .45% lower than yesterday's closing price.

The date and time of the quote is also displayed, usually along with the time that you requested the quote. Canadian and U.S. stock markets close each day at 4:00 p.m. Eastern Time. But that is changing. Several American companies already offer their U.S. customers after-hours trading in many New York– and NASDAQ–listed stocks. And in the fall of 1999, NASDAQ began a pilot program to keep its pricing and quote systems running until 6:30 p.m. to accommodate these new after-hours networks.

Different Classes of Stock Are Represented by Slightly Different Ticker Symbols

If a company has more than one type of share of stock, such as Class A and Class B, the letter of the class is usually appended to the end of the ticker symbol, sometimes by itself and other times following a period. Therefore, MDS Class A shares are known as MDS.A, and Class B shares are MDS.B.

You will also notice that the *last price* is always at least fifteen or twenty minutes old. That's because the exchanges charge steep fees for real-time prices. Because brokerage firms and investment banks can't do business without knowing the prices of securities at every second, they pay for the privilege. Brokers have to know how much a client must pay for shares—quotes that are a few minutes old are useless to them.

This also means that stock quotes that are a few minutes old have so little value to professionals that they can be given away for free by the quote servers. Most of the time, it's not a problem for individual investors to get their prices a little bit later, so everyone's happy. (You can pay for real-time quotes, or even get them for free from some new Web sites—but more about that later in this chapter.)

Back to the quote board.

The *high* and *low* are the highest and lowest prices that investors have paid for that security today. Some investors bought shares of TD at $33.75 today; others paid $33.25.

Volume is the total number of shares of the stock that have been bought and sold so far that day. A total of 663,557 TD shares have traded.

This quote from Globeinvestor.com shows the most recent price of TD Bank's stock, as well as other information about the security.

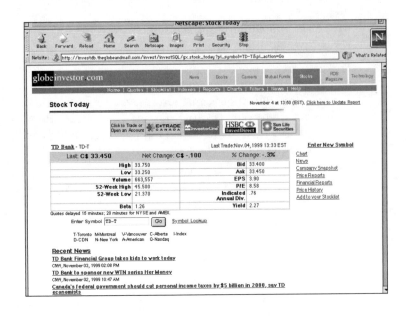

Bid and Ask Prices Aren't Reported for NYSE-Listed Stocks

Don't look for bid and ask prices for all stocks. You'll find them for TSE-listed stocks. But quotes on NYSE-listed stocks typically include the daily high and low prices rather than the bid and ask prices.

The *bid* is the highest price any investor is willing to pay for a stock at a particular time. You make your bid, just like at an auction.

The *ask* is the lowest price that any investor is willing to accept to sell a stock at that particular time. If you were selling your used car, for example, you would establish your asking price. That's the price you would ask a potential buyer to meet if he or she wanted to buy your car.

Buying a stock is really no different from buying a car. If you have a stock that you want to sell, you can establish your asking price. If you want to buy shares in a stock, you can make a bid. Unless you're one of the big players on the Street, however, you will usually have to resolve yourself to buying your shares at "the ask" and selling them at "the bid." If you placed an order with your broker to buy shares at a price lower than the current asking price of a stock, it's unlikely that any other investor would take you up on the offer. Why should they, when they can sell shares elsewhere for a higher price? Likewise, you could tell your broker to only sell your shares at a price higher than the current price that other investors are paying, but no one would jump at an offer like that! In the case of TD, the bid was $33.40, the price you could have sold shares at. The ask was $33.45, the price you could have purchased shares for.

Some people want more information than simply the bid and ask prices. They want to know the size of the bid and ask too. The bid size and ask size tell you how many shares are available for buyers and for sellers.

Across the Board: The Scoop on Board Lots

A *board lot* is a "grouped" number of shares for trading purposes. On the TSE, the board lot size depends on the price of the stock. If the security sells for less than 10 cents a share, the board lot size is 1,000 shares. For stocks selling between 10 cents and 99.5 cents a share, a board lot is 500 shares. And for stocks trading at $1 or higher, a board lot is 100 shares. Investors buying or selling less than a board lot are trading an "odd lot."

Let's try a site that gives bid and ask sizes. The Toronto Stock Exchange (http://www.tse. com) is one that offers these figures. Size is reported in blocks of one hundred shares, so a bid size of 70 means that bids have been made to buy 7000 shares of TD's stock. The ask size of 31 indicates that sellers have offered 31 blocks of one hundred shares (or 3100 shares) of stock at the ask price.

The TSE quote server also lists *open*, which is the opening price of the stock's first trade at the beginning of the day. An investor bought shares of TD for $31.20 in the first trade of this day.

You can see there's also an arrow beside the *last traded* quote. That's called the *tick*.

A tick is the change in the price of a security, and ticks come in two varieties. An uptick happens when the last trade in a security takes place at a higher price than the prior trade. A downtick happens when the last trade in a security takes place at a lower price than the prior trade.

With TSE's quote server, a green arrow pointing up represents an uptick, and a red arrow pointing down represents a downtick. Scroll down to the bottom of the page, and you'll find details on the last five trades of TD stock, including the time, the price, and the number of shares.

Most quote servers, the TSE's included, also give the 52-week highs and lows, so you can get a good picture of the trading range over the last year. Another popular bit of data is the *P/E ratio* (for Price/Earnings). This is a number that's obtained by dividing the

Make Sure You're Seeing the Latest Information on Your Browser Pages

When you're accessing quotes online, you will want to see the most current information available. Unfortunately, after you have viewed a page of quotes, pressing the Reload or Refresh button may load the page from the browser's cache instead of updating the prices from the Web site. If this happens using Internet Explorer, press the Ctrl (Control) key and Refresh button at the same time. This forces the browser to reload the page from the Web server, not from the cache. To do the same thing using Netscape Navigator, press the Shift key plus the Reload button.

earning per share (EPS) into the price of the stock at the close of trading the previous day. A low P/E ratio relative to other companies in the same sector can be one indicator of a good buy. The *dividend yield* is another useful statistic. That's the annual dividend divided into the share price at the previous close of trading. It's expressed as a percentage. Investors looking for steady income look for high dividend yield stocks.

In addition to stocks, the TSE site can deliver quotes for options, mutual funds, futures, and indexes. The one thing it can't do is give you quotes for stocks trading on other exchanges. That's why people who follow stocks in New York or NASDAQ pick other quote servers. Many will handle quotes from both Canada and the United States. Some, like Data Broadcasting Corporation (http://www.dbc.com) have overseas quotes. You can get the latest trading data for stocks listed on exchanges in nearly thirty cities around the world, including Prague, Sao Paulo, Bangladesh, Istanbul, and Shanghai.

One problem with getting quotes on international stocks is that ticker symbols aren't always standardized. That means some quote servers may use different symbols for the same stock. Another problem is that the same ticker symbol may be used on more than one exchange. "CAE" is the symbol for CAE Inc., whose shares trade on the Toronto Stock Exchange. But the Cascade Corporation also uses the ticker symbol "CAE." Its shares trade on the New York Stock Exchange.

When investors trade online, it's even more important that they get the trading symbol right. Guessing that "CIBC" is the symbol for the Canadian Imperial Bank of Commerce would be a mistake. It's actually the symbol for Citizens Bancorp of Indiana. The Canadian bank's ticker symbol is "CM" in Toronto, and "BCM" in New York. The company with the trading symbol "CIBC" trades on the NASDAQ bulletin board market.

Let's Go to the Ticker Tape

The phrase *ticker symbol* comes from the old, mechanical quote machines that ticked as they delivered stock prices to brokers by printing them on narrow, continuous rolls of paper called ticker tape. Even though the computer age has made ticker machines obsolete, electronic versions of tickers still deliver an uninterrupted stream of quotes in brokers' offices, on television, on the Web, or on pixel boards on the sides of buildings.

Also, some companies that trade on both sides of the border often have different symbols. The Canadian Internet auction company, Bid.com, trades under the symbol "BII" in Toronto, but "BIDS" on NASDAQ.

You may be wondering why some exchanges have shorter symbols than others. Generally, stocks that trade on established stock exchanges use one, two, or three letters. Stocks that are unlisted or trade over the counter in Canada have root symbols that are four letters long. In the U.S., the lettering system is a bit different for the over-the-counter market.

The TSE's First Century-and-a-Half

The Toronto Stock Exchange got its beginning in 1852, when a group of twelve businessmen formed the Association of Brokers to begin trading stocks.

NASDAQ (the National Association of Securities Dealers Automated Quotations) is the leading over-the-counter market in the United States, and in trading value, it's second only to New York. Such huge companies as Microsoft and Intel trade there. Some NASDAQ stocks contain five letters in their symbols. The fifth letter of a ticker symbol of a NASDAQ–listed stock has special significance. Here's a guide to help you decipher their meaning:

NASDAQ Fifth Symbol Meaning

A   Class A shares
B   Class B shares
C   Exempt from NASDAQ listing qualifications for a limited period
D   New issue
E   Delinquent in making required SEC filings
F   Foreign company

Give Me an "A"

Want to know how you can tell whether a stock trades in an over-the-counter market (such as on the Canadian Dealing Network or NASDAQ) or on a regular stock exchange? Just count the number of letters in its ticker symbol! A ticker symbol with one, two, or three letters is a stock that trades on a regular exchange like the TSE or the NYSE. If the ticker has four or five letters, it's an OTC or NASDAQ stock.

NASDAQ Fifth Symbol Meaning

G	First convertible bond
H	Second convertible bond (same company)
I	Third convertible bond (same company)
J	Voting shares
K	Non-voting shares
L	Miscellaneous situations, including second-class units, third-class warrants, or sixth-class preferred stock
M	Fourth-class preferred (same company)
N	Third-class preferred (same company)
O	Second-class preferred (same company)
P	First-class preferred (same company)
Q	Company is in bankruptcy proceedings
R	Rights
S	Shares of beneficial interest
T	Shares with warrants or rights
U	Units
V	When issued and when distributed
W	Warrants
X	Mutual fund
Y	American depository receipts
Z	Miscellaneous situations, including second class of warrants, fifth-class preferred stock or any unit, receipt, or certificate representing a limited partnership interest

Trading Floors: Some Have Them, Some Don't

On April 23, 1997, the Toronto Stock Exchange became the largest exchange in North America to abandon its trading floor. No more traders shouting out orders! Now, computers do everything. New York still has its trading floor, complete with seventeen separate trading booths and 8,000 phone circuits.

While looking up quotes, you'll find that many servers provide more information than just the quote. Some will give free reports like charts, news stories, company profiles, earnings reports, and links to filings with securities regulators. They're usually just a click away.

This feature is common to most quote servers on the Web. In addition to prices, you can quickly review other information about a stock. Although you are not likely to find extensive research on these sites, you can get a good snapshot of a particular company, especially if it's one you're not familiar with.

What's the Difference Between "Streaming Quotes" and "Snap Quotes" ?

If you look up the price of a single stock on the Web, you have used a method of delivering price data known as *snap quotes*. On the other hand, *streaming quotes* are a continuously delivered flow of prices automatically updated on your computer screen, usually on a real-time basis.

Now Available Live! Real-Time Quote Servers

So what do you do if quotes that are fifteen or twenty minutes old are just too old for you? Well, you can always pay for the real thing: real-time quotes.

If you have ever seen the terminal on a broker's desk, you will have noticed that the numbers and letters on the screen are in nonstop motion. The letters are the ticker symbols of stocks, and the flashing numbers are the prices of trades that have just happened in those stocks, continuously changing as a result of each trade.

Brokers and other investment pros pay a lot of money to have instantaneous access to all the action in the market. The prices are delivered to the broker's terminal in real time (or as close to real time as possible).

Now you can turn your desktop computer into a machine that resembles a broker's trading terminal, delivering real-time quotes and providing you with an immediate picture of the action in the market. All it takes is some special software, a link to the Internet, and a subscription to a data delivery service.

Several services can transport you to the trading floors of the exchanges (at least electronically!). Canada Stockwatch (http://www.canada-stockwatch.com) is one Canadian site that offers real-time quotes. For $4.95 a month, plus 2 cents per quote, you can have real-time quotes delivered to your computer. If you're really serious about real-time data, you can spend lots more. Canada Stockwatch has a variety of subscription options that can provide unlimited real-time quotes for all North American exchanges for up to 300 stocks at a time.

Quote.com (http://www.quote.com) offers a real-time quote package for all Canadian and U.S. exchanges, starting at US$24.95 a month plus exchange fees.

For most investors, however, these real-time quote services will be overkill. Do you really need a direct line into the stock exchanges to make your investment strategy work? Unless you're a day trader, the answer is probably no.

Still, there are times when it might be handy to be able to check the price of a stock and know that what you're seeing is the exact, current price per share. And that's why free real-time quote services have sprung up on the Web. These sites only allow you to look up a single price at a time, but the prices you see are absolutely timely—and you can't beat the cost!

Get Free Real-Time Quotes from Your Online Broker

Another source of free real-time quotes may be your brokerage. Online discount brokers usually give free real-time quotes to clients, typically in blocks of, say, one hundred quotes for each trade made by the customer. When you're placing an order, you would definitely want to know the most current price of that stock.

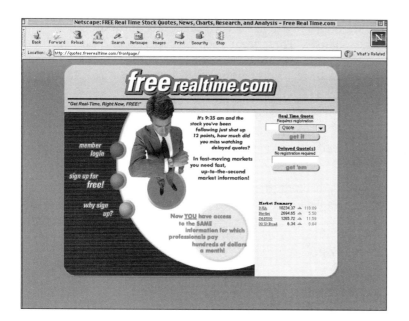

FreeRealTime.com gives you U.S. stock quotes without any delay.

You can take your pick of any (or all) of the half dozen or so free real-time quote servers now on the Web. That's the good news. The bad news is that, so far, none of the free services offer real-time quotes for Canadian-listed securities.

FreeRealTime.com (http://www.freerealtime.com), and Wall Street City (http://www. wallstreetcity.com) both offer access to free real-time stock prices. You can look up as many prices as you want each day. Wall Street City also lets you see the previous ten trades made in a stock (look for the link to register for free real-time quotes on their site).

Thomson RTQ (http://rtq.thomsoninvest.net) is a subsidiary of Canada's Thomson Corporation. It was the first online provider of free real-time quotes. Thomson also provides the quotes for two other free real-time services, Money (http://www.money. com/rtq) and Fox Marketwire (http://www.foxmarketwire.com). All three of these services limit you to one hundred free quotes per day.

You must register before you use each service, and the registration process is extensive. You need to provide your name and address and other contact information, and then pick out a username and password. Next, you need to answer a series of questions to

The Software May Be Free, but the Service Costs Money!

Don't be fooled by quote providers who offer "free software" on their Web sites. Although these programs often are free, they won't run unless you have a subscription to the site's services!

You Can't Fight the Tape

On Bay Street, professionals often repeat the adage, "You can't fight the tape." This word of advice is a reminder that there's nothing you can do to stop the momentum of a stock that's moving up or down in price on the ticker tape.

signify that you agree with the terms of the stock exchanges. These legal documents go on and on, but the exchanges require agreement from all investors who have access to real-time quotes.

After you register, you must log on before you access quotes from any of these sites. From there, the only thing that's different about these quotes is that they're not delayed—the same type of information is provided as you would get from a delayed quote server.

As mentioned, free real-time quotes are available only for stocks listed on U.S. exchanges. But as this book went to press, a couple of Canadian companies were exploring the possibility of offering free access to Canadian exchange–listed stocks.

Where to Find Historical and Daily Data

Although it's easy enough to find stock prices for today, it's another matter altogether to find prices for a specific date (whether it's last week, last month, or years ago).

If you're Marty McFly, you can always see whether Doc has enough plutonium pellets for the flux capacitor, hop in the DeLorean, and travel back in time to find the price of your favourite stock. (That's from the movie *Back to the Future*.)

But for the rest of you, what do you do when you need to establish the price of shares on a particular date, or want to know the highest and lowest prices of a stock in a particular year?

You turn to the Web, of course! A few sites are perfect for digging up the past.

The first site you need to know about is BigCharts (http://www.bigcharts.com). BigChart's database goes back to 1985. So if you're looking for a price from a date older than that, you're out of luck. Still, it is one of the best resources for information on past prices.

It is easy to use. Just click on Historical Quotes at the top of the page, and then enter the ticker symbol of any stock. And they do mean any stock: BigCharts has prices for thousands of Canadian and American stocks. Just remember to add the prefix "CA:" before any Canadian stock symbol.

Microsoft Investor (http://www.moneycentral.msn.com/investor) is another place to turn to if you are looking for historical price quotes. Investor will give you prices for a whole range of dates.

BigCharts can give you the closing price of 12,000 stocks for any date since 1985.

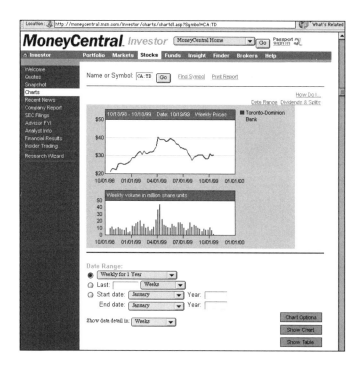

Microsoft Investor's stock charts can be created for a period that you select.

Click and drag on a Microsoft Investor price chart, and this bar appears, along with more details at the top of the graph.

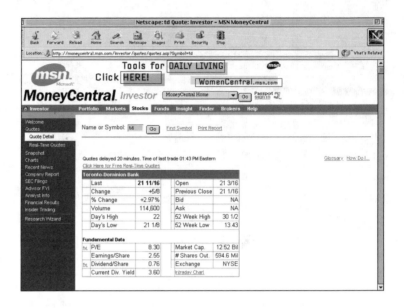

Move your mouse over a price chart at Microsoft Investor and this box appears, telling you the date and price.

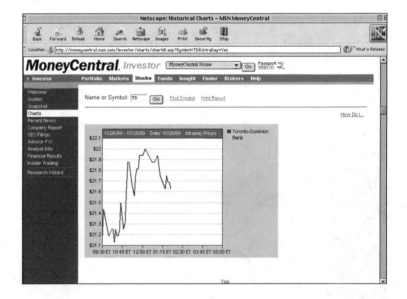

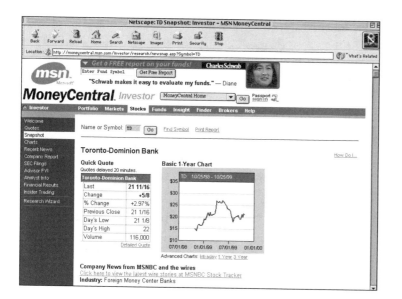

Microsoft Investor gives you the choice of customizing a chart for a particular period you specify.

When you go to the Investor site, enter a ticker symbol in the entry box at the top of the main page. If you're looking for a Canadian-listed stock, add the "CA:" prefix to the ticker symbol. This will display a price quote for the security. Next, click on Charts on the menu on the left side of your screen. This will display a chart for your stock. If you move your cursor over the line on the graph, you will see that the price is displayed in a box.

If you click on the price line, a vertical line appears on the graph. You can drag this line from left to right, and the price and date will appear at the top of the chart.

Splits

Split-adjusted prices have been adjusted for all stock splits and stock dividends that have happened in the past.

If you are looking for prices for a period not displayed on the chart, click the Period button and select the dates that you're looking for, anytime from the most recent trading day's intraday quotes to quotes from ten years ago.

Stock Splits Can Trip Up Your Data Collection

You need to watch out if your data source does not adjust for stock splits, or if you maintain your own prices. Until the data is adjusted for splits, you can't make valid comparisons between current and past prices.

Globeinvestor.com (http://www.globeinvestor.com) offers limited historical quote information too. After you look up your quote, click on Price History, and you'll be presented with the closing price of that equity for each of the previous thirty trading days.

Of course, you can always just call up price charts to get a feel for where the stock has been. Many quote servers that don't offer specific historical quotes still offer charts that will allow you to eyeball the information. So, if you don't require an absolutely precise figure, go the chart route.

Many people choose Canoe Money (http://www.canoe.ca/money) because you can see the price and the chart on the same page. When you look up a quote here, you enter the stock symbol along with the suffix (e.g., TD-T). You'll actually see two charts: one showing the price over the previous sixty days, the other showing the volume. You can further customize this chart to graphically show trading data from that day alone or from dates as far back as five years.

Canada Stockwatch (http://www.canada-stockwatch.com) offers a popular charting feature (the TSE site refers you to it). The chart goes back a full year, showing the high and low price of each trading day, with a red dot marking the close. That allows you to get a very good picture of your stock's recent trading history. And like the TSE's site, Canada Stockwatch will give you details of the last five trades, as long as you enter the symbol for a single exchange (T:TD, for example) and there have been fewer than 500 trades that day. The trading details include the time, the price, and the investment dealers that represented the buyers and sellers.

Ticks That Keep Check

The *uptick rule* prevents investors from selling a stock short unless the last tick was up or even. This rule helps maintain order in the market and keep short sellers from shorting a stock that's falling in price and therefore driving the price down even further.

And no mention of quotes with charts would be complete without a look at a rather amazing charting function from Quote.com (http://www.quote.com). Live Quotes gives you delayed charting of that day's trading action on a "tick-by-tick" basis with data that's updated as often as every minute. Once you enter the stock symbol (TSE:TD, for example), just watch the bids and asks being posted. It's a wonder to see. Just be sure to give it time to load. A real-time version is available, but it's US$79.95 a month, plus exchange fees.

What if you want to download historical price quotes into such popular personal finance programs as Quicken? At the present time, you can only do so with securities listed on U.S. exchanges. But Quicken says they may change that in the future.

Navigating for NAVs

It's just as easy to get prices of mutual funds as it is to get stock quotes. You have to remember, however, that fund managers figure the net asset value (NAV) of their funds just once a day, after the market closes, when they have the closing prices of all the stocks and bonds in their portfolio. Generally, you can get the NAV of a fund a few hours after the markets close each day.

The two most popular sources of Canadian mutual fund prices on the Web are Globefund.com (http://www.globefund.com) and The Fund Library (http://www.fundlibrary.com). Here's how to look up your fund prices. Mutual funds have tickers just

Your Fund Company May Provide NAVs on Its Site

Most mutual fund companies have Web sites where you can also find the latest net asset value for each of its funds.

like stocks. Fortunately, you don't need to know the specific ticker symbol for your fund with either Web site. Both have a search function that allows you to find the fund you're interested in by simply looking up its name, and then selecting it.

Let's say we're looking for information on a particular fund. Enter the name, and Globefund.com will generate a detailed profile. The closing net asset value of the fund is just the beginning of the numbers parade. Each profile also includes the fund's specs (size, management expense ratio, sales fee type) and the performance figures for the previous day or for the last ten years. You'll also find the fund's top ten holdings, and what percentage of the fund is invested in each sector (like financial services or consumer products). There's also a charting function that will allow you to generate a graph of the fund for time periods from three months to ten years. Once that's done, you can compare it with an index of your choosing. And for a subjective rating of each fund, Globefund.com assigns a letter grade based on the fund's five-year record.

The Fund Library offers much the same numerical data along with a charting function that goes from three months to two years. You can also find the rankings of each fund

You can find the net asset value of your mutual funds by using a quote server like The Fund Library.

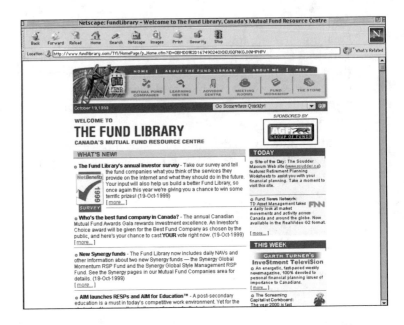

in comparison with others in the same fund type for periods ranging up to twenty-five years. Ratings here come courtesy of some well-known mutual fund authors (Gordon Pape, Stephen Gadsden, Jonathan Chevreau, Richard Croft, and Eric Kirzner).

The Least You Need to Know

➤ You can retrieve price quotes for stocks on a delayed basis during the day. You can find many quote servers on the Web, and many provide additional research, news, and charts, as well as prices.

➤ Several free real-time quote servers are available on the Web. Although registration is required, these services connect your computer to U.S. stock markets so you can see the most recent price of a stock.

➤ Several Web sites offer Canadian mutual fund quotes where you can find daily net asset values. Charts, performance figures, and ratings are also available.

Part 5

The Dark Side of the Web

When you've found a terrific deal, is there always a catch? Probably. On the Internet you've got to be alert to crooked deals and disreputable advisors. They are both out there in cyberspace waiting for you, but you've got good common sense and plenty of tips from this guide to help you avoid the danger.

Chapter 19

Hazards and Pitfalls of the Online World

In This Chapter

➤ Learn how to be a safe, secure, and private Web surfer

➤ Understand how cookies work and whether you should avoid them

➤ Realize the dangers of viruses and how to protect yourself from harm

"Is it safe?" "Are the private details of my financial accounts protected from prying eyes?" "How can I tell whether a tip I hear on the Internet is to be believed?"

As you begin to explore the Internet in search of investment information, you may be wondering about the answers to these questions. Or you may have your own questions about privacy, security, and investment fraud on the Internet. Now it's time to dispel the rumours and provide you with some straight talk about using the Internet and how to avoid getting tangled up in the process of navigating the Web.

This chapter provides some basic explanations of technical details, and also offers some practical advice to help you protect yourself.

Security on the Internet

When the Internet (or at least, the network that eventually became the Internet) was first designed, the creators never imagined that so many people would use their system or use it in the ways it is used today. A little history lesson would probably be helpful.

Back in the late 1960s, the ARPAnet was built by the U.S. Department of Defense to provide a way for the American military complexes to communicate in the event of a catastrophic attack on the United States. The ARPAnet was designed so that if any link in the network were to become disrupted, traffic would be automatically redirected to routes that were undamaged. As a result, communications among sites connected to the network would be able to continue.

Over the years, the ARPAnet expanded and was eventually replaced, but today's Internet was built on the framework forged by ARPAnet.

In the mid-1990s, a whole new crowd discovered the Internet. This was largely due to the development of a new method of sending information across the Internet, called the *Hypertext Transfer Protocol*. You are probably familiar with the abbreviation for this protocol, *http*, since it's used in every address on the World Wide Web.

The Web, with its capability to deliver formatted documents—and then images, and then music, and then movies, and then complete programs—has changed the way that people use the Internet. The developers of ARPAnet probably never imagined that users would listen to the radio or watch news broadcast over their network!

More importantly, despite the military beginnings of the Internet, it was never designed to be a "secure" network. The Internet is designed to work a bit like the old party-line system used by telephone companies. A number of customers would share the same line, and anyone who picked up the phone could listen in on any conversation that might be going on.

On the Internet, it is possible that someone could "listen in" on any information being sent across the network, whether it's sent by e-mail or to and from a Web site. Where your personal and financial information is concerned, that's a potential problem.

Fortunately, technology has come to the rescue with some solutions to this security problem. The makers of Web server and browser software have created versions of their products that use encryption to protect information as it is delivered from your computer, across the Internet, and to a Web server at the other end. *Encryption* is the process of scrambling information into a secret code and then unscrambling it after it arrives at a secured Web server. Encryption turns the Internet party line into a private line!

Archie and Veronica Are Popular No More

You have probably heard of e-mail and File Transfer Protocol (FTP), two common ways of sending data across the Internet. But maybe you haven't heard of Gopher, Archie, Veronica, or WAIS. These were once common methods of finding and retrieving information on the Internet, but they have by now fallen by the wayside.

Beware of Hacker Attacks

Hackers are individuals who try to secretly invade computer systems, and then steal private information.

The encryption technology used on the Web is called the Secure Sockets Layer protocol (or SSL). Web browsers that use it are often called secure browsers. Currently, two levels of encryption are in use in the SSL protocol: low or 40-bit encryption, and high or 128-bit encryption. (The number of bits refers to the strength of the encryption; the higher the number, the longer it would take any hacker to crack the code and read your information.)

To take advantage of SSL, all you have to do is use a secure browser. The site you connect to must also be a secure site. Versions of Microsoft Internet Explorer and Netscape Navigator higher than 3.0 can support secure transactions.

It is easy to know if you are connected to a secure Web site. First, the address of a secure Web server will always begin with https:// rather than http://, letting you know that the server will accept a private connection with your browser. Then, after you arrive at a secure site, your browser will give you a sign that it's properly connected. Have you

Keep That Credit Card Number Private

To be safe, you should never send a credit card number, bank or brokerage account number, Social Insurance Number, username, password, or other personal information via e-mail. This information could be intercepted on the Internet by a sniffer—a software program that scans traffic on the Internet looking for series of numbers that match a certain pattern, such as the series of numbers on a credit card.

ever noticed a small lock or key at the bottom of your Web browser's screen? When you connect to a secure Web site using Netscape Navigator 4.0, for instance, you will see a small, unlatched padlock in the lower-left corner of the screen and in the toolbar at the top of the screen. After you make a secure connection to the site, both these padlocks become latched and are highlighted with yellow backgrounds.

In Microsoft Internet Explorer 4.0, the locked padlock appears in the centre of the status bar at the bottom of the screen only when you connect to a secure Web site. Whenever you see this padlock, you know that your information is protected while it travels across the Internet.

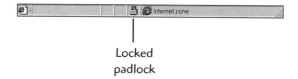

Locked padlock

The locked padlock in the status bar of Microsoft Internet Explorer indicates that you have connected to a secure Web site.

195

It's Browser Giveaway!

It's easy to get a copy of the latest Web browsers from Netscape or Microsoft. Just go to their Web sites, http://www.netscape.com or http://www.microsoft.com, and look for the browser downloading area. Both browsers are free!

Your online brokerage firm will require that you use a secure Web browser to access your account on its site. This makes it impossible for anyone to steal your password or account number when you log on to your broker's Web site, or to track your activity when you're on its site.

On the other hand, most of the portfolio trackers on the Web don't support secure Web browsers. That's because there usually isn't any significant personal information entered in these trackers, like your name or brokerage account number. Sure, some hacker might be able to find out that a user owns 500 shares of some stock, but it would be hard to trace that information back to you personally. So what if someone did? Most hackers would likely be interested in finding much larger fish to catch in the Internet ocean.

To be completely safe, any time you're asked to provide highly personal information on the Internet, such as a credit card number, account number, or your Social Security number, you should make sure that the site requesting that information is using a secure server.

Your Browser Needs to Handle the Highest Level of Encryption

Some online brokerage firms require that you use 128-bit encryption rather than 40-bit. If your browser doesn't support 128-bit encryption, you will have to upgrade your browser; otherwise, you won't be able to access your account information on your broker's Web site! Check on the firm's site to see which encryption level your browser must support.

Protecting Your Privacy

Software does a great job of providing the security that makes it possible for investors to safely use an online broker or make a purchase from a catalogue on the Internet. When it comes to protecting your privacy online, however, it takes more than technology to do the job. After all, ultimately you are in control of the personal information you reveal to anyone, whether it's your name or more intimate details of your stock portfolio.

If you have surfed around the Web for any amount of time whatsoever, chances are you've come across a site that asked you to "register," or that has special areas for "registered members only." Web sites ask users to register for many reasons, and registration could be voluntary or mandatory before you gain access.

For sites that are available only to subscribers who pay for the privilege, registration is the way they collect payment. Before they will process your credit card, you must provide your name, address, and telephone number.

On some sites, registration is used to make sure that you agree to some particular terms before you access certain information (protecting the site publisher from being sued, for instance). Other sites make you register so that you can be issued a unique username and password that you can use on a message board.

Another common reason for registration is for a site to collect demographic information about all its users. The site may ask such questions as your income range, your age, your gender, your employment status, and your education level. These sites aren't really interested in you personally. Their goal is to collect information about their user population as a whole. Then they can tell advertisers that "65 percent of our users are university graduates, 73 percent are women, and 87 percent have salaries above $50,000."

Other Web sites are interested in finding out as much about you as possible, however, so that they can target you with other services, promotions, or products. They want to know your interests so that they can target you with specific ad pitches.

Many users are concerned with keeping their e-mail addresses private. An unfortunate problem with the Internet is that your e-mail address can end up on a

Your Office Computer Network May Prevent You from Connecting to Secure Web Sites

If you connect to the Web at work, your office network may be protected by a firewall—a system of software that is designed to protect the network from intruders. If that's the case, you probably won't be able to connect to a secure site from your office computer.

Keep Personal Information to Yourself

The only people or organizations that need to know your mother's maiden name are you, your mother, your bank, your broker, and other trusted financial institutions. The same goes with your Social Insurance Number. If anyone else on the Web requests these personal details, politely refuse.

list that's used to send junk mail over the Internet. This unsolicited commercial e-mail is called "spam," and it can quickly fill up your mailbox with offers for various products and services.

Just Because They Ask Doesn't Mean You Have to Answer

Many sites that require registration don't necessarily *require* that you provide all the information they ask for. On some sites, required fields on a sign-up form will be indicated with an asterisk; the remaining fields are voluntary.

Companies that spam collect e-mail addresses from a number of places: Web pages, Usenet groups, or mailing lists. They use these sources to compile their giant databases of all those who will soon receive the spam. One way to keep your identity a bit more private is to use a free e-mail service, which you can get from a number of places. Just go to a free service's Web site and create your account. You will get an e-mail address that you can use. When you want to check your mail, just return to the site and log on.

After you sign up with this free e-mail service, rather than give out your main e-mail address to sites when you register or post to Web message boards, you can use the alternative address from one of these services. If you do begin to get an overwhelming amount of spam, you will know that your e-mail address was compromised.

Here are some popular free e-mail providers:

Try Skipping over Questions That Seem Too Personal

You might be able to circumvent a site's request for personal information by filling in only a few of the blanks on the form it supplies. If the site absolutely requires more information, you can just use your browser's Back button to return to the form and provide the additional answers.

Yahoo! Mail (http://mail.yahoo.com)

HotMail (http://www.hotmail.com)

MailExcite (http://mailexcite.com)

WhoWhere? Mail
(http://www.whowhere.com/MailCity)

RocketMail (http://www.rocketmail.com)

Uncheck the Check Boxes

When completing registration forms on a Web site, beware of check boxes that are already checked by default. Often, these give the site permission to e-mail you or even share your e-mail address with other sites. If you don't want to receive e-mail, uncheck the box before submitting the form.

One last note: Even though these services provide you with anonymity on the Internet, you should still strive to be a good Internet citizen. Unscrupulous Web surfers hide behind these services so that they can act rudely, indecently, or illegally; don't stoop to their level just because your true identity is hidden.

Dealing with the Cookie Monster

Would you like a cookie to go with your Web surfing? You may have heard talk about *cookies* on the Web, and are wondering whether this is something you should be worried about.

The answer is probably not. Here's the recipe for a Web cookie. Cookies are small text files sent to your browser from a Web site. Some of these cookie files are saved on your computer's hard drive, and other cookies are stored only temporarily in your computer's memory until you shut down your browser.

Cookies are generally good things. With cookies, a site could be customized according to your particular preferences. Cookies could indicate which parts of a site you've already visited, or which ad banners you've already seen.

Another helpful use for cookies is to streamline your visits to a particular site. A cookie could be used to indicate that you've read a disclosure statement so that you don't have to read it each time you visit the site. Your personal log-on information could also be saved in a cookie on your computer, making it easier for you to access a site.

Web Sites May Not Tell All

As of June 1998, only 14 percent of commercial Web sites provided users with any disclosure about their information collection practices.

Source: U.S. Federal Trade Commission

If You Log On in Public, Make Sure to Log Off, Too

If you use a shared computer—at a library, for instance—or if coworkers occasionally borrow your computer, you should take a little extra care when accessing a portfolio tracker or other site that stores log-on information on your computer. Choose not to have log-on information saved to your computer, or else make it a habit to log off the site after each use. Otherwise, your private portfolio may become a little too public.

Reject Those Cookies!

You can set your browser to reject all cookies, or to warn you when a site wants to deliver a cookie. Look for the cookie settings in your browser's options or preferences area. If you do reject all cookies, you may be surprised at how common they are!

You don't have to worry about any security issues with cookies. They can't be used to get your e-mail address, find data on your hard drive, or access other personal information. Only the site that originally sent a cookie can access or alter the information in that cookie; no other site or user can view or change it.

If you are an active surfer, you might build up quite a collection of cookies. You don't have to worry about them clogging up your hard drive, however, because cookies are very small (only 255 characters). Cookies sent from secure Web sites are encrypted, so there's an additional bit of protection there.

If you're wondering just how common the use of cookies is on the Web, you can try a little experiment. Tell your browser to reject all cookies or just to warn you whenever a site tries to give you a cookie. After your browser has warned you a dozen times about attempted cookie deliveries, you'll see that refusing cookies just isn't worth the frustration caused by the interruption to your surfing session.

Cookies are a way of life on the Web now, so the most practical way to deal with them is just to ignore them! But if you just have to know more about them, check out Cookie Central (http://www.cookiecentral.com), a Web site devoted exclusively to cookies! It's a great resource from which to learn more about cookies and how they work.

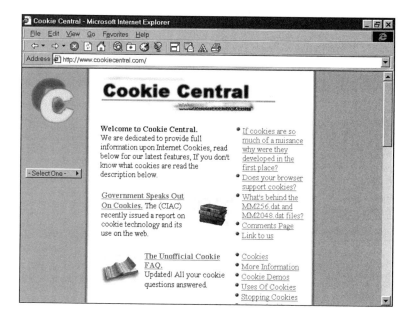

For answers to all your burning cookie questions, visit Cookie Central.

Warning: The Internet Can Be Contagious!

Another hazard that you must be prepared for when you venture onto the Internet is the risk of downloading a virus. A computer virus is a tiny program that hides itself in another file. After that file is on your computer, the virus can run without your knowledge, and possibly wreak havoc on your system.

The damage can range from displaying a silly message on your computer screen to wiping out your hard drive. Recently, viruses have been created that hide in Microsoft Word documents and Excel spreadsheets. These are called macro viruses. They execute automatically when you open the document, can damage your document template, and can then spread to any other documents you save or create.

On the Internet hazard scale, viruses are high on the list. You must do three basic things to protect yourself from a virus attack:

1. **Install anti-virus software.** There are a number of well-known programs, including Norton AntiVirus (http://www.symantec.com), McAfee VirusScan (http://www.mcafee.com), and Dr. Solomon's Anti-Virus Toolkit (http://www. drsolomon.com). All three of these products are easy to use and are effective at protecting your system. Chances are that one of these programs is already on your computer.

Don't Open Files Sent to You by Someone You Don't Know

If you ever receive an e-mail message from an unknown source that contains an attached program, avoid downloading the attachment if possible. If you have already downloaded the program to your computer, don't run it until after a virus checker has cleared it. Even then, if you suspect a virus, it wouldn't be a bad idea to throw out the program altogether and notify whoever sent it that the file was corrupt.

Viruses Can't Be Spread by an E-mail Message Alone

You can't get a virus from an e-mail message or a text file. However, an e-mail message could arrive in your mailbox with an attached file that contains a virus.

2. **Make sure the software is running.** Although this seems obvious, users sometimes have to temporarily turn off their virus checkers to install another software program, for instance. If you don't remember to turn the anti-virus software back on, it doesn't do you any good. You've got to use it if you don't want to lose it!

3. **Update the software's "virus definition file" regularly.** This is a list of all known computer viruses and how the anti-virus program can vaccinate your system against those strains. The problem is that hackers create new viruses nearly every day, so your anti-virus program needs to know about all these new viruses.

Periodically you should check the Web site of your anti-virus software and download the latest updates. (There may be a small charge or subscription fee.) After your anti-virus software is up and running, you can sleep comfortably knowing that you have greatly reduced the risk of a virus penetrating your computer.

Before You Spread a Virus Alert, Make Sure It's True

One problem that may be bigger than viruses is the spread of virus hoaxes. Dozens of well-known fake virus alerts are constantly travelling around the world by e-mail, with names like "Irina," "Good Times," and "Join the Crew." If you get messages warning you about these "viruses," ignore them—do not send them to others! Check with an authority such as the U.S. Department of Energy's Computer Incident Advisory Capability (http://www.ciac.org) to determine the accuracy of any virus warning.

The Least You Need to Know

➤ Online brokerage firms require that clients use a secure Web browser. This protects your private account information from prying eyes on the Internet.

➤ You need to take steps to protect your privacy online just as you would offline. Don't give out personal information unless it is unavoidable, and be sure to check a site's privacy policy to see how they use the information they do collect from users.

➤ Many sites use cookies to store information on your computer, usually for demographic studies or to track parts of a site or ads that you've visited or seen. In most cases, you don't have to worry about cookies. Often, they can make your Web surfing more convenient.

➤ You can download viruses from the Internet without your knowledge. These viruses can damage your computer—unless you use anti-virus software. Exercise extreme caution before running a program sent to you by a stranger, and check any new file for viruses before opening it on your computer.

Chapter 20

Online Schemes and Ploys to Get Your Money

In This Chapter

➤ Uncover some of the tactics used to promote stocks to gullible individual investors

➤ Learn how to protect yourself from scams and frauds

Newspapers and magazines love a sensational story, and the Internet seems to provide plenty of fodder for stories about the "dark side of the Web," murky tales of deception and blatant fraud. In reality, not much has changed since the days that quack doctors in travelling medicine shows hawked snake oil to gullible folks all across the country. The tools of the trade of the hucksters have merely evolved with the times, as scoundrels have discovered that many investors are all too willing to abandon any shred of common sense after they log on to the Internet.

But is the Internet really the problem? How many people are swindled out of money each year over the telephone? When photocopiers became popular, they were quickly put to use in coming up with schemes to defraud investors. Fax machines ensured that a rogue could send "urgent" (but phony) messages to thousands of people in a single day. When personal computers and laser printers arrived, anyone could create a professional-looking logo and letterhead.

It's a good bet that the medicine show quack of the 1800s would have embraced—had they been available—all these new tools and would have used them to come up with new schemes to prey on unsuspecting citizens.

Fraud Is as Popular as Ever

Every week, the National Fraud Information Center and Internet Fraud Watch programs receive an average of 1,500 calls and an equal number of e-mails from consumers seeking help about offers they have received or help with filing complaints about frauds they have discovered.

Source: National Consumers League

The point is this: Nothing has changed in the history of scams and schemes except the addition of a set of tools in the con handbook. You can now be swindled on a street corner, over the telephone, or on the Internet. Here's some practical advice that will alert you to the warning signs and help protect you and your nest egg when you're on the Internet.

First, you need to learn to identify some of the common ways that you can be deceived when it comes to "investment advice." Begin with the (American) National Fraud Information Center (http://www.fraud.org). The NFIC is a watchdog organization that works to educate consumers about fraud, both on the Internet and off. Founded by the National Consumers League, NFIC maintains an Internet Fraud Watch with tips, news, and alerts to help protect consumers from online fraud.

The Pump and Dump

One common ploy used to generate interest in a stock is the "pump and dump." A company or an individual can use this tactic to drive up a stock's price to new highs (the *pump*). After the stock's price has increased, the "pumpers" then sell their shares at the peak (the *dump*).

This tactic works only with shares of very small companies. These are typically shares that trade on the over-the-counter bulletin board—the market for stocks that don't

Anyone Can Create a Fancy Web Site—Even a Crook

Just because a company has a flashy Web site doesn't mean that it is a legitimate business. Anyone can create a Web site in a few days without a lot of money, so don't be fooled by appearances.

qualify for listing in the NASDAQ market. These stocks usually don't have a lot of trading activity, their shares have low prices, and they may not have a large number of outstanding shares. This combination of factors means that it's possible for a person or a company to drum up enough interest in the stock among individual investors to have a significant impact on the price.

On the Internet, it is relatively easy to promote a stock by posting messages on bulletin boards, by sending out e-mail messages, by publishing a "research report" on the stock, or by using many other methods. Today, it's possible to reach thousands of investors in a matter of minutes.

Investors who are anxious to make a quick profit are usually susceptible to buying stocks on the basis of hot tips. When they do purchase shares in the company, the stock price goes up and up. The more stocks investors buy, the more the price increases, and a vicious circle begins.

That is, the circle continues until the touting stops. After the price of shares increases, sometimes by as much as four or five times, all the activity that has gone into promoting the stock ends—but not before the promoters dump all their shares at an enormous profit.

With all the fanfare ended, the stock has nowhere to go but down. Because the increase in price was based on purely superficial "hot tips" and exaggerated claims, there's no way the price can remain at those inflated levels. And as the price falls, so does the value of the investments made by individuals, particularly if they got in at the end of the pump. If prices go back to the level they were at before the frenzy began, investors could lose up to 75 percent or 80 percent of their investment if they aren't able to sell in time.

For more on various schemes and investment fraud that have been used to victimize investors, visit the Web site of the U.S. Securities and Exchange Commission's Office of Investor Education and Assistance (http://www.sec.gov/invkhome.htm). Canadian provincial securities commissions also provide educational information to help you avoid investment fraud on the Internet and offline. If you have been a victim, you can file a complaint with the commission that governs that particular company; for example, contact the Ontario Securities Commission for an Ontario company or the SEC for NYSE stocks.

Don't Try to "Make Money Fast"

Trying to "make money fast" in any investment or business opportunity is a sure way to lose it faster.

Don't Let Greed Get in the Way of Making Good Investment Decisions

There's a saying on Bay Street that goes like this: "Pigs get fat; hogs get slaughtered." It means that it's okay to try to make money on your investments, but if you get too greedy, you're bound to make mistakes that can turn profits into losses.

Hot Tips and Sad Stories

It's time for a little pop quiz. (Your answer will be used to determine your suitability as a future investment maven.) Here goes:

> You're reading messages about technology stocks on a Web discussion board. You come across a well-written message by someone you've never heard of before. The message lays out an ironclad case for why investors should "jump all over" shares of a small-cap stock you've never heard of before, Mini-Micro-Macro Technology, Inc. This stock is "poised for a breakout" and "could be the next Microsoft." The author of the message urges investors to "back up the truck" before they lose the opportunity to "make some serious money" fast.

What do you do?

A. Log on to your brokerage account and buy several hundred shares of Mini-Micro-Macro Technology, Inc. What the heck! If it takes off, you could make a nice quick profit, even if you don't know what the company even does.

B. Put the stock on your watch list and make a note to do some of your own research.

The correct answer is B, unless you're determined to retire a pauper. It's surprising how many investors seem to believe that any "hot tip" they read on the Web must be true. A good dose of healthy skepticism can go a long way toward protecting your nest egg. Remember the adage "Do your homework" before you make any investment.

Don't Be Afraid to Report a Case of Fraud

Too many times, investors are too embarrassed to speak up after they have been swindled. If you think you've been taken in by fraud, it's important to put your shame behind you and report it to the authorities. You might prevent someone else from being conned.

It's probably safe to assume that anyone who posts a message to a discussion group on the Web about a stock has a vested interest in that stock. If you had a great stock idea, you would probably want to share it with the rest of the world, too. There's nothing wrong with that. The problem is that you have no way of knowing whether a message was written by an honest individual investor like yourself or by a promoter hiding behind a pseudonym.

Financial message boards, mailing lists, and newsgroups can be great ways to learn about new investing ideas. The best discussion areas are really small communities where ideas are openly shared and where the participants are respectful of the opinions of others. The advantage of these communities is that members get to know each other, and are naturally wary of outsiders. If someone swaggers into town with a "hot tip" in each holster and starts shooting off at the mouth down at the local watering hole, the other citizens will probably stand back and take in the spectacle for a bit.

Laws Regulate What Company Insiders Can Say to Outsiders

It's illegal for insiders to publicly talk about the nonpublic details of a company's operations. Insiders are people who own the stock of a company that also employs them, or on whose board they sit, or who otherwise have some formal connection that gives them access to privileged details about a company's operations. If someone claims to have "insider information," they're probably either breaking the law or spreading unfounded rumours.

Automatically Sign All Your E-mail Messages

Most e-mail programs enable you to set up a "sig" file. That's short for "signature," and it is a common practice on the Internet to have a sig automatically appear at the bottom of each e-mail message you send. Your sig could include your real name, your company, your Web site address, or any other information that can help others know more about you.

Like any small town, you will eventually find out who you can trust on a particular message board—you'll also find out who is merely blowing hot air. The key is that it takes time for you to learn about the people in a new neighbourhood. So look for an online community where you're comfortable, one that fits your investing style.

Newsletters Aren't Always What They Seem

When is a newsletter not a newsletter? When it's purely an advertisement that's trying to sell you a stock.

Many Web and e-mail newsletters or research services promote stocks. But these are usually not independent publications. Usually, the company whose stock is being promoted is also paying for the newsletter!

Here's how these ventures usually work. A publicly traded company hires a promoter to help increase awareness of its stock among investors. The promoter will issue press releases, write research reports, publish a newsletter, create a Web site, or use any other method to stir up interest in the stock. In return, the promoter may be paid in cash, stock, stock options, or some combination of all three.

The problem is, the disclosure about the promoter's interest is often nonexistent or difficult to find on the site. In one well-publicized case, the SEC settled a 1997 case with online stock promoter George Chelekis, the publisher of several popular Internet newsletters. The SEC charged that Chelekis did not properly disclose to subscribers that he received substantial payments in return for promoting several stocks. Chelekis paid $163,000 to the U.S. Securities and Exchange Commission to settle the civil case, without admitting or denying the commission's charges. He also agreed to a permanent injunction barring him from violating securities laws (an oxymoron if there ever was one!).

Since 1997, the SEC has stepped up enforcement. But this isn't enough. You should make it a practice to read the fine print on any investment newsletter you come across—on the Web, in your e-mail messages, or in the postal mail. Even though a report on a stock may not be completely invalid if written by someone paid to do the analysis, you have the right to know the situation before you invest.

If you have questions about a small-cap Web site, pay a visit to the Stock Detective (http://www.stockdetective.com). The Stock Detective uncovers the truth about stock "newsletters" that provide analyses of small-cap stocks and whether those services are providing adequate disclosure about any compensation that they have received.

Watching Your Step: How to Protect Yourself and Your Money

Now that you know some of the ways that investing could fool you, how do you protect yourself from falling victim? You can start by sticking to a consistent investment methodology, and avoid making decisions on the basis of tips. In addition, here are a few simple rules to make sure you won't lose money in an investment for all the wrong reasons:

1. The first rule is to be especially wary of "penny stocks," those low-priced, small-cap stocks that trade on the over-the-counter (OTC) bulletin board. These stocks are particularly susceptible to pump-and-dump schemes, and you should always view these investments on a speculative basis.

2. If you read messages on a discussion board or mailing list recommending an OTC bulletin board stock, ask yourself what you know about the author of the message. Is he or she someone you know, or whose past advice you know to be reliable? Is

the message signed with a real name, or does the writer use a nickname? Is the person using a free e-mail service such as HotMail, Yahoo! Mail, or RocketMail? Although many people use these services as their primary e-mail accounts, these services also offer an anonymous way of posting messages on boards.

3. Does the tip sound "too good to be true" ? Don't be lured by promises of big returns in a short period—that's the route to a sure money-losing proposition.

4. What's your hurry? Take your time; there's no investment opportunity that's so great you have to take advantage of it right now. Even if you do miss your chance to invest in a stock that subsequently increases in value significantly, there will be other stocks to buy—it's guaranteed!

5. Read the fine print. If a Web site is promoting stocks, read to see whether they are an independent analysis firm or whether they are being paid by the companies they are touting.

6. Finally, there's no replacement for doing your homework when it comes to investing. Can you substantiate the claims made about a stock that's been recommended to you? Remember that the best defence is a good offence. Do your homework before acting on any tip.

The Least You Need to Know

➤ Don't be a "hot tips" investor. Take the time to do your homework before you take the plunge.

➤ Don't believe everything you read, particularly in small-cap "newsletters"—these may be nothing more than paid advertisements.

Part 6

Putting It Together

Everyone has big goals in life: buying a home, paying for your kids' education, and on top of all that we want to retire wealthy—not an easy feat. But, with sound, long-term investment strategies these goals—your goals—are within reach.

Chapter 21

How to Retire a Millionaire

In This Chapter

➤ Learn about the various sources of retirement income

➤ See how important it is to take advantage of an RRSP

➤ Use online financial calculators to help you with your RRSP and retirement planning

➤ Request an estimate of the Canada Pension Plan benefits you will receive when you retire

➤ Build a plan to save and invest for your retirement

One of the most common reasons that people start investing is because they're worried about their retirement. Today, fewer and fewer companies offer pension plans that guarantee retirement payments to workers. Not only that, but many workers routinely move to new employers four or five times during their working lives, so even if company pensions are available, they may be very small for mobile workers. Add to that the angst of worrying whether there will be money for you from the Canada Pension Plan when you're ready to retire, and you have all the incentive you'd need to save for your "golden years."

A million dollars for retirement? It's not so far-fetched anymore—if you begin early enough.

Don't Take Your Severance Pay in Cash—Roll It Over Instead

When you leave a job, your employer may give you a retiring allowance or severance pay. If you take it in cash, you'll pay tax on it. But you may be able to shelter a lot of it in your RRSP. You're allowed to "roll over" $2,000 for every year of service (or part of a year) before 1996. You can also shelter an extra $1,500 for every year prior to 1989 that you weren't a member of a company pension plan.

It doesn't have to be just a dream. Many people are actually surprised to find out that it's really not so hard to put together a retirement plan that will make them millionaires by the time they retire.

You don't need to be an investing genius to reach your million-dollar goal, either. You just need to invest regularly in the stock market and let the power of time do its trick. As your returns compound over the course of twenty or thirty or forty years, your nest egg will grow considerably.

You don't have any time to waste, however. You have to get started today if you want to have a fighting chance of retiring a millionaire. Fortunately, the Web has tools that can help.

The Rule of 72

Wondering how long an investment will take to double? Divide the interest rate into 72. So an investment that earns 8 percent a year will take nine years to double. How long to triple? Divide the interest rate into 113. And to quadruple? Go back to the rule of 72 and multiply your answer by 2.

RRSP Contribution Deadline

The RRSP contribution deadline is sixty days into the new year. So it's February 29, 2000 for the 1999 tax year and March 1, 2001 for the 2000 tax year. Any contribution made during January or February can be applied to the previous year or the current year, or you can carry it forward and claim it in a future year when your income may be higher.

The Registered Retirement Savings Plan (RRSP)

These plans began modestly back in the 1950s. Millions of Canadians now have one. But millions more don't. And that's a shame, because the RRSP is quite simply one of the most generous tax shelters any government offers its citizens.

First, the basics. An RRSP is a special, government-approved savings vehicle that allows you to save for retirement with the help of two big tax breaks: (1) You can deduct allowable contributions from your income; (2) All the income earned inside an RRSP

TaxWeb provides an online answer to how much tax you'll save by making an RRSP contribution.

(that includes interest, dividends, and capital gains) is allowed to accumulate tax-free until you withdraw the funds. That's a powerful and unbeatable combination.

Under current rules, you can contribute up to 18 percent of your *previous* year's income, to a maximum of $13,500. Those maximums are set to rise to $14,500 in 2004, and $15,500 in 2005. If you have a company pension plan, you have to subtract your pension adjustment from that maximum contribution figure. Any unused contribution room can be carried forward indefinitely. And anyone who is 69 years old or younger may contribute, as long as they have earned income.

You're free to invest your contributions in almost anything, with a few exceptions. No more than 20 percent of the book value (what you originally paid) can be invested in foreign investments (although there are a growing number of derivative-based "foreign" investment products that are considered 100 percent RRSP-eligible). You can't invest in stamps and coins or other collectibles; real estate (although real estate investment trusts are okay); or gold bullion or any other precious metal (but gold stocks and precious metals mutual funds are approved). Foreign currencies are a no-no too.

Designate Your Spouse as the RRSP Beneficiary

If you name your estate as the beneficiary of your RRSP, it will take longer for your spouse to get access to the money. And it will have to go through probate, with fees in some provinces that can approach 1.5 percent of the RRSP's value. Far better to name your spouse as the beneficiary. No probate, and a quicker transfer of funds.

The rules surrounding RRSPs generate a lot of questions. And there are many Web sites to provide the answers. Many companies that sell RRSP-eligible investments have this information. So do many media sites. Let's start with the financial "supersites": ilmoney (http://www.imoney.com) and Quicken.ca (http://www.quicken.ca).

Ilmoney's Knowledge Base deals extensively with the subject. The All You Need to Know section features fifteen RRSP subcategories where you can get more details: everything from RRSP Loans to Spousal RRSPs to Self-Directed RRSPs. There's also a particularly useful category dealing with the latest rule changes. The section on Frequently Asked Questions features many of the ones financial advisors hear a lot: for example, "What happens if I overcontribute?" and "Can I take money out of an RRSP before retirement?"

The Quicken.ca site puts RRSP material in its RRSP Planner. It groups its information into four broad subcategories, such as Why Do I Need an RRSP? These, in turn, are further subdivided, with hands-on tools that will help you figure out how much you'll need to live on in retirement, and how inflation will affect your savings. There's also a good Retirement Tips section.

If You Withdraw, You Will Pay

If you withdraw money from an RRSP, you'll be liable for tax on that amount. The trustee will withhold tax on a sliding scale, depending on how much you take out. On amounts up to $5,000, the withholding tax is 10 percent. On amounts from $5,000 to $15,000, the rate is 20 percent. And on amounts over $15,000, it's 30 percent. The rates are higher in Quebec.

Both Quicken.ca and ilmoney feature several RRSP-related calculators (more about these later in the chapter).

The non-profit Investor Learning Centre (http://www.investorlearning.ca) provides easy-to-understand answers to some RRSP Frequently Asked Questions, such as "When should a young investor consider opening a self-directed RRSP?" Just click on Investment FAQs and enter RRSP in the search window.

The Financial Pipeline (http://www.finpipe.com) has a Retirement section with useful primers on RRSPs, pensions, and annuities.

Many newspapers and magazines archive their RRSP articles, and these can be great sources of up-to-date information. For instance, *IE:Money* (http://www.iemoney.com) publishes an RRSP issue every February. Several articles from that issue are posted online. *The Financial Post* has dozens of RRSP-related articles, as well as relevant columns that can be searched from its site (http://www.nationalpost.com). And *The Globe and Mail*'s Report on Business can be searched online for its many RRSP-related features (http://www.globeandmail.com/hubs/rob.html).

How Much Tax Will I Save?

Human nature being what it is, the most powerful incentive to contribute to your RRSP is usually not the fear of eating dog food in your golden years. No, what really interests RRSP contributors is the tax refund they'll get in the spring.

Instead of guessing how much that refund will be, there's a Web site that will do the calculation for you. TaxWeb (http://www.tax.ca) is co-sponsored by Ernst & Young and

Borrowing from Your RRSP Carries a Long-Term Cost

Ottawa allows people to borrow from their RRSPs for only two purposes: to buy a home, and to go back to school. The Home Buyers Plan allows people to borrow up to $20,000 from their RRSPs, and pay it back over fifteen years. The Lifelong Learning Plan allows people to raid their RRSPs for higher education (see chapter 22). Just be sure to repay the money as soon as possible, so that the money has time to compound in that tax-free environment. And if you withdraw money for any other purpose, you can't repay it at all.

the Canadian Institute of Chartered Accountants. Click on Tax Tools, and then choose the RRSP Savings tax calculator. Enter your income and RRSP contribution, and you'll find out how big that refund would be in each province and territory.

How Long Will I Live?

Who isn't interested in how long they're going to live? And for retirement planning, it's a question you need to ask yourself. After all, the money you've saved over your lifetime has to last as long as you do. So how long will that be? If your answer is 110, try a calculator or two to nudge you towards a more realistic figure.

RetireWeb (http://www.retireweb.com) is the work of a Montreal actuary. His life expectancy calculator is very simple: Just enter your gender and age, and voila! You find out the number of years the mortality tables suggest you'll have left. For instance, the calculator says that a 40-year-old man can expect to live 38.5 more years—to age 78.5.

Now let's try a more detailed calculator. The Quicken.ca (http://www.quicken.ca) life expectancy calculator is found in the RRSP Planner section under the Why Do I Need an RRSP section. Click on the brutally direct question, When Am I Going to Die? This time, you'll be asked about your height, weight, blood pressure, and education, and whether you wear a seat belt. This time, our average 40-year-old male was handed a life expectancy of 78.4 years. So does this mean that the typical 40-year-old male should assume that he'll die just after his 78th birthday? No! Mortality tables provide a median figure. In our example, the figures mean that half of all men who are now 40 can expect to live beyond 78.5...and half can expect to live less than that. Many financial planners recommend that you assume you're going to live to 90. Good news, indeed. But it means you have to save more. And that brings us to our next section.

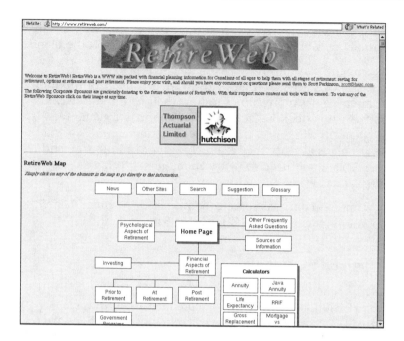

RetireWeb is a comprehensive source of retirement information—before, during, and after.

Other Sources of Retirement Income

RRSPs are just one of the three pillars of retirement income. The other two are company pension plans and government plans (like Old Age Security and the Canada Pension Plan). Let's deal first with company plans. About five million Canadians are now members of registered pension plans at work. That means that the majority of workers don't belong. Employer-sponsored pension plans are traditionally much more prevalent in the public sector (e.g., teachers, government employees, police officers). Some large private employers offer them; many more do not. And most smaller companies don't have a pension plan for their workers.

The two main types of company pension plans are Defined Benefit (DB) plans and Defined Contribution (DC) plans. Defined Benefit plans guarantee workers a specific pension at a specified age after a given number of years of service. A typical government pension provides a pension equal to 2 percent times the number of years of pensionable service (to a maximum of thirty-five

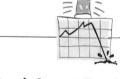

Don't Invest Too Heavily in Company Stock

Some companies give employees an incentive to invest in that company's stock. If you invest too much in shares of your company, however, you can throw your portfolio out of balance, and put your retirement at risk.

years), times the average pensionable salary over the best three or five earning years in your career. This may be partially or fully indexed to inflation, depending on the plan.

Most Canadians who have company pensions have Defined Benefit plans. But the number is shrinking as more employers switch their plans to the Defined Contribution variety. In these plans, the employee has more choice in how their contributions and their employer's contributions are invested. But he or she has no income guarantees. If the investments do well, the pension will reflect that. If the investments sink, so will the pension. Employers like DC plans because they're much easier to administer, and shift the risk to the employee. They don't need to worry about guaranteeing a certain pension to an employee thirty years away from retirement.

The ilmoney site (http://www.imoney.com) has some good primers on Defined Benefit and Defined Contribution pension plans. Click on Knowledge Base, then RRSPs.

Government Retirement Programs

The two main income security programs for seniors in Canada are the Old Age Security (OAS) benefit and the Canada Pension Plan (CCP). As of September 1999, Old Age Security payments were worth $413.70 a month. Payments go to most Canadians age 65 or over. But once income rises above $53,000 or so, the OAS starts getting "clawed back."

By late 1999, the maximum Canada Pension Plan retirement benefit was $751.67 a month at age 65. CPP retirement benefits only go to those who paid into the plan and are no longer working. Ten million people contribute to the CPP. And another three million contribute to the Quebec Pension Plan (which is administered separately, but has similar benefits). You can start to receive benefits as early as age 60, but the CPP will then be reduced by 6 percent per year (a 30 percent reduction if the CPP starts at age 60).

Is Your Old Age Security Cheque in the Mail?

In 1999, 3.7 million Canadians received Old Age Security benefits.

Source: Human Resources Development Canada

The one source that has all the details about what these programs pay and who's eligible is Human Resources Development Canada. Its Web site (http://www.hrdc-drhc.gc.ca) is a must-see for people with questions about either the OAS or the CPP. Be sure to use this site to check the current rates whenever you use retirement calculators on the Web. Some calculators still have pre-programmed benefit details from years gone by.

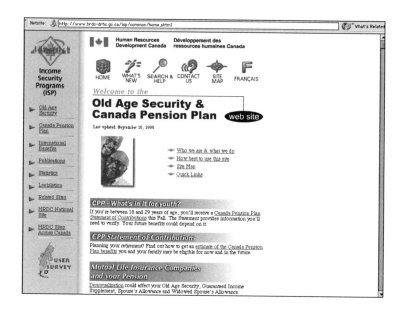

The Web site of Human Resources Development Canada has all you need to know about the Canada Pension Plan and Old Age Security benefits.

And lastly, if you want to find out how much you're likely to get from the CPP, you can request an estimate of your CPP benefits. You can download an online application form at http://www.hrdc-drhc.gc.ca/isp/cpp/soc/soc2_e.shtml.

Let's Start Planning

There are so many retirement calculators on the Web, that if you were to try every one, you could spend much of your waking life just plugging in numbers. The key is to find one you like and then check in every year or two to see how you're doing and whether a mid-course correction is in order.

Enter "RRSP Calculator" in most Web browsers and you'll receive a list of many sites to choose from (perhaps too many!).

Most banks and mutual fund companies offer RRSP calculators of one sort or another. Some are excellent, others less so. And just because a company has a good calculator does not necessarily mean its products are as good. Remember too that

Pay Down the Mortgage or Top Up Your RRSP?

Some people use extra cash to top up their RRSPs, and then use the refund to pay down their mortgage. RetireWeb (http://www.retireweb.com) has a calculator that will allow you to figure out which move makes more financial sense for you.

with some sites, there isn't much of a separation between the calculator's message and the RRSP product. If every financial dilemma exposed by your calculations is answered by a suggestion to buy a certain mutual fund, it's time to raise those eyebrows! Also, make sure that the assumptions the calculator uses and the choices you make are realistic. Hoping for a compound average annual 12 percent return on your investments isn't realistic if you're a conservative investor. Hoping that inflation will average 1 percent may not be realistic either. The better calculators will suggest a figure of 3 percent to 5 percent.

All right, enough with the warnings! Let's try a couple.

Spectrum United mutual funds has a simple calculator that just tells you how much money you'll likely end up with in your RRSP, based on the information you plug in. For instance, let's say our current RRSP savings are $25,000. We're going to contribute $3,000 a year. We plan to retire in twenty-five years. We'll estimate the average inflation rate during that time at 4 percent. And we'll assume our investments will grow at an annual average compound rate of 8 percent. Press Calculate and we have our verdict. The RRSP will be worth $408,000 in twenty-five years (or the equivalent of $191,000 in today's money). Impressive numbers. But what do they mean? Will that be enough to survive? Time now to go up the calculator sophistication ladder.

Let's try Scotiabank's Reality Check (http://www.scotiabank.ca/RealityCheck.html). This is a little more elaborate than most. It will end up delivering a seven-page report that analyzes your RRSP savings, tells you whether you're saving enough to meet your goals, and suggests moves you can make to erase any shortfall. Let's use the example from above and see how we're faring.

Spectrum United offers a basic retirement calculator that tells you how much you should be contributing to your RRSP to reach your goal.

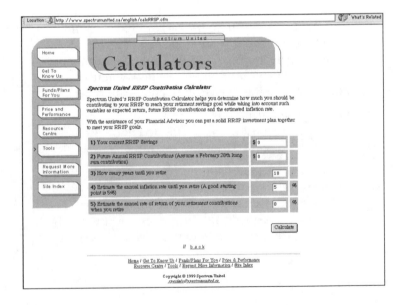

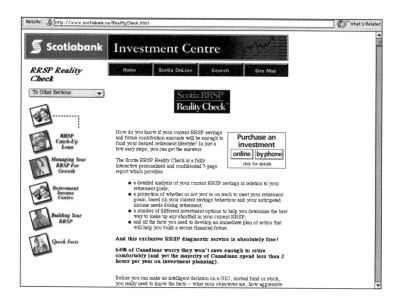

Answer the questions posed by Scotiabank's Reality Check online retirement planner and find out if you're on track for a comfortable retirement.

You'll quickly notice that it asks you questions the Spectrum calculator didn't (like what income you think you'll need to retire on, in today's dollars). We'll enter 70 percent of our pre-retirement income of $50,000 (that's $35,000). Next, it asks if you expect to get a company pension. We'll say yes and go along with the default percentages that suggest where the income will come from (RRSP, company pension, and government). We're 35 now, and want to retire at age 60. Our current RRSP contribution limit is $4,000. Our total unused RRSP contribution room is $10,000. Our current income, as

How Much Java Do You Need?

Many Web sites use a programming language called JavaScript to create calculators and handle other basic interactive functions. Microsoft Internet Explorer and Netscape Navigator provide different levels of support for JavaScript, so a particular browser may occasionally give you an error message that it can't run a script that's built in to some Web site. This is one reason why heavy-duty Web surfers install both Explorer and Navigator. With both installed, they can access any site.

above, is $50,000. We're then asked to describe our investment objective. We'll enter Conservative Growth. Our investment knowledge is moderate. And the risk we're willing to take is also moderate. Press the button, and we embark on a seven-step analysis. It all ends with a finding that we'll have a surplus of $136,000!

Now go back and fiddle with the variables and you'll see what a difference one change can make. Remove the company pension plan from the equation (and most Canadians will be doing this), and suddenly that surplus turns into a deficit of almost $190,000! The calculator then suggests ways to overcome that deficit (like contributing more to the RRSP, trying for better performance numbers, saving outside the RRSP, or perhaps settling for a little less retirement income). You could also retire later.

There are other retirement calculators worth mentioning. Canada Trust (http://www.canadatrust.com) has one that takes into account both kinds of registered pension plans (Defined Benefit and Defined Contribution). The retirement calculator from Dynamic Mutual Funds (http://www.dundeefunds.com) takes into account both RRSP and non-RRSP savings.

And for people who want the kind of retirement calculator they can really sink their teeth into, try the one put out by seclonLogic Inc. (http://www.seclonlogic.com). This one allows you to vary the age at which you start to receive the CPP (at 60, for instance). It also takes a spouse into account, and allows you to select the pension income option for that spouse.

Don't Be Too Aggressive with Your Projections

When you make projections about the future growth of your portfolio, it can be tempting to plug in a high growth rate. But consider that as you get older and closer to retirement, you might not want to invest in aggressive, high-growth stocks. You will probably be more interested in bonds and other fixed-income investments so that you can protect all the wealth you have built up over the years. That also means that your portfolio's growth will slow down the closer you get to retirement. You can account for this by using a lower average annual growth rate when you make projections about your portfolio.

When You're 69

RRSPs must be wound up by the end of the year in which you turn 69 (you can wind things up sooner, if you want). You have three main choices:

1. **Take the money in cash.** This is a bad choice in almost every situation. You'll probably lose half the money to Revenue Canada, and you won't have a retirement income. Choose this only if your bookie is about to break your legs for nonpayment of gambling debts.

2. **Buy an annuity from a life insurance company.**

3. **Transfer the assets into a Registered Retirement Income Fund (RRIF).**

Let's take a closer look at options 2 and 3.

Annuities

When you buy an annuity, you're handing over all the money in your RRSP to a life insurance company. In return, they promise to pay you a guaranteed income for as long as you live. That can be comforting. But there are some restrictions.

For one thing, you have no control over how the money is invested. And with today's relatively low interest rates, annuities aren't as attractive as they once were. They're also irrevocable. Once you've bought one, you can't ever change your mind. You're locked in to that steady payment forever. Not only that, but when you die (unless you buy one with an extra guarantee) your estate is left with nothing. Conditions like that have made RRIFs the overwhelming favourite among people converting their RRSPs.

Registered Retirement Income Funds (RRIFs)

RRIFs are really like RRSPs in reverse. All during your working life, you've put money into your RRSP and watched it grow. When you convert to a RRIF, you don't need to sell any of your investments. They can continue to grow tax-free. But instead of adding to the pile of money, as you did in your RRSP years, you now have to take out a set amount each year. The government specifies a minimum withdrawal schedule you must adhere to.

RetireWeb (http://www.retireweb.com) has a RRIF calculator that's easy to use. Just enter the age (we'll say 70), the amount of money ($100,000) and the interest rate you feel the investments will earn (8 percent).

You'll notice that you'll also be asked if the RRIF was established before January 1, 1993. That's because RRIFs set up before that date have a different withdrawal schedule. Back

Quicken.ca offers a life expectancy calculator that asks you to answer medical and lifestyle questions.

then, Ottawa calculated RRIF withdrawal minimums so that the funds would be exhausted by the time you were 90. The problem was, too many people were living longer than that, and running out of money. So now, the schedule goes to age 100. You'll see that, under the new schedule, annual RRIF payments rise steadily until age 93, and then start easing back.

SeclonLogic (http://www.seclonlogic.com) has a calculator that will let you compare retirement income from a RRIF and an annuity. It will also compare those sources to the income produced by a LIF. What's that, you say? Next paragraph, please.

The Alphabet Soup Continues: LIRAs, LIFs, and LRIFs

When people leave a company that has a pension plan, they usually have two choices. They can leave their contributions with the company's plan and eventually get a pension from the company. Or they can transfer the value of their pension to a LIRA—a Locked-In Retirement Account (sometimes called a Locked-In RRSP).

As the name suggests, these funds are locked in until retirement. But you're free to invest them in much the same way as you would with a regular RRSP. But unlike an RRSP, you can't convert this money into a RRIF. Instead, you set up a Life Income Fund (LIF). This is like a RRIF. But there are some added restrictions. Not only is there a minimum payout each year, there's also a maximum. And you must buy a life annuity with the balance of the LIF by the end of the year in which you turn 80.

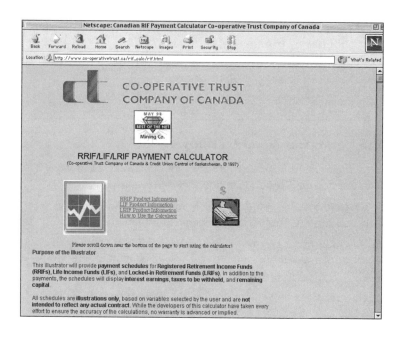

Co-operative Trust has a calculator that can compare RRIF, LIF, and LRIF rates.

In Alberta, Saskatchewan, and Manitoba, there's a new option—an LRIF. This is a Locked-In Retirement Income Fund. Unlike LIFs, LRIFs do not require people to buy annuities. Retirees can continue to manage their money as long as they want.

Co-operative Trust and Credit Union Central in Saskatchewan have developed a calculator that compares RRIF, LIF, and LRIF payments. Try it at http://www.co-operativetrust.ca/rif_calc/rif.html.

A Million-Dollar Strategy

We began this chapter talking about a million dollars. And if you've been plotting sample retirement strategies, you've probably noticed how easy it is for a nest egg to reach the high six-figures or even a million...if you start early enough.

Consider this. Imagine that you're 19 again. Get a part-time job and set up an RRSP. Save a dollar a day. At the end of each month, take the $30 and

It May Be a Good Idea to Overcontribute to Your RRSP

You're allowed to overcontribute up to $2,000 to your RRSP during your lifetime. The contribution will not be tax-deductible. But it will be allowed to grow on a tax-deferred basis inside the RRSP in the meantime. You can always claim the overcontribution as a regular contribution in a subsequent year if you find yourself $2,000 short.

invest it in something that will earn an average annual compound return of 12 percent a year. By the time you're 69, you'll have...trumpets please...$1,171,750.

A million-dollar strategy—with just a dollar a day.

The Least You Need to Know

➤ There are three main sources of retirement income: your RRSP, your pension plan at work, and government benefits like the Canada Pension Plan and Old Age Security.

➤ The RRSP is by far the best retirement savings vehicle available for Canadians. Anyone with a job should have one. Many sites offer useful RRSP and retirement information.

➤ After an RRSP is wound up, you must make a choice about whether you want to buy an annuity or convert to a Registered Retirement Income Fund. These days, most choose the RRIF because of its flexibility.

➤ You can request an estimate of your Canada Pension Plan benefits from Human Resources Development Canada's Web site.

➤ A good plan can help you set and reach goals for your retirement savings. Online calculators can help you to understand how much you need to save and invest regularly to retire a millionaire. But the most important thing is to start planning for retirement now, no matter what your age.

Chapter 22

Paying for a College or University Education

In This Chapter

➤ Project how much a college or university education is likely to cost when your child is ready to enroll

➤ Navigate the array of options available to help you save for higher learning

➤ Map your plan to save and invest for your child's post-secondary education

One of the most common fears parents have is how they'll ever be able to pay for college or university for their children. And with the costs of a post-secondary education increasing faster than the rate of inflation, it's not likely to get any easier down the road.

For much of the 1990s, governments gradually shifted the burden of education financing from their shoulders over to the students (and their parents). And the figures only hint at the depths of this crisis. How bad is it now? According to a survey done by USC Education Savings Plans, the average cost of a single year at an average university in Canada tops $6,500 in the 1999/2000 school year. That figure includes tuition, fees, local travel, books, supplies, and incidentals. Notice that the list doesn't include residence. Throw in an eight-month stay in the average campus dorm, and the new total comes to a whopping $11,587. That's per child, per year. And some organizations put that estimate even higher.

An Education Is Worth It

Are you wondering whether a college or university education is worth it after all? It's estimated that university graduates will earn almost twice as much over their lifetimes as high school grads ($2.37 million versus $1.2 million).

Source: Statistics Canada

College and University Tuition Go Up and Up and Up

According to Statistics Canada, from 1980 to 1998, average tuition fees in Canada rose 115 percent, while average family income rose just 1 percent (after accounting for inflation).

If education costs continue to grow (and that seems likely), how much will a year of university cost when your child is ready to enroll? The Web, as you might expect, is a great place to start looking for the answers. Let's try the Education Savings Calculator developed by Human Resources Development Canada (http://www.hrdc-drhc.gc.ca/cgi-bin/english_calc_page1_cesg.cgi), and you get a not-so-pleasant glimpse into the financial future. We'll figure out how much you might need to fork over for your child's bachelor's degree in 2014.

Let's assume you have your heart set on sending three-year-old Nelson to college away from home. Enter $11,587 (the USC estimate for the average present cost of a year studying away from home) as the "Total Costs, Education and Living, This Year," and enter an expected inflation rate for those total costs (try 4 percent), with fifteen years to enrollment. Click the Next button.

The results of your projection might be a little overwhelming at first. In this case, four years of college study away from home are projected to cost $88,700 in fifteen years.

You can go ahead and experiment with different rates of inflation, or try using the average costs of a stay-at-home college or university experience. But you will have to face up to the fact that you've got some work to do! The most important thing to realize is that the time to start worrying about paying for your kid's college education is not when he or she is three years into high school, but before the little one learns to walk! As with any investment, time can be your ally or your enemy.

Understanding the Available Options

Saving and investing for university is often different from saving for retirement or other goals. A number of special options are available to help you find the money for higher education. You may want to rely on more than one of these options to help meet those costs.

Your first step is to understand just what's available. After that, you can put together a strategy that works best for your particular situation.

Registered Education Savings Plans (RESPs)

The late 1990s finally saw these plans come into their own. The federal budgets of 1997 and 1998 made these plans much more attractive and flexible savings vehicles, and sweetened their tax-saving opportunities too. They can be set up at most financial institutions and mutual fund companies. They're also sold by a handful of non-profit "scholarship trust" organizations.

No matter which you choose, the basic rules are the same. You can contribute up to $4,000 per year, per child, to a lifetime maximum of $42,000. The contributions are not tax-deductible. But the earnings inside the plan are allowed to grow on a tax-sheltered basis. Not only that, but when the money is finally withdrawn when the child is in college or university, the earnings will be taxed in the hands of the student...usually at a much lower rate because the student will have little other income.

There are two main kinds of RESPs. With an *individual* plan, you decide how to invest the money. Stocks, bonds, GICs, mutual funds—the choice is yours. And unlike RRSPs, there are no restrictions on how the money is invested (other than any limitations imposed by the plans themselves). So you could invest 100 percent of the money in foreign equities or mutual funds if you wanted. There are also family versions of these plans that can cover all the kids, and make it easier to switch beneficiaries in case one of the children doesn't want to pursue post-secondary studies.

The other main type of RESP is the *pooled* (also called *group*) RESP. Scholarship trust organizations will make the investment decisions for you. Your money goes into a giant investment pool that will ultimately be tapped to provide a series of scholarship

What if the Child Doesn't Go on to College or University?

Recent changes to RESP rules have made it easier to substitute another child as a beneficiary if the original beneficiary doesn't attend past high school. And if plans have been open for at least ten years, and the intended beneficiary is at least 21, you are permitted to roll up to $50,000 of the plan's earnings into your own RRSP (provided you have the room). But the grant must then be repaid (see the next page for information about the Canada Education Savings Grant). And anything you can't roll into your RRSP will attract special tax penalties. Be sure to check the terms and conditions of the RESP you're thinking of buying, as some are more flexible than others.

Ask Your Parents to Help Their Grandkids

Grandparents can set up and con-tribute to RESPs (both the individ-ual and pooled varieties) for their grandchildren. They might also want to make direct gifts of cash or Canada Savings Bonds.

payments for each college- or university-bound child who qualifies. By law, pooled plans must put the money to work in safe investment products, like GICs and government bonds. But beyond that broad requirement, the terms of each pooled plan vary greatly. So find out exactly what you're buying, and what happens if your child doesn't end up being college or university material. These plans can be quite complex.

So that's where things stood as of early 1998, when the whole RESP world was suddenly given a major performance-enhancing rule change. That year's federal budget announced free money...also known as the Canada Education Savings Grant (CESG). From 1998 on, Ottawa is giving a tax-free grant equal to 20 percent of the contributions made to an RESP, to a maximum of $400 per year, per child, with a lifetime grant maximum of $7,200.

The grant is paid directly to the child's RESP. And that brings up one key point: all children must have a Social Insurance Number to get a CESG. So it's a good idea to apply to your local office of Human Resources Development Canada for that all-important SIN as soon as the future grad is born. You can download an application form at HRDC's Web site: http://www.hrdc-drhc.gc.ca/sin/download.shtml.

Another couple of key points: The CESG doesn't reduce your overall $4,000 contribution limit. And, as with your contributions, the grant is allowed to grow

Use this directory on the Human Resources Development Canada site to find organizations authorized to sell RESPs.

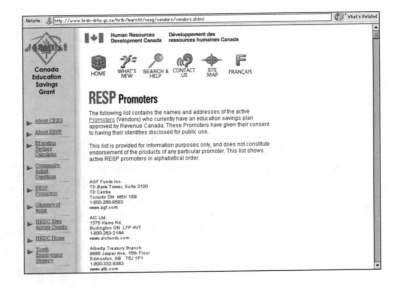

tax-free inside the plan. And what a boost that can give your savings. $400 a year, invested for eighteen years at an average annual compound rate of 8 percent, will grow to almost $15,000! That's prompted an explosion of interest in these plans. Still, as we'll see, RESPs aren't the only way of saving for higher learning.

For more information on the rules and restrictions surrounding Registered Education Savings Plans, pay a visit to Revenue Canada's RESP page at http://www.rc.gc.ca/E/pub/tg/rc4092ed/ rc4092ed.html or link to HRDC's informative RESP/CESG site at http://www.hrdc-drhc.gc.ca/ hrib/learnlit/cesg/about/about.shtml.

It's Always Better to Save

Some people think that they will be eligible for more financial aid if they don't save anything for university. In fact, your household's income is a much bigger factor when a financial aid package is determined. It's best to save, save, save!

In-Trust Accounts

In-trust accounts, also known as informal trusts, are another common way for parents or grandparents to save for a child's post-secondary education. There's no free grant from Ottawa with these. But they may be a better idea than RESPs for parents who are sure that their children aren't heading for any kind of higher education. They can also supplement an RESP.

Like RESPs, in-trust accounts can be set up at virtually any financial institution or mutual fund company. Money is deposited and invested "in trust" for a child's future use. What you are doing is transferring assets and their potential growth to your child. But these accounts must be set up properly, or a nasty tax surprise could await. And the tax benefits are what make them worth considering.

Don't Forget the Age Limitations

RESPs must be wound up within twenty-five years after they're set up. But the federal grant (CESG) is only for children 17 years of age and under.

Here's what Revenue Canada will look for to see if they pass muster. For one thing, the donor and the person who manages the money (the trustee) can't be one and the same. And for an actual transfer to take place in the eyes of the tax department, the money must be irrevocably given to the child. Dipping into an in-trust account to take a Florida holiday will render it a mere savings account. And you don't want that, because in-trust accounts have some real tax benefits, even though the contributions don't compound tax-free. With a properly constructed in-trust account, just the interest and income is attributed back to the donors. The capital gains is taxed in the hands of the

**Avoid Borrowing
If Possible**

You may be able to take out student loans to help pay for college, but remember that it's better to be paid for saving instead of having to pay to borrow.

child when he/she turns 18, probably at a much lower rate than what Mom, Dad, or the grandparents would be taxed. For this reason, in-trust accounts usually invest in the types of growth securities that generate healthy capital gains, but little income (things like growth stocks or growth equity mutual funds). One other thing: Irrevocable means exactly that. Once the child turns 18, the money is theirs to do with as they please. That could mean a college or university education. It could also mean buying a Porsche Boxster. Choices…choices….

The Child Tax Benefit

The Canada Child Tax Benefit (CCTB) is aimed at modest and middle-income families. It replaces the old Family Allowance system, which sent out a cheque for the parents of each child, no matter how wealthy the family.

The basic benefit is $1,020 per child per year for each of the first two children. Third or fourth children get a slightly higher benefit. As of July 2000, the full benefit will be paid only to families whose net income is under $29,590. The CCTB will be gradually clawed back at incomes above that level. At $70,390 it will disappear altogether. A supplemental benefit was introduced in 1998 for families with net incomes below $21,000.

Child Tax Benefit payments enjoy a unique status among government income-support programs.

And it's something parents can potentially use to their advantage. If these payments are invested "in trust" for the child, the money earned is the child's. All the interest, all the income, and all the capital gains will be taxed in the child's hands.

The only problem with trying to save these payments for college is that they're meant to help the family meet day-to-day expenses right now. So while the potential to use the Child Tax Benefit as a long-term education savings vehicle is there, the reality of present-day living costs may torpedo that plan.

Revenue Canada administers the Child Tax Benefit program. Its Web site has what you need to know: http://www.rc.gc.ca/cctb-gstc/.

Canada Savings Bonds

For more than fifty years, Canada Savings Bonds have been one of the most popular ways for people to tuck away a little something for the kids. More than seven million Canadians now own CSBs. And about a million of us buy them every year through payroll savings plans at work. Entire generations of moms, dads, grandpas, and grandmas have been attracted by their flexibility and ease of purchase.

Canada Investment and Savings is the place to go for details about Canada Savings Bonds.

CSBs can be put into some self-directed RESPs set up through investment dealers, or just stashed in a safety-deposit box. The CSBs' earnings will compound tax-free if they're held inside an RESP. But remember, we're talking savings bonds here. They're not spectacular growth investments. Recent bond offerings have offered interest rates around 4 percent.

There's generally no advantage in putting CSBs into an in-trust account because of the attribution rules mentioned earlier. After all, interest income from in-trust accounts is taxed in the hands of the person who bought the bonds, not the child. But there is one exception. If the bonds were bought with money that came directly from Child Tax Benefit payments, then those bonds could be held in trust and the interest would be considered the child's.

You have two kinds of bonds to choose from: regular interest (R-Bonds), and compound interest (C-Bonds).

Regular interest bonds deposit interest directly to your bank account or pay you by cheque on the anniversary of the issue date, until the bond matures. They're available in denominations as low as $300.

Compound interest bonds automatically reinvest the interest until the bonds are redeemed or they mature. Available denominations start at $100.

Whichever you choose, be sure to keep track of the maturity dates. They don't earn any interest at all once they mature.

Several provinces also offer savings bonds of their own, although some are not as instantly cashable as CSBs.

Student Loans

Figures from the Canadian Federation of Students show that many of today's grads haven't been able to keep their heads above the ever-rising waters of current education costs. The average debt owed by graduating students in 1999 was $25,000. Quite a financial albatross to begin your working life with.

Still, for those without enough resources to head to college or university, these loans have become a very popular way of getting there. The Canada Student Loans Program Web site (http://www.hrdc-drhc.gc.ca/student_ loans/engraph/index.html) provides general information on federal loan and grant programs, as well as links to provincial aid programs, the lenders who deliver them, and Student Need Assessment Software (SNAS), a program that estimates your Canada Student Loan.

Students and Bankruptcies: Part 1

Twenty-five percent of all bankruptcies in 1997 listed student loans among the bad debts. In 10 percent of those cases, student loans were the main factor that triggered the bankruptcy. In 1996/97, student loan bankruptcies cost the federal treasury $70 million.

Students and Bankruptcies: Part 2

Students hoping to escape repaying student loans by declaring bankruptcy now are in for a rude surprise. As of 1998, student loan debt cannot be discharged by bankruptcy until ten years after studies are finished.

The Feds' "17 Percent Solution"

Full-time students can claim a 17 percent education tax credit (take the number of months you're in full-time attendance at school, multiply by $200, and take 17 percent of that figure). Students can also claim a 17 percent credit on their annual tuition fees. And there's now a 17 percent tax credit on the interest portion of payments to federal and provincial student loan programs.

The Lifelong Learning Plan

Beginning in 1999, eligible students have been able to borrow from their RRSPs to help pay for post-secondary education costs. The Lifelong Learning Plan (LLP) allows students to borrow up to $10,000 a year from their RRSPs, to a maximum of $20,000. The money must be paid back to the RRSP over a ten-year period, with at least one-tenth of the amount repaid each year. Any installment not repaid will be added to your income for the year, and you'll pay tax on it.

The LLP isn't for everyone. But for people who have RRSP funds (mature students) and especially for those who think more schooling will eventually help them earn a bigger salary, this might be one option.

More information on the Lifelong Learning Plan can be obtained at http://www.rc.gc.ca/E/pub/tg/rc4112ed/rc4112ed.html.

The Hidden Costs of Borrowing from Your RRSP

Even though the federal Lifelong Learning Plan (LLP) allows you up to ten years to repay the money you borrowed, you should try to repay it as soon as possible. The sooner you can get that money back into the warm and fuzzy tax-sheltered environment of the RRSP, the faster your retirement nest egg will grow.

Scholarships

It's always nice when someone gives you money. And scholarships, bursaries, and grants can really fill that funding gap when savings, student loans, gifts, and lottery wins don't quite do the trick.

Universities hand out these awards by the fistful; so do colleges, corporations, unions, government agencies, charitable foundations, and individuals. Millions upon millions of dollars. Free for the asking. And every year, lots of it goes unclaimed, simply because people don't know what's out there. And what's out there is truly amazing. Would you

The Web site of the Canadian Millennium Scholarship Foundation has information on who's eligible for these awards.

Interest Relief and Debt-Reduction Programs

If students find they're having trouble repaying their loans, Ottawa will pay up to 100 percent of the loan's monthly interest, depending on the borrower's family income. Some provincial aid programs also offer some kind of interest relief. Lenders can also be asked to extend the repayment term of a loan from ten to fifteen years. And when that isn't enough, governments will, in certain circumstances, reduce the borrower's loan principal.

Beware of Scholarship Application Deadlines

A recent ScholarshipsCanada survey found that more than 60 percent of scholarships have deadlines in the spring or summer. Only 4 percent, for instance, have December deadlines. If you're late applying for many awards, you'll have to wait a full year before being considered again.

believe there are 60,000 scholarships available for Canadian students? That's how many awards are listed in ScholarshipsCanada's Web site (http://www.scholarshipscanada.com). A subscription to this site costs $25. That entitles you to ten sessions on the scholarship database anytime within a year of registration.

Another useful site belongs to studentawards.com (http://www.studentawards.com). This one is free, and offers a searchable database of up to 15,000 scholarships, bursaries, grants, and fellowships, with the majority available to average students.

The Association of Universities and Colleges of Canada has its own list of scholarships and awards on its site (http://www.aucc.ca).

And the National Educational Association of Disabled Students (NEADS) has also published an online list of awards (http://www.indie.ca/neads/scholarships.html).

But the prize for the richest scholarship jackpot by far belongs to the federal government. Beginning in the 1999/2000 academic year, the federal government will start handing out 100,000 Millennium Scholarships a year, each averaging $3,000. The total handed out over ten years is expected to be $2.5 billion, with the vast majority of that money earmarked for full-time undergrad students in financial need. The Canada Millennium Scholarship Foundation site is at http://www.millenniumscholarships.ca.

Putting Together a Plan

So how are you going to put all this together? Now that you know more about the options, you need to put together a plan. You will need to know when you need the money, which options you will be able to use, how much you need to save, and whether you can tolerate the risk of investing the money or whether you would rather lock in a guaranteed (but lower) rate of return.

When it comes time to start saving and investing for college or university, just remember: It's important that you start early, and save and invest regularly, no matter which savings plan you select.

Online Tools to Put Together Your Plan

Many banks and mutual fund companies offer RESP calculators on their Web sites. Some of the more sophisticated ones require you to download and install the software first (for example, the Royal Bank's RESP calculator at http://www.royalbank.com/resp/ calc.html). Whichever one you choose, be sure it takes into account the latest RESP changes. Some still don't factor in the 1998 announcement of the Canada Education Savings Grant.

Let's use the Education Savings Calculator discussed at the start of this chapter to map out a plan of attack (http://www.hrdc-drhc.gc.ca/cgi-bin/english_calc_page1_cesg.cgi).

We've already used this RESP calculator to show us how much we'd need to save to pay for little Nelson's college education ($96,300 to live away from home for four years).

Let's review the assumptions and calculations that got us there: We've entered Nelson's birth year as 1996, and entered 2014 as the year in which he's likely to start post-secondary studies. After that, we entered the average annual cost increase at 4 percent, and out came that $96,300 figure.

This time, we'll keep going. The calculator asks how much you plan to save towards those costs. We'll leave the default figure of $96,300 (after all, we want to cover everything!).

The Education Savings Calculator can project the cost of four years of post-secondary education when your child will be ready to enroll. It also tells you how much you need to save and invest each year to cover those costs.

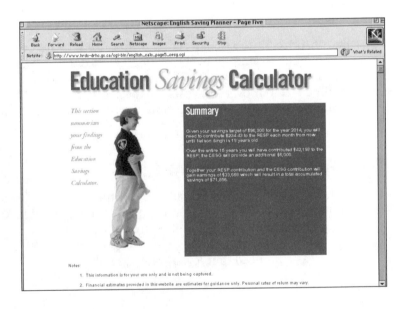

Now, estimate the annual return you can make on your college savings portfolio. Although you may be tempted to use a high rate of return, you should use a lower figure to be on the safe side. Let's assume you're hoping for a return of about 8 percent annually over the long term.

Click the Next button one last time and you'll receive an outline of how much you must save each month from now until Nelson enrolls in college.

In this example, you will need to contribute $234.43 to the RESP each month from now until Nelson is 18. Over that fifteen years, $42,196 will have come from you, and the Canada Education Savings Grant will have provided an additional $6,000. Together those two amounts will have earned another $23,668 for a grand total of $71,668. If you use an in-trust account instead of an RESP, you'll need to save more (there will be no Canada Education Savings Grant).

You can experiment with various rates of return, inflation, and costs to see different scenarios. If you have more than one child, you will have to run each projection separately and then do some addition to figure out how much you need to save. And after you know how much you need to save, the final step is to get started.

The Least You Need to Know

➤ College or university tuition, fees, and other expenses are likely to increase at a rate faster than inflation. You can use a calculator on the Web to see just how high costs may be when your child is ready to enroll in college.

➤ Many plans are available to help you save for college or university, among them, RESPs and in-trust accounts. Scholarships, loans, and other savings programs can help fill the gap. You will probably need to use several of these to reach your university savings goal.

➤ You can build a plan using a tool on the Web that will demonstrate how much you need to save and invest regularly to reach your goal. Investing in the stock market, either in stocks or mutual funds, may need to be part of your plan.

Chapter 23

Planning to Take Care of the "I Wants"

> **In This Chapter**
>
> ➤ Build a plan to meet short-term goals
>
> ➤ Learn why the stock market is not suited for goals that don't have a long-term horizon
>
> ➤ Find the best products for your short-term savings

Funding your retirement and saving for a post-secondary education are two goals that are (or at least should be) essential components of your overall financial plan. Chances are that you have some other goals in life besides helping your kids through college or university and making a comfortable retirement plan for yourself. Maybe you have your eye on a huge sailboat, or you want to throw a big wedding bash for one (or more) of your children.

You can include these other nonessential goals in your savings and investing plan, too, but you need to approach them somewhat differently than your long-term savings. The following sections introduce you to some Web tools that can help you create the best plan for your short-term goals.

Planning for a Home, Boat, or Dream Vacation

No matter what goal you're saving for, you will still need a roadmap to get you there. You need to figure out the amount of money you will require, how much you will need to save, how much you can earn on your savings, and how you will put together all these components.

You Need Time for Your Savings to Grow

Way back in chapter 2, you learned about compound interest and how it works. Here's a refresher: When you invest for many, many years, most of what you end up with in your portfolio will have come from the profits that you earned over the years (and the profits earned on those profits). On the other hand, when you have your money working for only a few years, the biggest part of your account will come from your own contributions, the money you socked away. The conclusion? A heavy-duty savings plan is required when you have short-term goals. It's the only way you will get there.

There are lots of savings calculators on the Web. But many of them don't take into account the income tax you have to pay on the interest your money earns. Altamira's Web site features an easy-to-use Capital Builder Calculator that takes taxes into account, so let's start there (http://www.altamira.com).

After clicking on Toolkits, select the calculator titled Capital Builder. Let's say you would like to save $10,000 to buy a new car over the next five years, and you have already got $1,000 in the bank. In the appropriate places on the calculator, fill in the amounts requested: Under Current Savings, enter $1,000. Then, estimate the rate of return you can achieve on your savings. You should probably start with about 5 percent. (You will learn later in this chapter how to get the best returns for your short-term savings.) Under Number of Years, enter 5.

Next, you need to estimate how much you can put away each month—let's say $100— and be sure to leave the Payment Frequency at Monthly. We'll leave the Inflation Rate at 0 for this example, although you might want to enter 1 or 2 percent.

Finally, enter your Taxation Rate. This will give you an idea of how much you will have to pay in taxes on your interest earnings each year. You can enter zeroes in these fields if you like, if you're not worried about the effect of taxes on your savings or if you aren't going to be paying any taxes out of those funds. (Some people make a point not to touch any of the money they have set aside for a specific purpose, not even to pay taxes.) In this example, a marginal tax rate of 45 percent was entered.

After you have entered all these variables, click the Calculate Future Value tab. You will be presented with the figure of $7,571.42.

In this example, your $100 a month won't get you to your goal in five years. So what can you do? Well, the Capital Builder Calculator is actually five calculators in one: a

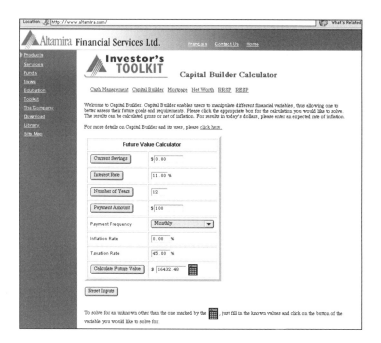

Altamira's Capital Builder Calculator allows you to calculate current savings, future value, rate of return, the payment required, and the number of payments required.

Future Value Calculator (the one we've just used), a Current Savings Calculator, a Rate of Return Calculator, a Number of Payments Calculator, and a Payment Amount Calculator. Let's assume you want to find out how big your monthly payment needs to be to get to that $10,000 figure. For this, go down to the $7,571.42 figure and replace that with $10,000. Then go back up to the Payment Amount line and erase the $100 figure and just leave it blank. Then click on the Payment Amount bar, and voila! It turns into a Payment Amount Calculator, and tells you that you'll need to put aside $137.80 a month to reach your goal. You can try different scenarios, perhaps trying to reach your goal in three years rather than five, or trying to eke out a slightly higher rate of return.

Where to Save and Invest for Your Short–Term Goals

After you have figured out how much you need to save, you can turn your attention to finding the best places to stash the cash. Obviously, with a short-term goal, you want the highest return for the least amount of risk. Where do you turn?

Before you begin your online search, stop for a moment to take this quick quiz. Let's say you just won the lottery at the county fair, and are driving home in your Ford F150 pickup with a picnic basket filled with $5,000 in fives, tens, and twenties. Do you

    A. stuff the cash under your mattress?

    B. stuff the cash in your cookie jar?

C. bury the cash in a Mason jar in the backyard?

D. put it in the bank?

The answer should be fairly obvious, but just in case, the right answer is D. The problem with answer A is that lumpy mattresses make for a bad night's sleep, even neglecting the fact that Canadian currency is notoriously combustible in the event of a fire. B can't be right; where do you think the burglars will look first when they rob your house (or at least second, after they look under your mattress)? And you need to remember the specific location of choice C, particularly when the worker with the backhoe is about to dig a new hole to relocate your septic tank.

You have to face all sorts of risks like these whenever you're dealing with your savings. You may have other dreams you would like to fulfill, but you need to tackle them with a somewhat different strategy.

Take Inflation Into Account

Even when planning for short-term goals, you can't completely ignore the impact of inflation. It's a good idea to build in a little bit extra when you're estimating the total cost of whatever goal you're trying to reach. That way you will help ensure that you won't come up short.

Here's why. When it comes to investing in the stock market, you must have a long-term approach. You need to have at least five years for your investment in stocks or mutual funds to really pay off and to weather any occasional storms the markets may provide.

As a result, if you need access to your savings in less than five years, you probably shouldn't be putting your money into the stock market. There's just too much risk involved, and it might not sit too well with your family if you have to postpone moving to a bigger home because the stock market declined 30 percent and you no longer have enough money for a down payment.

For short-term goals, you will have to put your money to work in some other way. Besides a savings account at your neighbourhood bank, you might consider purchasing a term deposit or GIC with a great rate that you found offered on the Internet.

Term deposits are typically for very short periods of time: from thirty days to less than a year. They're available from banks, trust companies, credit unions, and some life insurance companies. There's typically a minimum amount you must invest, sometimes as little as $1,000. But the minimum is usually more like $5,000. The interest rate is fixed and guaranteed.

GICs are available in terms that run from one to five years, and sometimes longer. There was a time when GICs always paid a fixed interest rate. But more and more companies are marketing new twists to these products, offering "step-up" or variable rate GICs that change rates from time to time. GICs can be bought in amounts as small as $500.

Calculate the Impact of Inflation

Inflation is currently running below 2 percent annually in Canada. To get a better idea of how inflation erodes the value of money (even over a short period), you can find out with the help of the Bank of Canada's Inflation Calculator. Select any two years from 1914 to the present, enter a dollar amount, and you'll instantly see inflation's effect on the value of money. For instance, a basket of goods and services that cost $100 in 1994 cost $108.76 in 1999. The calculator tells you that the average annual rate of inflation over that time was 1.69 percent.

Now let's go a bit further back. We'd also find that a $100 basket of goods from 1914 now costs $1,556.34 to buy. Over the eighty-five-year period from 1914 to 1999, that represents an average inflation rate of 3.28 percent.

For nervous investors, the main advantage of GICs is that you can lock in an interest rate and know exactly what your return will be while you hold onto it. But that's also the disadvantage. If interest rates should increase while you hold your GIC, you will miss out on that higher rate of return.

GICs can sometimes be cashed before their maturity dates. But then you either pay a penalty or settle for a lower interest rate.

Although many individuals are content dealing with their personal bank when they're in the market for a term deposit or GIC, it might pay you to shop around in your community for the best deal you can get. Or you can search for rates from institutions across the country using the Web. One of the most useful things you can do on the Web, in fact, is to comparison shop for the best rates for your short-term savings from financial institutions all over the country.

Term Deposits and GICs

CANNEX Financial Exchanges (http://www.cannex.com) is an independent supplier of interest rate information from dozens of financial institutions across Canada.

Click on Canada and then select Term Deposits/Guaranteed Investment Certificates (GICs). You'll see that the site divides its survey into short-term and long-term rates. The short-term section lists the rates paid for money you're willing to invest for thirty

Search for the best term deposit and GIC rates from financial institutions all across the country at the CANNEX Web site.

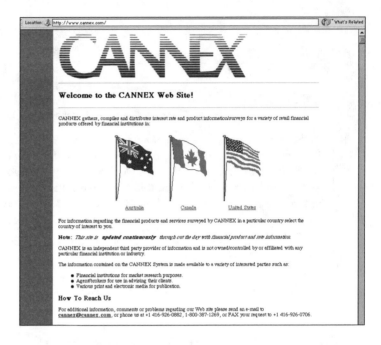

to 270 days. Use the long-term rates section for GICs of one year or more. The site lists the minimum amount you must invest, whether the product is redeemable or cashable before maturity, and, of course, the interest rate.

Savings Accounts

There was a time when bank savings accounts paid such poor interest rates that anyone serious about saving would only do that through term deposits or GICs. But in the last couple of years, several "virtual" or "supermarket" banks (like ING Direct, mbanx, and President's Choice Financial) have sprung up with rates so attractive, they're giving the "brick-and-mortar" banks a real run for their money.

The prize for the most exhaustive list of what financial institutions will pay for money in savings accounts still goes to CANNEX (http://www.cannex.com). Click on Deposit Accounts and you're presented with a list of every conceivable deposit account from dozens of financial institutions (under the Bank of Montreal, for instance, thirty different types of accounts are listed!). CANNEX tells you how the interest is calculated (daily, monthly), when it's paid (monthly, semi-annually), whether you can write cheques, whether any minimum account balance is required, and lastly, what interest is paid. This may be more information than you need to know. If you're just looking for a quick list of who pays the best rates for a daily interest savings account, try iImoney (http://www.imoney.com). Go to the Shortcuts section, find Timely Info, and then use the drop-down menu to find Savings Accounts. If you want to rank order this list, showing the best-paying daily interest savings accounts at the top, click on Daily

Long-Term Savings: Don't Shoot Yourself in the Foot

Don't make the mistake of thinking that putting all your money in the bank is enough of a plan to help you reach your financial goals. Investors who won't touch their savings account money for ten to twenty years and who are too conservative, are shooting themselves in the foot. They are likely to fall far short when retirement arrives. For short-term goals, however, a savings account or money market mutual fund might be just the place.

Interest, and the list will be reordered to show you who's on top. You'll notice that you have to look down—way down—to find the big banks.

Money Market Mutual Funds

Another option for your short-term savings might get you a slightly higher return: buying shares in a special kind of mutual fund called a money market fund. These funds invest in a variety of very short-term, high-quality securities, like Government of Canada Treasury bills (T-bills), investment-grade corporate paper, and bankers' acceptances. You can buy them through any company that sells mutual funds.

Money market funds are great for investors looking for a safe place to park some cash. You can redeem your units at any time, and some money market funds offer investors cheque-writing privileges. And you can often get a higher yield than you can with a regular bank account.

Globefund (http://www.globefund.com) is a good resource for unearthing the best current money market rates. The site's Fund Selector (under Tools) takes you to a page with four options. Choose Option B and use the drop-down menu to select Canadian Money Market funds. You'll find more

Money Market Funds Are Growing in Popularity with Investors

Money market funds have been around for decades, but started exploding in popularity with investors in the early 1980s, when short-term interest rates hit all-time highs (even more than GICs). Today you can choose from more than 160 money market funds, which, as of August 1999, held total assets of over $43.7 billion.

Source: Investment Funds Institute of Canada

Let Your Broker Sweep Up for You

Usually, brokerage firms automatically invest any cash in their clients' accounts into shares of money market funds. Many will "sweep" any cash into these funds on a daily basis, ensuring that your money is always working for you.

than 160 funds listed. Then, it's just a matter of selecting one. To find the ones that have managed the best return over, say, three years, just click on the 3-Year category, and Globefund will reorder the list from best to worst.

The Least You Need to Know

➤ You need to determine your saving goals, and then build a plan to help you get there. Use a calculator on the Web to figure out how much you need to save on a regular basis.

➤ Decide where to invest your savings. You will probably want to buy a term deposit or GIC, invest in a money market mutual fund, or open up a higher-interest savings account available from the "virtual" banks. You can find the best returns by searching on the Internet.

➤ No matter how you plan to reach your short-term goals, the key to success is the ability to save money on a regular basis and put it away where you won't touch it.

Chapter 24

More Investments to Consider

In This Chapter

➤ The hard, cold truth about options and commodities, and why you should avoid them

➤ Where to begin to search for information about bonds on the Web

➤ Questions you should ask before you invest

You can find thousands and thousands of investment-related sites on the Web, each one vying for your dollars. So how do you make sense of everything that's out there? It's not easy, but here are some tips to help you ferret out the truth—whether it's an opportunity to invest in commodities, options, or bonds, or some other exotic offering you may come across on the Web.

How to Lose a Bundle Fast in Commodities

In recent years, a whole new category of outrageous sports has become popular, from street luge to sky-surfing to downhill inline skating. These sports make pro football look downright tame in comparison. These events are known as extreme sports because the risks involved go way beyond the traditional sporting life.

In the same way, it's probably a good idea to put commodities and options into the category of extreme investing. Some of the material in this chapter could be so hazardous to your long-term financial plan that it ought to carry a warning label, something like this:

Caution! Investing in commodities and futures can result in really, really big losses of money.

We're operating under a yellow caution flag right now for a couple of reasons. First, on the Complete Idiot's Guide Investing Risk Scale, commodities and options jump off the top of the charts. In general, investing in derivatives is risky business. How risky? Consider this: You can lose all of your money...and very quickly. Now you're probably saying, "But I could lose all my money buying a stock or mutual fund!" True, but not likely. Mutual funds provide built-in diversification that limits your losses. And as for stocks, they don't often lose all their value on a particular day. But options can. They have expiry dates. And if that date comes and you're on the wrong side of the market, you've lost. Every penny you invested.

When you invest in commodities, your potential for loss is even greater. It's actually possible for you to face unlimited losses dabbling in commodity futures. That's right, you could lose all of your original investment and be on the hook for even more. Remember this point, especially if you find an attractive Web site that seems to lay out a clear plan for you to make a lot of money trading commodities.

Second, any Web site that suggests that beginners can make a fortune trading options or commodities should be viewed with suspicion. It's certainly possible that you could be a profitable commodities trader, and it's also possible that you could win the 6/49 lottery. It's possible, all right, but it's certainly not very likely.

The Toronto Stock Exchange site tells you just about everything you'd want to know about options and futures trading.

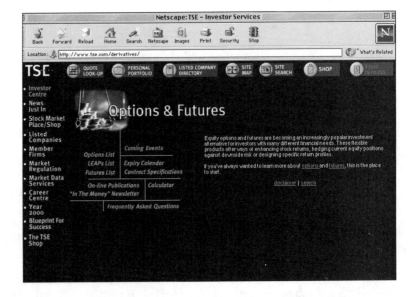

If you decide to investigate commodity trading, even after these warnings, you need to understand a lot about how they work. You need to understand the different commodities that are traded on futures exchanges (in Canada and around the world). Each exchange specializes in one or more commodities, including contracts on wheat, black tiger shrimp, butter, cheddar cheese, cocoa, coffee, corn, fresh pork bellies, and platinum (to name a few). Just about any raw material can be sold as a commodity, as long as a formalized market is established on a futures exchange.

And what does one do when one trades futures? Basically, you're dealing with a contract to buy or sell a commodity on a set date for a predetermined price. A futures contract on wheat is really a bet on which way wheat prices will head. Farmers use futures to hedge—to reduce their risk. They're able to lock in a current price, so if wheat prices plunge before they deliver the grain, the farmer will still get the price originally locked in. Investors who speculate in futures like the huge leverage these contracts provide. For example, you can control $25,000 worth of a commodity for only 10 percent of its value: $2,500. The potential for gains (or losses) is enormous. The "miracle" of leverage could suddenly look like the work of the devil if the price moves against you.

The only commodity exchange in Canada is in Winnipeg. And in a word, it's about grain.

The Winnipeg Commodity Exchange (http://www.wce.mb.ca) trades futures contracts for canola, wheat, flaxseed, oats, barley, and rye.

The commodity futures market in the United States is much bigger. The two largest exchanges are both in Chicago (the Chicago Board of Trade and the Chicago Mercantile Exchange). New York also has several big exchanges, including the Commodity Exchange (also known as COMEX).

In the U.S., commodity exchanges are regulated by the U.S. Commodity Futures Trading Commission. Its Web site (http://www.cftc.gov) provides some useful articles from an American perspective.

For Canadians, the Web site of the Investor Learning Centre (http://www.investor learning.ca) is a good place to start if you want to learn more about futures and options. Click on Education, then Investment Products, then select either Futures or Options.

In Canada, options and futures contracts have historically traded in both Montreal and Toronto. But a proposed reorganization of Canada's stock exchanges will eventually see all options and futures trading end up in Montreal, with all stock trading in the big, established companies taking place in Toronto.

The Toronto Stock Exchange (TSE) site (http://www.tse.com/derivatives/) maintains a good explainer on the inner workings of these derivative products ("derivative" because they "derive" their value from underlying securities).

Are Options a Choice for You?

Options are first cousins to commodity futures, in that both exist only on paper. Options provide the holder with the right, but not the obligation, to buy or sell a certain security (usually a stock, index, bond, or currency) at a specific price within a specific period.

A stock option contract represents one hundred shares of the underlying stock (an index option's value is determined by multiplying the index by $100). When you buy or sell an option, the price you pay for the right to eventually buy or sell the underlying shares is called the premium.

Unlike commodity futures, the extent of your potential losses when trading in options is the amount of the premium you paid. Commodity futures are an obligation to buy or sell the underlying asset; options are a right that you can exercise or not—it's your option! If the price of the stock or index didn't move in the direction that you predicted, you merely ignore the option when it expires.

One thing you will notice when you get interested in options is that you will see the same warning label popping up all over the place. The companies in the industry have all agreed to make sure that individual investors understand the risks involved with options trading. Prior to buying or selling an option, a person must receive a Risk Disclosure Statement. It summarizes some of the risks of trading in options. A sobering statement on the front says it all: "A high degree of risk may be involved in the purchase and sale of options, depending to a large measure on how and why options are used. Options may not be suitable for every investor." The risks are so high, and the strategies so complex, that investment advisors who want to sell exchange-traded options must first pass a special course.

The Difference Between Employee Stock Options and Exchange-Traded Options

Don't confuse employee stock options, such as those that your company might issue to you, with stock options that trade on an exchange. Employee stock options generally can't be sold, and so they are only valuable to you (and you only) when you cash them in and as long as the stock price exceeds the exercise price (but you wouldn't cash them in if the price were lower than the exercise price).

Blessed Be the Bonds That Yield

Bonds are another security that you might like to invest in at some point in your lifetime. When you get right down to it, a bond is really nothing more than an IOU. When you buy a bond, you are lending money to a corporation or government agency, or to a provincial or federal government. In return, the borrower agrees to repay the loan to you with interest.

Although the basic idea about bonds is pretty simple, there are thousands of variations on this idea. Bonds that are offered for sale to the public can have quite different features. These differences stem from such factors as who is offering the bond for sale (a corporation, government, or government agency), when the bond matures, and many other factors.

What Is a Debt Security?

Bonds and Treasury bills are some-times called *debt securities*. This is just a fancy term to describe how a promise to repay the loan becomes a financial instrument that can be bought and sold in formalized marketplaces.

The most important thing to understand about bonds is this: Interest rates affect bond prices. When rates go up, bond prices go down. And when bond prices go down, the yield goes up. The yield is the average annual compound return you would get if you kept the bond until its maturity date. But you can usually sell it before that date. So if you bought the bond when interest rates were high, and rates are now lower, you would make money.

Don't confuse Government of Canada bonds with Canada Savings Bonds (see chapter 22). Government bonds can rise or fall in price and can be sold to other people in what's called a secondary market. CSBs, on the other hand, don't rise or fall in price and can't be transferred to another owner—you just cash them in for their full face value plus any interest they've earned.

Bond mutual funds invest in a variety of bonds (both government and corporate) and can be bought or sold at any time.

One of the most thorough sites for Canadian bond information is Bondcan.com (http://www.bondcan.com). It's the work of John Grundy, who's been working the fixed income side of the street for more than thirty-five years. The site provides a good introduction to the bond marketplace (in the Bonds 101 section) and includes a glossary that goes a long way toward explaining the huge amount of bond-related jargon out there. You'll also find a commentary on the day's bond-trading activity, as well as daily quotes on a variety of federal, provincial, municipal, and corporate issues. You must register for full access to the site, but it's free.

Bondcan.com provides an independent look inside Canada's bond market.

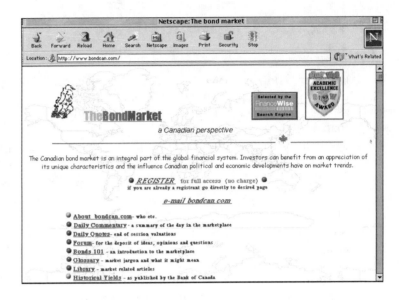

Every day, the Bank of Canada posts Government of Canada bond yields on its site.

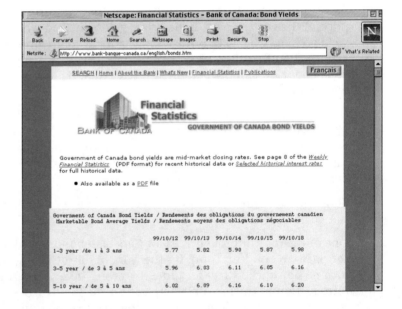

If you want to learn more about bonds and the countless varieties, or about how bonds might fit in your portfolio, the Financial Pipeline's site (http://www.finpipe.com) can give you a good grounding. And the Investor Learning Centre can again help, in the Education section of its Web site (http://www.investorlearning.ca). Go to Investments 101 and then to Bond Market.

Compared to the plentiful amount of information available on the Web about stocks, mutual funds, commodities, and options, only a handful of sites are devoted to bonds. Are bonds that boring? Not really, but a couple of reasons conspire to limit the amount of information you can find on the Internet about bonds.

The first is that you can determine what a bond is worth with a fair degree of certainty. The prices of stocks, on the other hand, rise and fall due to a multitude of factors. After you know when a bond comes due (its maturity date), the interest rate it pays, and its face value, most experts will agree pretty closely on the value of that bond. Without a lot of differing opinions about the prices of stocks, you won't find people who are interested in arguing about bonds in the same way.

Another reason for the lack of information about bonds is that, up until recently, you usually needed to work with a broker if you wanted to include bonds in your portfolio. Sure, you could buy Canada Savings Bonds directly from the government or your bank. However, if you wanted to buy municipal debentures, corporate bonds, or Government of Canada thirty-year bonds, you had to employ the services of a full-service broker. But as with so much else in online investing, this too is changing. In October 1999, E-BOND Ltd. (http://www.e-bond.ca) became Canada's first online discount bond broker. The service allows people to buy and sell federal and provincial bonds, along with a selection of corporate debt issues. Watch for more firms to follow E-BOND's lead in this area.

Full-service brokers have been slow to provide any kind of research on their Web sites—and that includes information about bonds. Discount brokers aren't much better, although some do give Web surfers access to market commentaries on bonds (TD

A Crash Course in Treasury Bills

➤ Canadian T-bills have original maturities of 91 days, 182 days, and 364 days.

➤ T-bills don't pay interest. They're sold at a discount and mature at par. The difference is taxed as regular income, not at the more favourable capital gains rate.

➤ Retail investors may buy them at financial institutions in denominations as small as $1,000.

The Canadian Bond Rating Service is one of Canada's two bond rating agencies.

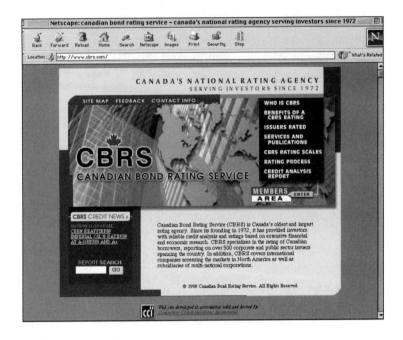

Everything you always wanted to know about a publicly listed Canadian company is available from Carlson Online.

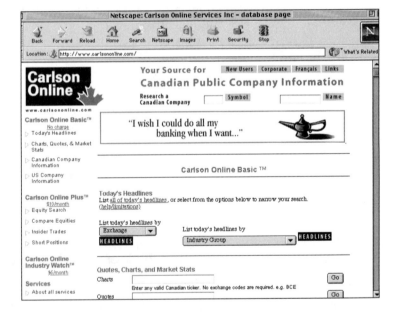

Waterhouse, www.tdwaterhouse.ca, for example, allows non-clients to access its Green Line Newsletter, which features a Bond Corner commentary every month.)

Bond trading in Canada is dominated by the large financial institutions, and until recently, their dealings have remained beyond public scrutiny. But as of mid-1999, market dealings on some Government of Canada issues were being made available at CanPX (http://www.canpx.ca).

If you want current ratings (but not quotes) of corporate and government bonds, you can try Canada's two bond rating services. The Dominion Bond Rating Service (http://www.dbrs.com) and the Canadian Bond Rating Service (http://www.cbrs.com) each rate hundreds of corporate and government bonds. They assign a letter grade to each security, along with an outlook for that debt instrument (such as "AA with negative trend").

The U.S. Bond Market Is Enormous!

The bond market in the United States is the world's largest securities market. It's even bigger than the New York Stock Exchange! The total value of the U.S. bond market the first six months of 1999 was $5.3 trillion. In all of 1998, the total trading volume in New York was $7.3 trillion.

Source: The Bond Market Association/NYSE

The Carlson Online Web site (http://www.carlson online.com) keeps an excellent database on more than 4,200 Canadian companies. You'll be able to search for press releases, research reports, and other tidbits that can tell you a lot about a company's financial health and its ability to keep paying the bond's interest.

To research American companies, a good first stop is Invest-O-Rama! (http://www.investorama.com).

Ten Things to Consider Before You Invest in Anything!

Now that you're nearly finished reading this book, does that prepare you to tackle any potential investment and wrench the profit from it? Unfortunately, no. For every legitimate investment that you will find on the Web, there are dozens of shady deals, overly complex schemes, and probably inappropriate "opportunities" that are best avoided.

At some point in your investing career, you may be offered the chance to "invest" in diamonds, eel farms, vending machines, or time-share real estate. You may be offered a sure-fire method of investing in "rolling stocks" or a "guaranteed" program to profit from seasonal commodity trading. Some investors may find these schemes to be profitable, or even lucrative. But chances are just as good that you'll never see your money again.

Most investors do just fine sticking to stocks, bonds, mutual funds, or perhaps real estate. But if you're ever tempted by some flashy opportunity to "make money fast," here are some final words to help you protect yourself. Answer these questions honestly, and if you find yourself trying hard to justify the answers, you should recognize that as a sign of trouble.

1. **Is this an investment or a gamble?** If you find yourself saying, "Oh, what the heck?" as you write out a cheque, you're probably throwing good money out the window. Investing isn't a game of chance, and when you invest with a sound long-term strategy, the odds are overwhelmingly in your favour. If you sense the odds tipping against you, think twice. And if you want to gamble, book a trip to Las Vegas and get it out of your system!

2. **How does this opportunity fit into your investment plan?** Is it part of your retirement strategy, to help you reach your education savings goal, or are you just "taking a flier" with your hard-earned cash?

3. **Do you have reasonable expectations for a return on your investment?** Greed is a powerful force, and sometimes greed can make you think that an outlandish promise of profits is reasonable. Remember that you can't "make money fast" without facing a whole lot of risk.

4. **Who regulates the market in this security or opportunity?** Most securities investments in Canada are regulated by provincial securities commissions. That means you can verify the legitimacy of any offer with the appropriate authorities. Find out who regulates a particular investment and check it out.

5. **Who is the individual or organization selling this investment?** What are their credentials? Do they need to be licensed or registered? And if so, are they?

6. **What happens if you change your mind?** It's a simple question, but find out what happens if you decide to pull out after you write the cheque. Can you get your investment back? Is there a penalty? Or are you locked in for a specific period of time?

7. **What happens if you need to sell your investment?** Is there a market where this investment is regularly bought and sold by other investors? Maybe you can make a bundle by investing in an eel farm (although that's dubious); but if you need to sell your investment, where are you going to go to find potential buyers? Are you going to have to find a buyer on your own?

8. **Does this opportunity require you to sell anything to other people?** "Multilevel marketing" is the term used to describe businesses that are built on individuals who sell to others, and then move up the pyramid to become distributors. Amway is the best known example of a multilevel marketing firm. You

shouldn't confuse these with investing, however. If you're required to sell to others to realize a profit, it should be taken as a sign to take a pass.

9. **What did your lawyer say about the paperwork that you were asked to sign?** You did get legal advice, didn't you? Don't sign anything without having a lawyer review the documents first.

10. **Is it okay if you "sleep on it" for a day or a week?** There's no opportunity so great that it won't wait for you—and there will be plenty of others down the road. If anyone tries to use high-pressure tactics to get you to act right away, it's time to beat a hasty retreat and think about it, starting with question No. 1!

If any of these questions start to bring on "reasonable doubt" about the "investment" that you're considering, that's a good enough sign that you should probably move on. There is plenty to learn about investing in stocks and mutual funds—enough to keep you busy and occupied for a lifetime! After you have mastered stocks and funds, then (and only then) should you consider alternative investments.

The Least You Need to Know

➤ Commodity trading and options trading are risky and probably not suitable for beginners. Period.

➤ Canada's bond rating agencies post their ratings, research, and analysis of hundreds of government and corporate bond issuers on the Web. Bond quotes are not as readily available as stock quotes.

➤ Most investors will never have a need to invest in anything other than stocks, bonds, or mutual funds. If you have an urge to expand the range of your portfolio, you should ask some important questions—before you invest.

Index